Theodore Roosevelt Jr.

Brigadier General Theodore (Ted) Roosevelt Jr. in Italy in early 1944. His aide named the jeep in honor of the "Rough Riders" cavalry led by Ted's father during the Spanish-American War. Note the bullet hole in the windshield. (Theodore Roosevelt Collection Harvard College Library)

Theodore Roosevelt Jr.

The Life of a War Hero

H. Paul Jeffers

PRESIDIO

Published by Presidio Press, Inc.
505 B San Marin Drive, Suite 160
Novato, CA 94945-1340

Library of Congress Cataloging-in-Publication Data

Jeffers, H. Paul (Harry Paul), 1934–
    Theodore Roosevelt, Jr. : the life of a war hero / H. Paul Jeffers.
      p. cm.
    Includes bibliographical references (p.).
    ISBN 0-89141-739-7
      1. Roosevelt, Theodore, 1887–1944. 2. Generals—United
States—Biography. 3. United States. Army—Biography. 4. Children
of presidents—United States—Biography. 5. Politicians—United
States—Biography. 6. World War, 1939–1945—Biography. I. Title.
E748.R68 .J44 2002
973.91'1'092—dc21
[B]

2001055163

Printed in the United States of America

For Jake Elwell

We'll start the war from right here.
                                    —Brig. Gen. Theodore Roosevelt Jr.
                        Utah Beach, Normandy, France, June 6, 1944

Contents

Part 1: Father and Son

What we have a right to expect of the American boy is that he shall turn out to be a good American man.

—*President Theodore Roosevelt,*
The American Boy,
St. Nicholas Magazine, *May 1900*

1

"We are starting on the great venture of war," wrote Brig. Gen. Theodore Roosevelt to his wife, Eleanor, on the night of June 5, 1944, "and by the time you get this, for better or worse, it will be history."

Forty-five years, eleven months, and sixteen days before the second in command of the 4th Infantry Division penned these words on the eve of the greatest invasion ever attempted from the sea, his father had sailed from Tampa Bay, Florida, in command of a cavalry regiment called the Rough Riders. On the troopship *Yucatan* for an expedition to liberate Cuba from Spain, on June 14, 1898, Lt. Col. Theodore Roosevelt, whom all but his family and friends called "Teddy," had said in a letter to his wife, Edith, that he faced a "nearing future" that held "many chances of death, honor, and renown." If he failed, he wrote, he would "share the fate of all who fail."

On the date that Colonel Roosevelt experienced what he called his "crowded hour" in Cuba, his namesake had been three months and two weeks shy of his eleventh birthday. Now, on the evening before a date that Gen. Dwight D. Eisenhower's invasion plan called "D-day" and future historian Cornelius Ryan would name "the longest day," the oldest son of the man whose heroism in Cuba had paved the way for him to become twenty-sixth president of the United States wrote to his own wife, "We've had a grand life and I hope there'll be more. Should it chance that there's not, at least we can say that in our years together we've packed enough for ten ordinary lives. We've known joy and sorrow, triumph and disaster, all that goes to fill the pattern of human existence."

There is no way of knowing how many men jammed into ships bobbing on the churning English Channel were writing similar letters as they anticipated bloody hours ahead on a stretch of beach with the code name "Utah" at a place in France named Normandy.

"We are attacking by daylight the most heavily fortified coast in history, a shore held by excellent troops," Ted Roosevelt's letter continued. "We are throwing excellent troops against it, well armed and backed by good air and naval support. We are on our transports, buttoned up, our next stop France. The ship is dark, the men are going to their assembly stations."

After leading his Rough Riders cavalrymen to fame and into legendary glory in Cuba, Colonel Roosevelt had written, "All men who feel any power of joy in battle know what it is like when the wolf rises in the heart."

What thousands of seasick soldiers from all over America felt rising in them on the night of June 5, 1944, was vomit.

Aboard the attack transport USS *Bayfield*, their commander was Maj. Gen. Raymond O. Barton. In a letter written months earlier to Eleanor, Roosevelt had said of him, "He is a very fine character of a real American type. His nickname is 'Tubby.' He's so square. Not only is he sound on military tactics but he's a real leader. I've seen so much of generals who were neither that it's a joy to be with him."

That Barton would approve of his deputy going ashore on Utah Beach with the first wave of troops had been in doubt. The reticence was based on the state of Roosevelt's physical condition. In 1941 he had been diagnosed with arthritis. The condition resulted from a World War I leg wound that had been aggravated by years of playing squash on hard courts. While the ailment had not prevented him from participating in the campaigns in North Africa, Sicily, and Italy, he needed a cane.

Complications regarding his health had occurred in late February 1944 when he'd arrived in England to take up a post at Eisenhower's headquarters. En route from Italy he came down with a fever that reached 103 degrees. The diagnosis was pneumonia, requiring three weeks of hospitalization. Nevertheless, General Eisenhower's chief of staff, Walter Bedell Smith, promised that he would be given a combat command as soon as he was well.

Accordingly, upon release from the hospital, he was ordered to report for maneuvers that included amphibious training in preparation for the invasion. After spending a day in a small boat, shivering-cold in raw, bleak weather, he wrote to Eleanor that he believed he was being physically tested. "I knew I was well," he said, "and now I've proved it."

Appointed deputy commander to General Barton, he asserted readiness and eagerness for battle during a conference of field officers. It was held a few days before the scheduled date of the invasion. When its commander, Gen. Omar Bradley, told the generals and colonels that they would have ringside seats at the greatest fight in history, the son of the hero of San Juan Hill whispered to those seated around him, "Ringside, hell! We'll be in the arena."

Another man would have echoed the prizefight analogy. But Ted Roosevelt was the firstborn son of the man who a quarter of a century earlier in an address at the Sorbonne in Paris had spoken of "the arena" and provided his son and historians the Roosevelt measure of manhood. He lauded the man "whose face is marred by dust and sweat and blood . . . who knows the great enthusiasms, the great devotions, and spends himself in a worthy cause; who at least knows in the end the triumph of high achievement; and who, at worst, if he fails, at least fails while going greatly, so that his place shall never be with those cold and timid souls who know neither victory nor defeat."

For the son of the author of those words, being "in the arena" on D day meant going in with the first assault wave and hitting Utah Beach at H-Hour. After a verbal request to do so had been denied, a formal, written request had followed. When General Barton voiced reservations about what troops would think of being led by an officer who needed a walking stick, Roosevelt replied, "They'll figure that if a general is with them, it can't be that rough. It will steady the men to know I'm with them, to see me plodding along with my cane."

Barton wavered.

Roosevelt pleaded, "I would love to do this."

Barton relented. "When I said good-bye to Ted in England," he recalled, "I never expected to see him alive again."

Roosevelt did not report the result of the decision to Eleanor until the June 5 letter. He did so in an offhand way. "I don't think I've told you," he wrote, "that I go in with the assault wave and hit the beach at H-Hour. I'm doing it because it's the way I can contribute most."

Half a century earlier, astride a horse named Little Texas at the foot of Kettle Hill in the San Juan Heights, Lt. Col. Theodore Roosevelt had inspired soldiers whom he had found hunkered down against Spanish rifle fire behind a protective mound of earth by shouting, "Are you afraid to stand up when I am on horseback?"

On the morning of June 6, 1944, Brigadier General Roosevelt's letter to his wife was in a mail pouch along with thousands of others that had been hurriedly written in the hope, if not in confidence, that the writers would one day be reunited with the loved ones to whom they were addressed. The final lines of Ted's letter to Eleanor read, "Soon the boats will be lowered. Then we'll be off."

When he stepped out of a Higgins landing craft into waist-deep water along with the men of E Company, 2d Battalion, 8th Infantry, the only general to land on a Normandy beach in the first wave carried his cane in one hand and a Colt .45 automatic in the other. Because he hated heavy army helmets, he wore a knit olive-drab cap. Short and slender, with a nose that seemed to have been dented during childhood, perhaps by another boy's fist or in a tackle on the Harvard football gridiron, he was fifty-seven years old.

2

On September 13, 1887, a few hours after Edith Carow Roosevelt gave birth to her first child, the father of the eight-and-a-half pound boy had written a letter to a friend to announce the blessed event and proudly added to his signature the word *Senior.* This was despite the fact that the father of the Theodore penning the birth announcement had also been named Theodore, thus entitling the newborn Theodore to put *III* after his name.

The grandfather of the baby whom Edith cuddled had died on February 9, 1878. Of the death his shattered and grieving son, then a student at Harvard, had written in his diary, "He was everything to me." At no time in his life had Theodore Roosevelt Sr.'s son been known as "junior." As a child he was "Teedie." When he outgrew the nickname, he was either "Theodore" or "TR." Only the people who did not know him personally—journalists, cartoonists, political foes, and the general public of his adult years—referred to him as "Teddy."

That he chose to enter politics had surprised nearly everyone. Rejecting warnings of his friends that politics was "low" and the province of "saloon keepers, horsecar conductors, and the like" who would be "rough and brutal and unpleasant to deal with," he believed that a moral duty rested upon a man of education to take an active part in political life "without regard to the effect it has upon his own fortunes." His plunge into politics in the fall of 1880 resulted in his election to the New York legislature. That year he provided family and friends a second surprise when he married Alice Hathaway Lee. But three years later, it seemed to everyone that his political career was over when, less than twenty-four hours after the death of his mother, Alice died after giving birth to a daughter. Leaving little Alice Lee in the care of a sister, he left New York to become a rancher in the Dakota Territory and stayed for two years. After losing as the Republican candidate for mayor of New York in 1886, he again surprised everyone by marrying a childhood friend, Edith Carow. He settled down with her in a house he had expected to share with his first wife. Atop a hill at Oyster Bay on the northern shore of Long Island, it was named after a local Indian chief, Sagamore.

With the birth of a brother in the sprawling house in the fall of the following year, pretty, perky, blond Alice plunked herself next to his crib in her little rocking chair and would not be moved. She told their father she thought the little boy's squeals and cries made him sound like "a howling polly parrot."

When the child reached the crawling stage, his beaming father wrote to one of the child's aunts that he was "just like one of Barnum's little seals" and that he "plays more vigorously than anyone I ever saw."

Two years later, Alice and Ted gained a brother called Kermit, named after their father's brother. During the next decade, Kermit would be followed by Ethel, Archibald, and Quentin. They lived in a house crammed with souvenirs of adventures in a land of cowboys and Indians. Most of these thrilling objects were kept in a large room on the top floor that the architect's plan designated as "the den." Ted called it "the gun room," a name that stuck.

In it, Ted recalled, were "relics of the time when Father as a young man wished to dress as well as act the part of a dashing young cattleman" in the rugged hills of Dakota. Among the artifacts were a pair of dueling pistols in a mahogany box, a brace of six-shooters with ivory grips, cartridge boxes, leather cases, and ramrods. Behind glass in big cases were three shotguns, several rifles, six-shooters with ivory handles, a brace of dueling pistols, swords, and scimitars from TR's sojourn to Egypt when he was eleven years old. Displayed on the walls of the room that filled the Western gable of the house were heads of game shot by TR on numerous hunting trips, each with an exciting tale to be told. The floor was scattered with rugs of animal hide.

Bookcases held volumes whose pages brimmed with stories of gallant soldiers, intrepid sailors, and fighters in the American Revolution and the Civil War, including relatives. Among them in Edith Carow Roosevelt's family tree were four ancestors who'd sailed to America on the *Mayflower*. Another member of her family, Benjamin Lee, had been a midshipman in the British navy. Serving in the Caribbean during the American Revolution, he had been commended for gallantry during a sea battle off the island of Guadeloupe. After protesting inhuman treatment of prisoners of war and challenging his lieutenant to a duel, he was court-martialed. Condemned to death for insubordination, he was saved when a petition for clemency signed by fellow officers persuaded the admiral to commute his sentence. Dismissed from the navy, he changed sides and joined the American Merchant Marine.

While Edith's *Mayflower* ancestors had left England seeking religious freedom, the first Roosevelt to set foot in America, Klaes Martensen van Roosevelt, had been motivated by the health of his pocketbook. His father, Mareten Cornelissen Geldersman, was a landowner on the Dutch island of Tholen. Among his holdings was a farm called "Roosevelt" (Field of Roses). Listed in records of the town of Poortvliet as "Mareten Cornelissen Geldersman van Roosevelt," he'd fallen upon hard times. Losing the farm to creditors, he fled the island for the mainland with the town bailiff in hot pursuit. Evidently out of a combination of a son's embarrassment and financial necessity, Klaes departed Holland for America in 1644. Settled in the colony of New Amsterdam, he founded a family of substance and achievement that gave the United States of America two presidents.

When the father of the first of the Roosevelts who would occupy the White House took a bride in 1853, he chose a vivacious Southern beauty from a distinguished family of Georgians. Her name was Martha Bulloch. Her great-grandfather, Archibald, had been a delegate to the Continental Congress in 1775, first revolutionary president of Georgia, and a signer of the state's first constitution. But far more exciting to Martha's grandson Ted were her two brothers. James Dunwoody Bulloch had been an admiral in the Confederate Navy and also a Confederate agent in England, where he arranged for construction of the warship *Alabama*. As a midshipman serving aboard her, James had fired the last gun before she was sunk in a duel with the Yankee warship *Kearsarge*. Because the brothers were not included in a postwar amnesty, they had settled in exile in England and thrived as cotton merchants.

Among the exciting volumes in TR's Sagamore Hill library was a memoir of James's war exploits as a Confederate agent. Titled *The Secret Service of the Confederate States in Europe*, it stood on a shelf next to TR's book on sea battles of an earlier war, *The Naval War of 1812*. Begun as TR's senior thesis at Harvard, it had been expanded for publication in 1881.

Should young Ted seek other stories of warfare outside the pages of books, he had only to ask about his father's uncle who had lived next door to the Roosevelt house on East Twentieth Street. A veteran of the Union Army, Robert Barnwell Roosevelt, known to TR as "Uncle Barnwell," had been a swashbuckling adventurer, hunter, fisherman, conservationist, and a writer on all those topics. He differed from the Roosevelts next door politically, being a Democrat, and in social reputation by being widely known as a womanizer who had fathered children by one of his mistresses. One of her sons would join TR's Rough Riders in Cuba.

While gladly regaling Ted with accounts of his uncle Barnwell and the Bulloch brothers during the Civil War, TR had no such daring exploits to relate regarding his father. With a wife and children to support, he had taken advantage of a law that permitted him to hire a substitute soldier. Rather than taking up arms, he'd lobbied in Washington for passage of a law to establish a means by which soldiers could set aside part of their pay to send home to their families. The act established allotment commissioners who went to military camps to persuade troops to take part in the program.

Family friend William E. Dodge wrote in *A Tribute to TR Sr.* that as one of the commissioners Theodore spent "long, weary months in the depth of a hard winter" going from camp to camp, urging men to take advantage of the plan. He described Theodore "on the saddle often six to eight hours a day, standing in the cold and mud as long, addressing the men and entering their names." This resulted in many millions of dollars sent to homes where the money was greatly needed and kept the memory of wives and children fresh in the minds of the soldiers as they went into battle. But to TR, his father's enduring long hours of discomfort while wearing civilian clothes to persuade soldiers to send money home was not the same as donning a uniform and bearing arms, and therefore, not the stuff of stories for the amusement and instruction of his son in the room at the top of the house on Sagamore Hill.

More impressive to Ted than his father's souvenirs in the gun room, and shelves of books, was the man to whom they belonged. "His knowledge," Ted recalled of his father, "stretched from babies to the post-Alexandrian kingdoms and, what was more, he could always lay his hands on it. It made little difference in what channels the conversation turned. Sooner or later he was able to produce information which often startled students of the theme under discussion."

TR's education of his son extended beyond the walls of library and gun room to the woods surrounding the house. The house was for sharpening the mind. The outdoors was for honing the body. Determined to toughen Ted, TR took him on tramps that tested both strength and spirit.

On these outings the father became, in the words of TR biographer Hermann Hagedorn, "a combination of deity and friend, his mystical heroes brought to life, King Arthur and Daniel Boone rolled into one."

After observing the father and son one day, Edith noted in a letter, "Ted is such a piece of quicksilver that I am in constant anxiety about his life and limb. Theodore thought his neck was broken the other day and declares he will never live to grow up."

Fear for the boy's life had been very real when at two and a half he was felled by a fever. "It has just been heart-breaking," TR wrote to a sister, "to have the darling little fellow sick; and the first forty-eight hours I really look back to with a shudder. When he would rally at times and come out of his stupor, and begin to say the cunning things he always says, it was about as much as Edith and I could stand."

As Ted grew, a certain "irregular independence of the eyes" that TR had noted soon after Ted's birth continued to manifest itself in a squint and frequent headaches. Although Ted was fitted for eyeglasses, the problems persisted. When an oculist recommended an operation, Edith refused to allow it. "It would be mortal agony to me," she wrote to her sister Emily, "to see the knife touch Ted's eyes."

Having to wear glasses did not interfere with the strenuous life Ted's father demanded of him. TR wrote to Edith's mother, "It is an awe-inspiring sight to see him, when Alice has made a nice nest in a corn-stack, take a reckless header in after her, with sword and spectacles, showing a fine disregard both of her life and his own."

On October 10, 1889, Ted lost the distinction of being his father's only boy with the birth of Kermit, named after TR's older brother who also was father of an ungainly girl named Eleanor. When Kermit was born, TR was serving in Washington, D.C., as a civil service commissioner. He rushed back to Sagamore Hill and found the yellow-haired child cuddled in Edith's arms. She later wrote to her sister of Kermit's "big dark eyes, full of poetry." While Ted was rambunctious, Kermit proved to be so quiet that Edith described him as a "good deal of a hermit" who "never need retire to a cloister for a life of abstraction."

Because his governmental position kept TR away from Sagamore Hill for long periods, the times when he returned to New York were occasions of rejoicing for the children. Of Ted's greetings he wrote, "I really think he loves me, and after I come back from an absence he greets me with wild enthusiasm, due however, I fear, in great part to the knowledge that I am sure to have a large paper bundle of toys, which produces the query of 'Fats in de bag,' while he dances like an expectant little bear. Ted is a most warm, tender, loving little heart; but I think he is a manly fellow too."

The Roosevelt family of Sagamore Hill expanded again in 1891 with the birth of Ethel, in 1894 with the arrival of Archibald, and on November 19, 1897, with Quentin. TR delighted in calling his brood "my bunnies." When he watched them frolicking each summertime with the numerous Roosevelt cousins who lived nearby in Cove Neck, he called the noisy tableau "the seventh heaven of delight." Edith joyously observed her husband full of "life and energy" as he acted as their guiding spirit and the inventor of activities and games meant to provide fun and a strengthening of bodies and a character based on self-esteem and courage.

Doting on the children without spoiling them, he saw himself as "their special friend, champion, and companion." He was beside them when they rode horseback, raced, hiked, swam, hunted, and climbed. As their role model, he presented a straightforward example. His message was that if they wished to be like him they had to be enthusiastic about life, physically active, and brave.

"Don't let anyone impose on you," he lectured. "Don't be quarrelsome, but stand up for your rights. If you've got to fight, fight hard and well."

When he gave Ted a pocketknife, Ted considered it "an accolade." Of the gift he wrote, "I felt about it much the way a young medieval knight must have felt about his spurs. It was one of those combination knives with everything from a pair of tweezers to a gimlet folded into its corpulent body. I called it 'Bowie' because I had lately read of Colonel Bowie at the Alamo, and thought that anything that bore his name smacked of romance. In some magical way that bit of steel transmuted the knife for me from an ordinary little boy's knife to the trusty blade of an adventurer. All I needed when I had that knife in my hand was a horse to make me a cowboy."

At the age of ten he was given his own gun. The presentation of the Flaubert rifle was made just after dark as TR was dressing for dinner.

"I wanted to see if it fired to make sure it was a real rifle," Ted recalled in a book of family memories, "but Father was not dressed to go outside at the moment."

Picking up the rifle and slipping a cartridge into the chamber, TR whispered, "You must promise not to tell Mother." Ted gave his word and TR shot the bullet into the ceiling.

"The report was slight, the smoke hardly noticeable," Ted recalled years later, "and the hole in the ceiling so small that our sin was not detected."

Practice in using the gun was on a makeshift firing range set up across a gully with the butts of logs as targets. Noting that the shooter fired while lying in a shallow pit, Ted recalled, "It was almost as exciting to be snuggled in the pit and to hear the bullets strike the butts as it was to shoot. We used to dig the spent bullets out of the bank and keep them as treasures."

On the subject of acumen with firearms, TR wrote in his autobiography, "There are men whose eye and hand are so quick and so sure they achieve a perfection of marksmanship which no practice will enable ordinary men to attain. There are other men who cannot learn to shoot with any accuracy at all. In between come the mass of men of ordinary abilities, who, if they choose resolutely to practice, can by sheer industry and judgment make themselves fair rifle shots." He observed with pleasure that Ted quickly became a good one.

Of learning how to handle firearms Ted wrote in *All in the Family,* "If I got on the target at fifty yards I was happy. Above two hundred yards the element of luck plays the greatest part in shooting. The rifle may be accurate but the sportsman is not."

Three or four years after the gift of the rifle, an admirer of TR presented Ted with a sixteen-gauge Scott shotgun. In order to "christen fittingly this new possession" TR took him hunting for ducks. Up before daylight on a cold winter morning and fortified by "gulping some coffee," they tramped through woods to Eel Creek. With a gray dawn breaking they paddled out from shore in a small boat, and "with numb fingers" set wooden decoys.

"Soon the ducks began to flight," Ted recalled. "After much expenditure of ammunition I succeeded, more by good luck than good management, in killing one female old-squaw. Meanwhile, Father had practically duplicated my performance by killing one male. In triumph we returned to the house in time for a regular breakfast. In spite of their very fishy taste and leathery toughness we had the birds cooked and ate them for dinner."

The children of a father who advocated "the strenuous life" were expected to take part in all kinds of sports, both individual and team. As a family they competed at tennis. "We had a dirt court near Sagamore," Ted remembered. "It was in a hollow. The moles traversed it regularly, which gave it an uneven surface. In addition, it was so well shaded that moss grew over it. The branches of the trees were so low that we had a special rule that when a ball hit a branch and might have gone in it was a 'let.' There were no professionals in those days, so we batted the ball in whatever fashion seemed best to us. Father played with us whenever he had the time, and was always welcome. His method of playing was original, to say the least. He gripped the racquet halfway up the handle with his index finger pointed back. When he served he did not throw the ball into the air, but held it in his left hand and hit it from between his fingers. In spite of this, and in spite of his great weight, he played a surprisingly good game. We used him as a sort of milestone of progress. When we were able to beat him in singles it was equivalent, so to speak, to having passed the entrance examinations to college."

In winter the children's strenuous life included hikes through the snow, sledding, and snowball fights. When their father came home one day with "snowshoes" that had been given to him by a Norwegian diplomat, they were introduced to a new sport that would be known in the future as skiing.

Although Ted was small for a boy his age and had to wear glasses, TR described him to a friend as "exceedingly active, normally grimy." His advice to the boy concerning bigger boys who might try to take advantage of him was to be prepared to fight. "If you fight hard enough," he advised, "you are perfectly certain to secure the respect of your playmates."

Testing of this counsel was not long in coming. Almost immediately after Ted entered the one-room Cove Neck School, he found himself in a class with the children of gardeners, horse grooms, and coachmen who teased him about his good manners and courtesy to girls. After a scrap with an older schoolboy named James Gallagher, who called him a sissy, TR proudly reported to a friend that Ted had "despatched" him.

Writing in *All in the Family*, a memoir of growing up at Sagamore Hill, Ted noted that his father "liked some of our toys as much as we liked them ourselves." These were generally of a warlike nature. Occasionally, TR made toys from whatever was at hand. Among them, created out of pillboxes, Ted recalled, was a pair of Civil War–type warships known as Monitors. One was given to Ted, the other to Alice. Supervised by their father, they were shown how to enact the Battle of Mobile Bay. The problem was that neither Ted nor Alice wanted his or her ship to be sunk. When Ted moved to attack, Alice shouted, "Leave my Monitor alone." Picking up her boat, she declared, "My Monitor has gone to bed. It always goes to bed at six o'clock and it's half past six now."

Edith wrote to a friend in 1894 that seven-year-old Ted "grows like a Century Plant. He is more like his father every day."

That "Father" was an important man was evidenced by guests who called at Sagamore Hill. Some came only for a dinner. Others spent a day or weekend. A few stayed for a week or month. Men and women with brilliant minds and animated spirits, they talked about politics and the great issues of the day. As they assessed the characters of the leading personalities in the government in New York, city and state, and in the national capital, Ted could not fail to observe that the person who shaped and dominated the lively conversations was his father. Nor was it lost on him that most visitors expressed the opinion that one day Theodore Roosevelt would be president of the United States.

Not *should* be president, mind you, but WOULD BE.

3

In the spring of 1895 the "bunnies" got the thrilling news that Father was giving up his job as civil service commissioner in Washington, D.C., to become one of four commissioners who supervised New York City's police department. The new position meant that they would return to Sagamore Hill. Appointed to the post by the newly elected mayor of New York City, William L. Strong, who had been swept into office on a reform ticket to clean out scandalous corruption in city government, especially in the police force, TR was immediately chosen by the others to be president of the police board.

Because of the demands of the job the children had little more than a glimpse of him in the morning before he set out on a three-mile ride on a bicycle to catch a train into the city. But Ted knew he could expect Father home in time to romp with all of them and to chat with him as he changed clothes for dinner. Then came dinnertime and everyone around the table as Father talked with whatever guest he'd brought home.

"The table talk was over the children's heads, of course," wrote William H. Harbaugh in *The Roosevelt Family of Sagamore Hill,* "but the sparkle of it was not lost on them. Their father bubbled with ideas, many of them challenging; he had a remarkable vocabulary, moreover, and delighted in using it to castigate his enemies or to characterize some 'amiable old fuddy-duddy with sweetbread brains' who had crossed his path; he had a quality of wit, besides, which inspired wit in others."

These dinners with the entire family around the table at Sagamore Hill were still warm in Ted's memory in 1929. In *All in the Family* he wrote,

"In times of happiness or sorrow, in times of stress or in the everyday oc-
currences of life, the dinner table plays its part. A building rests on its
cornerstone. In much the same fashion a family may be said to depend
on its dinner table."

At such times TR expected the bunnies to speak up. "We always told
him everything," Ted recalled, "as we knew he would give us a real and
sympathetic interest."

Conversations included all the current issues and controversies concerning the national debate over the gold standard versus the coinage
of silver, the tariff question, the forthcoming 1896 presidential election,
and whether the United States should intervene in a revolution in Cuba
on the side of rebels in their fight to free the island from Spain. A name
for one who urged such action, Ted learned, was "jingo." The word came
from an English music-hall song. Written by G. W. Hunt in 1878 in reference to Britain's resistance to Russian designs on the Turkish port of
Constantinople, the song asserted:

> We don't want to fight,
> But by Jingo if we do,
> We've got the ships,
> We've got the men,
> And got the money too.

In America, *jingo* had come to mean a bellicose patriot or warmon-
ger. No individual embodied the definition more than Theodore Roosevelt. In 1886, a year before Ted's birth, when newspapers had been
filled with predictions of war with Mexico, he had offered to organize a
cavalry battalion made up of cowboys from the Dakota Territory. On July
4th of that year he told an audience that he hoped to see the day "when
not a foot of American soil will be held by any European power." In 1894
he had been the first to call for annexation of the Hawaiian Islands and
had endorsed building of an ocean-linking canal through Nicaragua,
whether Nicaraguans agreed or not. Speaking to the National Republican Club on May 28, 1895, he had called for a navy "that will sustain the
honor of the American flag" and ensure that the Monroe Doctrine would
be "upheld in its entirety."

Writing on that subject in March 1896, he declared, "The United
States ought not to permit any great military powers, which have no

foothold on this continent, to establish such a foothold; nor should they permit any aggrandizement of those who already have possessions on the continent. Every true patriot, every man of statesmanlike habit, should look forward to the day when not a single European power will hold a foot of American soil."

When Great Britain had sought settlement of a boundary dispute with Venezuela without considering the interests of the United States, he all but welcomed a war. If it should come, he predicted, Canada would be "wrested from England" and never restored. In a letter to his friend and political mentor Henry Cabot Lodge he exclaimed, "This country needs a war."

Espousing his opinion that the United States had not only the right to take the side of the Cuban rebels, but a duty to do so, he called anyone who disagreed "anti-American." Claiming they were "too shortsighted or too unimaginative to realize the hurt to the nation that would be caused by the adoption of their views," he dismissed such persons as timid individuals "who undervalue the great fighting qualities, without which no nation can ever rise to the first rank."

While TR expressed these beliefs at the dinner table with like-minded guests Ted sat by, quietly listening and recalling the feats of Civil War daring and bravery of uncles that had been recited in the gun room. In all the stories, and in the books about history's heroes on the shelves in the library, war was pictured romantically with valorous scenes of man-to-man combat, dashing figures in uniforms, blaring bugles, flags flying, cavalry charges, and many brilliant tactical maneuvers. War was his father reciting a poem written by TR's friend Rudyard Kipling:

"What are the bugles blowin' for?" said Files-on-Parade.
"To turn you out, to turn you out," the Color-Sergeant said.

The battlefield, according to Father, was a place to exhibit one's bravery and reap honor and glory, as had the valiant cavalrymen in Tennyson's "The Charge of the Light Brigade":

Cannon to the right of them,
Cannon to the left of them,
Cannon in front of them,
Volley'd and thunder'd.
Into the jaws of death,

Into the mouth of hell
Rode the six hundred.

One evening at the table when Ted interrupted the adults to declare,
"Someday I'm going to be a soldier," TR looked at his jingo friends and
beamed with pride.

In the age that the nation's most popular author, Mark Twain, had dis-
dainfully termed "Gilded" and other social commentators called "the Gay
Nineties," lettered men found romance in going to war, and none more
so than TR's friend Brooks Adams, who never shunned a chance to ex-
tol its glories. In the words of another occasional Sagamore Hill dinner
companion, naval historian Alfred Thayer Mahan, war was "a necessary
evil" that provided "a remedy for greater evils, especially moral evils."

In the view of the guests at Theodore Roosevelt's dinner table at Sagamore Hill in the summer and fall of 1896, there was no greater evil than
continued Spanish subjugation of Cuba. In hope of fostering the ouster
of the "Spaniards," these men looked to the Republican candidate for
president, William McKinley. A veteran of the Civil War, he had ended
his service with the rank of brevet major and returned to civilian life to
study law. Attracted to politics, he had won election to Congress, serving in the House of Representatives from 1877 to 1883 and again from
1885 to 1891. Defeated for reelection in 1890, he returned to Ohio to
win election as governor.

Although Theodore Roosevelt considered McKinley an "upright and
honorable man of very considerable ability and good record as a soldier
and in Congress," he worried that he might not embrace the cause of
Cuba libre by intervening militarily. Notwithstanding his doubt, he campaigned for McKinley's election in a series of speeches throughout the
Midwest. He did so not only because he was a loyal Republican, but in
the hope that President McKinley would reward him with a significant
position in the administration. With McKinley victorious, he asked
friends to inform the president-elect that the post he coveted was assistant secretary of the navy. If appointed, he would be in direct command
of all naval operations and in a position to encourage and supervise a
rapid expansion of the fleet, especially in its number of modern, long-
range battleships.

With an expressed reluctance to endorse the jingoists' demands for
a declaration of war against Spain and a preference to obtain Cuban lib-
eration through negotiations with Spain, and nervous about adjectives

he heard applied to Roosevelt—*robust, strenuous, active, vigorous,* and *pug-nacious*—the president-elect yielded to pleadings from TR's allies. In naming him to the navy post, McKinley said to Henry Cabot Lodge of TR, "I hope he has no preconceived plans which he would wish to drive through the moment he got in."

Appointment in March 1897 followed by confirmation by the Senate meant a return to Washington. But the family's move to the capital had to be delayed because Edith was pregnant. For the time being, it was decided, she and the children (Alice, Ted, Kermit, Archibald, and Ethel) would remain at Sagamore Hill and TR would be a guest in the Massachusetts Avenue home of Henry Cabot Lodge. When the family joined him in October, they took up residence at "a very nice house, just opposite the British Embassy," at 1810 N Street.

November nineteenth brought the birth of Quentin. But the glow of this happy occasion was soon dimmed by complications in Edith's recovery. She suffered fever and pain that puzzled her physician, and other doctors who were called in. The malady persisted until Friday, February 25, 1898, when TR requested the services of a celebrated Canadian physician on the staff of Johns Hopkins University, Sir William Osler. Declaring Edith "critically ill," he discovered a large abdominal abscess and recommended surgery.

TR wrote to his sister, "She behaved heroically; quiet, and even laughing, while I held her hand until the ghastly preparations had been made."

As Edith recovered, she worried about the health of ten-year-old Ted. For several weeks he had been suffering with severe headaches and what appeared to be an extreme nervousness. When an examination by a doctor did not result in an explanation, TR wrote to his sister-in-law, "We have been very much worried over the little fellow, for doctors are utterly unable to find out the ultimate cause of the trouble."

Convinced that she knew the cause, Edith whispered her diagnosis to an old friend who was a doctor. Might it be possible, she asked, that Ted was overwrought from trying to measure up to his father's excessive expectations? The doctor examined Ted and agreed with Edith's theory.

When he informed TR of his conclusion, the shocked and embarrassed father mulled over the notion, reviewed the manner in which he'd raised the boy, and responded to the doctor, "Hereafter I shall never press Ted either in body or mind. The fact is that the little fellow, who is particularly dear to me, has bidden fair to be all things I would like to have been and wasn't, and it has been a great temptation to push him."

• • •

Ten days before TR sent the urgent request to Dr. Osler, the Cuban situation had taken a dramatic turn. On the sultry night of February 15 in the harbor of Havana, Cuba, the liner *City of Washington* had sailed into port with her passengers standing on deck to get a view of the United States Navy's battleship *Maine*. She lay at anchor on the twenty-first day of a "friendly call" in keeping with President McKinley's interest in averting American entry into the strife between the Spanish colonial government and the Cuban rebels. Two hours after the tourist ship dropped anchor at its berth, a bugler on *Maine* sounded taps and the white warship fell silent. The time noted in the log of her captain, Charles D. Sigsbee, was 9:40 P.M. As he laid down his pen, the battleship exploded.

Outraged Americans who believed the ship had been blown up by Spaniards screamed, "Remember the *Maine*," and demanded a declaration of war. A still reluctant McKinley asked for it from Congress on April 11, 1898, the day after Easter. Eight days later at three o'clock in the morning Congress granted it in a resolution demanding that the government of Spain withdraw its land and naval forces from Cuba at once and "directing the President of the United States to use the entire land and naval forces of the United States" to drive the Spaniards from Cuba.

As war fever swept the nation, the phenomenon also touched Sagamore Hill. After seeing an operetta in Manhattan, Ted and Alice paraphrased one of the songs in the show. As they cavorted on the lawn, they sang:

Unleash the dogs of war!
The enemy will find us unrelenting,
When our cannons roar,
The little king of Spain
Will be repenting.

In Washington their father left his Navy Department office in a building adjacent to the White House to see McKinley. "I have the navy in good shape," he reported proudly. Adding that he would be useless to the war effort on a ship, he asked to be allowed to raise a regiment of cavalry. Admitting that he had little experience, he proposed he be appointed second in command, with the rank of lieutenant colonel, and that the unit be led by Leonard Wood. A physician by training, he had joined the army and become a hero, receiving the Congressional Medal of Honor for valor during the army's recent campaign to capture the Indian renegade Geronimo. Officially named the First United States Volunteer Cavalry, the regiment was organized at a training camp near San Antonio, Texas. Consisting of an unlikely mixture of former college footballers and polo players from the east and scores of rough-and-ready cowboys, the unit was immediately nicknamed "Roosevelt's Rough Riders."

When four-year-old Archie heard that Father would be going off to war, he asked, "Will he bring back a bear?"

One day while taking rifle practice at Sagamore Hill before departing for Texas, TR lay flat on the ground taking aim at a life-size paper image of a man tacked to a tree. Eleven-year-old Ted watched and waited for the bang of the gun. When the bullet punched a hole in the target, he exclaimed, "Excellent shot, Father!"

"Bunnies mustn't talk," TR admonished. "Father needs to concentrate on shooting if he is to kill enough Spaniards to win the war."

When he departed Sagamore Hill for San Antonio, he told the bunnies they were not to cry. Soon after he arrived in Texas, the first of many letters arrived with vivid descriptions of the training camp and about Rough Riders who exhibited all the qualities he had taught his bunnies to value and live by. The soldiers he and Colonel Wood were training, he wrote, were "obedient and yet thoroughly self-reliant and self-helpful, not afraid of anything and able to take care of themselves under all circumstances."

The second in command at the camp (known as Camp Wood, after the number-one in command) wrote home that he was happy to report that he was "fully measuring up." He noted that he felt "both astonished and pleased at my own ability in the line of tactics."

Not all his letters were so self-confident. Edith read one aloud to Ted and Kermit in which their father coldly calculated his chances of survival at one in three. When he said that if he did not survive he wanted Ted and Kermit to have his sword and revolver, the boys buried their heads in her lap and cried.

Along with the letters Ted and his siblings could turn to vivid accounts in newspapers of the adventures of "Teddy Roosevelt's Rough Riders" as they trained in Texas and then as they camped near Tampa Bay, Florida, awaiting orders to embark for Cuba. When Edith showed Ted where Tampa Bay was on a map of Florida, he said proudly, "I suppose Father will get the war wind full in his face."

In relating this in a letter to TR, Edith wrote, "He says he should think every boy should want to go to war and wished you could have taken him just to clean your guns for, of course, he would not expect a shot at the enemy! He subsequently remarked he was sure he would be angry in a battle and ping away at the foe as fast as he could ram in cartridges. Ted hopes there will be one battle so you can be in it, but come out safe. Not every boy has a father who has seen a battle."

When the calendar of war afforded time for Edith to travel to Tampa to spend a few days in a hotel near TR before the Rough Riders sailed for Cuba, he wrote home to the children, "It has been a real holiday to have darling mother here. Yesterday I brought her out to the camp, and she saw it all—the men drilling, the tents in long company streets, horses being taken to water, my little horse Texas, the colonel and the majors, and finally the mountain lion and the jolly little dog Cuba [regimental mascots]. The mountain lion is not much more than a kitten as yet, but it is very cross and treacherous. . . . Mother stays at a big hotel. . . . There are nearly thirty thousand troops here now, besides the sailors from the war-ships in the bay. At night the corridors and piazzas are thronged with officers of the army and navy, and now they are all going to Cuba to war against the Spaniards."

On the evening of June 13, 1898, the War Department in Washington, D.C., flashed to the troopships at Tampa to sail. Of this energizing and exhilarating spectacle, the author who had penned *The Naval War of 1812* and had regaled his namesake with tales of heroic men going into battle wrote:

Ship after ship weighed anchor and went slowly ahead under half-steam for the distant mouth of the harbor, the bands playing, the flags flying, the rigging black with the clustered soldiers, cheering and shouting to those left behind on the quay and to their fellows on the other ships. The channel was very tortuous; and we anchored before we had gone far down, after coming within an ace of a bad collision with another transport. The next morning we were all again under way, and in the afternoon the great fleet steamed southwest until Tampa Light sank in the distance.

Before sailing he had written to his brother-in-law, Douglas Robinson, "Those of us who come out of it safe will be bound together all our lives by a very strong tie."

American history had recorded no greater armada.

The world would not witness anything like it until an even larger fleet ferried the firstborn son of Theodore Roosevelt and thousands of other men across the English Channel to storm the beaches of Normandy on the sixth of June 1944.

4

When the transport *Yucatan* and other troopships anchored off the small port of Daiquirí in the eastern Cuban province of Oriente on June 22, 1898, Theodore Roosevelt and his Rough Riders found themselves in the company of a handful of newspapermen who called themselves "war correspondents." Among them was Richard Harding Davis, an employee of newspaper magnate William Randolph Hearst. Clad in khakis, a pith helmet, and a white turban sash, Davis peered from the deck of the *Seguranca* and saw an island "all brilliant, gorgeous, and glaring" and a sea of "indigo blue, like the blue in a washtub" and the green of the mountains like that of "corroded copper" beneath a sun "like a limelight in its fierceness." In the coming days he and his journalistic companions would furnish the war-hungry people at home with unvarnished descriptions of a reality that had nothing in common with tales of glories of war that Ted read in Tennyson and Kipling.

Two days after Roosevelt and the Rough Riders went ashore and into their first battle, the front page of Mr. Hearst's *New York Herald* offered Ted the account by Davis of a battle at a place called Las Guasimas. "After ten or fifteen minutes of hot work the firing fell off some," he wrote, "and Lieutenant Colonel Roosevelt ordered his men back to the trail, narrowly escaping a bullet himself which struck a tree at one side of the road."

A correspondent for the magazine *Leslie's Illustrated Weekly* caused Ted's chest to swell with pride as he read of the Rough Riders:

It is a very typical American regiment. All have the spirit of adventure strong within them, and they are in the Cuban chapparal because they see the perils, because they are patriotic, because, as some think, every gentleman owes a debt to his country, and this is the time to pay. And all these men, drawn from so many sources ... have been roughly, quickly, and effectively moulded and formed into a fighting regiment by the skillful discipline of Leonard Wood, and by the inspiration of Theodore Roosevelt, their lieutenant-colonel, who has laid down a high place in the administration at Washington and come hither to Cuba because thus only can he live up to his idea of conduct by offering his life to his country when war comes.

As word came that the Americans were arrayed to attack the city of Santiago, Edith wrote to her sister, Emily, that the "suspense is hard." Noting that Alice "is a great comfort," she continued, "The three older children suffer greatly from apprehensions."

At one o'clock in the afternoon, July 1, 1898, as Edith ate lunch with the children on the veranda at Sagamore Hill, Richard Harding Davis was observing her husband in action again. Waving his hat with the blue-and-white polka-dot bandanna of the Rough Riders dangling from it, Roosevelt led a charge up Kettle Hill in the San Juan Heights overlooking Santiago.

Davis's account, published the next day, read:

They had no glittering bayonets, they were not massed in regular array. There were a few men in advance bunched together and creeping up a steep, sunny hill, the top of which roared and flashed with flame. The men held their guns pressed against their breasts and stepped heavily as they climbed. Behind these first few, spreading out like a fan, were single lines of men, slipping and scrambling in the smooth grass, moving forward with difficulty, as though they were wading waist high through water, moving slowly, carefully, with strenuous effort. It was much more wonderful than any swinging charge could have been. They walked to greet death at every step, many of them as they advanced, sinking suddenly or pitching forward, and disappearing in the high grass, but the others waded on, stubbornly, forming a thin blue line that kept creeping higher and higher up the hill. It was inevitable as a rising tide. It was a miracle of self-sacrifice, a triumph of bulldog courage, which one watched with breathless wonder.

• • •

No more breathtaking and wondrous to witnesses such as Davis had been the sight of the man at the head of the attack. "One's instinct was to call them back," Davis reported. "You felt that someone had blundered and that these few men were blindly following some madman's mad order." Correspondent Stephen Crane wrote, "It was the best moment of anybody's life."

Eleven-year-old Ted Roosevelt's father would call it his "crowded hour."

Although newspapers were filled with accounts of the charge, it was a letter to Edith from a family friend, Bob Ferguson, that couched the event in personal terms. Beginning with "Dear Mrs. Theodore," he wrote, "No hunting trip had ever equalled it in Theodore's eyes. All the way down to the next line of entrenchments he encouraged us to 'look at these damned Spanish dead!'"

When the city of Santiago fell a few days later, and with the Spanish fleet sunk before the withering fire of guns as it tried to escape blockading American battleships, Spain was driven out of the Western Hemisphere. John Hay, the secretary of state and close friend of TR, called the conflict "a splendid little war."

Roosevelt wrote to Edith, "For three days I have been at the extreme front of the firing line. How I escaped I know not."

Ted would learn later that in the race toward the top of Kettle Hill his father had fired his pistol twice, killing one fleeing foe. By TR's accounting, out of the 490 Rough Riders who had marched into the battle for the San Juan Heights, 89 were killed or wounded. He regarded the fact that no regiment in the cavalry division suffered heavier losses a point of pride.

He wrote to Ted that "a great many" of his men had been killed. Of those who survived, he promised Ted, "you will see some at my house often."

In reading accounts of the assault, Ted noted that men who had taken part in it agreed that the victory was attributable to the man who led them. Captain C. J. Stevens of the 2d Cavalry attested, "By his gallantry and strong personality he contributed most materially to the success." Major M. J. Jenkins of the First Cavalry asserted that "unhesitating gallantry in taking the initiative against intrenchments lined by men armed with rapid fire guns certainly won him the highest consideration and admiration of all who witnessed his conduct throughout the day."

General Samuel S. Sumner urged the Department of the Army that "as a reward for conspicuous gallantry at the battle of San Juan," Roosevelt be given the Congressional Medal of Honor. In support of the recommendation, Leonard Wood, who had been promoted to general, wrote that in leading "a very desperate and extremely gallant charge" TR set "a most inspiring example" by encouraging the troops "to pass over the open country intervening between their position and the trenches of the enemy."

Unfortunately, as these and other letters supporting the Medal of Honor made their way toward the War Department, Secretary R. A. Alger seethed with anger over another letter that had appeared in the newspapers following the close of hostilities. Signed by Roosevelt, it cited outbreaks of yellow fever and malaria in army camps. Writing, "The whole command is so weakened and shattered as to be ripe for dying like rotten sheep," TR demanded the immediate withdrawal of the entire army from Cuba to Puerto Rico.

While praising Roosevelt in a personal letter as "a most gallant officer and in the battle before Santiago," Alger felt insulted and undermined. He bristled at the criticism and refused to endorse the recommendation for the Medal of Honor.

Although TR remained silent on the rejection, Edith later told Ted that his father's being denied the nation's accolade for bravery was "one of the bitterest disappointments of his life."

Early in August, Edith informed the Sagamore Hill bunnies that their father was on his way home. On the fifteenth of the month, he bounded down the gangplank of the transport ship *Miami* tied to a pier at Fort Pond Bay at Montauk, New York. Suntanned and twenty pounds lighter than when he had boarded the *Yucatan,* and with the pistol he'd used to kill a Spaniard belted to his hip, he told a reporter he was "feeling disgracefully well" and that he'd had "a bully time and a bully fight." He added with a toothy grin, "I feel as big and strong as a bull moose!"

With the Rough Riders settled into an encampment for the process of being disbanded, Edith took Ted, Kermit, and fourteen-year-old Alice to Montauk for an overnight visit. When their heroic father allowed the boys to sleep in his tent, they were thrilled. Ted took the cot, and Kemit sprawled on an air mattress. Father made a bed atop a table that served as his desk.

On September 15, 1898, the hundred thirty-third day since he'd said good-bye to the bunnies to go off to war, TR watched through teary eyes as Color Sgt. A. P. Wright struck the regimental flag and the Rough Riders passed into history and, as their "colonel" would write in a book about them, "to their homes in the North and South, the few going back to the great cities of the East, the many turning toward the plains, the mountains, and deserts of the West . . . as gallant fighters as ever wore the United States uniform."

TR went back to Sagamore Hill. One day not long after his return, a reporter appeared on the front porch and asked Archie, "Where is the Colonel?"

The little boy eyed the man suspiciously and replied, "I don't know where the Colonel is, but Father is having a bath."

As though Father had never been away, Ted noted, the rambling hilltop house was again peopled by visitors who stayed for dinner and talked about politics. What they had in mind, Ted learned, was that the hero of San Juan Hill, now the most famous man in America, run as a Republican for governor of New York. In a lifelong Theodore Roosevelt–habit of seeing gloom ahead, he wrote to a friend, "I haven't bothered myself a particle about the nomination, and have no idea whether it will be made or not. In the first place, I would rather have led this regiment [the Rough Riders] than be Governor of New York three times over. In the next place, while on the whole I should like the office of Governor and would not shirk it, the position will be one of such extreme difficulty and I shall have to offend so many good friends of mine, that I should breathe a sigh of relief were it not offered to me."

When the offer came in the form of the Republican nomination, the bunnies shared what Alice would describe years later as "indescribable excitement of our father running for office." They also shared the loss of his company as he traveled across, up, and down the state making speeches, shaking hands of voters, and granting interviews to reporters. They also struggled to get used to hearing Father addressed as "Teddy." Great fun was had in singing campaign songs and chanting slogans. And they delighted in mocking Father's Democratic opponent, a judge named Augustus Van Wyck.

A few days before the people of New York were to decide if they wanted Theodore Roosevelt as their governor, the candidate returned to Sagamore Hill for a day of rest. Edith noted, "Theodore is under such a strain. Last week he made a hundred and two speeches, most of them in the open air." The children welcomed him as always, and as usual, he came home with a bag of presents for them.

On the night of Election Day as Ted and the other children slept, their father, mother, and Alice had dinner and retired to the library to await the outcome. When a reporter declared that Roosevelt had won, Ted was awakened by a shout from Alice.

"The jubilation thus heralded, went on all day," wrote William Harbaugh in his book on the Roosevelt family of Sagamore Hill. "The children in the school caught the general contagion and started their morning exercises with a demonstration their teachers had difficulty in bringing under control."

A second, more formal celebration occurred at the Cove Neck School on the afternoon of Christmas Eve. It had been a custom of Theodore Roosevelt to come to the school at Christmas for the students' holiday program, and to make a speech. This year's occasion was to feature a recitation by Ted, but he had come down with the grippe and was unable to perform. Kermit's contribution was a recitation of "Higgelty Piggelty Went to School." One of the speakers was James Gallagher, whom Ted had once vanquished in a fight. When the guest of honor got up to address the group, Ted whispered, "Father, don't speak long."

TR's message was the one he had given each year: have a good time as long as you live, but do something worthwhile. "Work hard and do the things you set out to do."

When he'd finished to louder-than-customary approval, he delighted in helping Edith hand out the Christmas gifts they'd brought for every student.

Seven days later, on New Year's Eve, Ted and the other bunnies found themselves on a train bound for the state capital and the governor's mansion. The next day, January 1, 1899, the air was so cold in Albany that it froze the brass instruments of the band that escorted the new governor to the Capitol.

While Governor Roosevelt rapidly adapted to his new role, Edith quickly settled the family in their new home and arranged for their education. Archie and Quentin were too young for schooling. Alice and Ethel were placed in the keeping of an English governess. For Ted and Kermit it was the Albany Military Academy. All but Alice enjoyed their new surroundings. She found Albany so dull that, Edith wrote, "she cares neither for athletics nor good works, the two resources of youth in this town."

A constant source of diversion for the younger children remained their ever-ready-for-a-game father. One day when political leader Gifford Pinchot arrived for a meeting, he found the governor of New York helping a group of giggling children "escape" by lowering them out of a second-story window with a rope. But Father's being governor, the requirements of schooling, and the strictures of living in the Executive Mansion placed severe limits on the rambunctious play they were used to enjoying at Sagamore Hill. Consequently, parent and children looked forward to the end of the legislative session in late spring and a return to such outdoors delights as swimming, riding, hiking, and tennis at Oyster Bay.

Especially thrilling for Ted in that first summer respite from Albany was the family's annual Fourth of July celebration. He led seventeen boys tossing firecrackers as they pretended to be Rough Riders in a parade from Cove Neck to Sagamore Hill. That evening saw a dazzling display of fireworks. A pyrotechnic picture of the hero of San Juan Hill, noted Edith in a letter, was "accompanied by the national salute of twenty-one bombs which quite overcame some of the smaller children." An added thrill for the children was helping TR and other adults in stamping out grass fires kindled by rocket sparks. When the last Roman candle had lit up the sky, the children sat in a circle on the ground to listen to Theodore Roosevelt's adventures in the wild and woolly west, from roping cattle to sitting around a campfire under a sky sparkling with a hundred million stars. Wrote one observer, "He knew how to tell such a story so boys would feel the sting of the smoke in their eyes."

All too soon summer was over and Ted found himself back in Albany and returning to studies. Mindful that much was expected of a Roosevelt, he understood that his precollege schooling was to be at the Groton School in Massachusetts and then college at his father's alma mater, Harvard. He also understood from his father's lectures that while social status afforded the opportunity to obtain a superb formal education, he must "beware of associating only with people of his own caste." That was TR's purpose in enrolling him in the Cove school. It would assure that Ted would be with children of working-class families. Theodore Roosevelt Jr. was expected by his father to realize "that he must deal with the mass of men; that he must go out and stand shoulder to shoulder with his friends of every rank, and must bear himself in the hurly-burly." At the same time, Ted had been taught, he must not be frightened by "unpleasant features of the contest," and he "must not expect to have it all his own way." He should expect to meet with checks and to make mistakes, but if he persevered he would "achieve a measure of success and do a measure of good "such as is never possible to the refined, cultivated, intellectual men who shrink aside from the actual fray."

There was also an obligation of the educated man, TR believed, to involve himself in politics. Believing this, he had come straight out of Harvard and into the fray of running for a seat in the New York State Assembly, been elected, and "risen like a rocket" in his second term to be chosen Republican leader. When called upon to run for mayor of New York in 1886, he had given it his all, and although he lost, he did not abandon his belief that the educated man of means must remain committed to public service. Now, he was governor of New York and in a position to change people's lives for the better. At the July 4th celebration he addressed the people of Oyster Bay on their "duty of being true to ourselves; the duty of bringing up our children to be good citizens."

At the start of the ceremonies in Audrey Park on that Independence Day, the Reverend Mr. Henry Washburn, rector of the Episcopal church attended by the Roosevelts of Sagamore Hill, had electrified the townspeople by declaring that they were welcoming into their midst not only the governor of New York, but a future president of the United States. When the sentiment was echoed by the Reverend John L. Bedford, a Roman Catholic priest, a reporter for the *New York Times* noted, and wrote for his readers, "The Governor's expression was ludicrously like that of a boy trying to keep an impassive face while something pleases him."

Enthusiasms of two clerics and the people of Oyster Bay notwithstanding, whatever plan the governor might have with regard to seeking the presidency as a Republican would have to wait. The party's nomination in 1900 would go to the present occupant of the White House, William H. McKinley. However, there were indications that McKinley's vice president, Garret A. Hobart, might not choose to run again. When political allies such as Henry Cabot Lodge inquired if TR might be interested in seeking the nomination, he replied that the office was "about the last thing for which I would care."

Pressure on him to change his mind increased after November 21, 1899, when Hobart died. Asked by a newspaper reporter if he would accept the vice-presidential nomination, TR was emphatically negative: "I would rather be in private life than be vice president. I believe I can be of more service to my country as governor of the state of New York."

This adamant position remain unchanged in June 1900 when he said good-bye to Ted and the rest of the family to travel to Philadelphia for the Republican National Convention. Called upon to second the nomination of McKinley, he galvanized the delegates with rousing rhetoric that exhorted an America "glorious in youth and strength" to look to the future "with fearless and eager eyes, rejoicing as a strong man to run a race."

When he finished speaking, reported the correspondent of the *New York Times,* the band struck up the theme song of Teddy Roosevelt's Rough Riders, "There'll Be a Hot Time in the Old Town Tonight." The conventioneers reacted with "wild spontaneous roars and tumults of applause" and let it be known that they would not be satisfied until he accepted the nomination.

Yielding to their demand, TR said to Republican Party chairman Mark Hanna, "I am as strong as a bull moose, and you can use me to the limit."

A result of the nomination was a flood of visitors to Sagamore Hill, including a horde of reporters and photographers. But when two cameramen hid in bushes to snap photographs of the bunnies as they were swimming, Father lost his temper. Threatening to take "legal steps," he thundered that he would not have the innocent freedom of his children trampled. "I am a public man and free game," he said, "but my house is my castle. In my home I will be let alone."

After his return from Philadelphia to Sagamore Hill, the children learned that he would be leaving immediately for Oklahoma City and a Rough Riders reunion, with a stop on the way back to call on President McKinley at his home in Canton, Ohio. When the children learned that the trip would coincide with the traditional Sagamore Hill July 4th celebration, he promised them that the festivities would occur as usual, but a few days later. Less than a week after the delayed fireworks illuminated the skies above Sagamore Hill, he was gone again to campaign throughout the West.

The summer for Ted was a period of the combined emotions of missing his father and anxiety about leaving home in September to go to Groton. Edith wrote to her sister, Emily, that getting him ready for school "is rather sad work for me and has to be done with a very smiling face for fear of working on his feelings unduly."

The plan had been for TR to escort Ted to Groton, but because he was on the campaign trail, the bittersweet task fell to Edith. A week after leaving him in Massachusetts she wrote to Emily, "You can't think how we miss Ted. The house seems so empty without him."

On the Nashua and Squannacook Rivers about thirty-five miles northwest of Boston, the town of Groton was rich in colorful history. It had been settled and incorporated in 1655, destroyed twenty years later by Indians during King Philip's War, and rebuilt. According to legend a man named John Chamberlain of Groton killed Paugus, chief of the Pequawkets, and then killed Paugus's son when he came to town seeking revenge. Chamberlain threw the body into the mill brook. Consequently, the stream had been named Paugus Brook. Interred nearby in the Old Burying Ground were the remains of Capt. Job Shattuck, a hero of the American Revolution. When he later took part in Shay's Rebellion, he was tried for treason and condemned to be hanged, but was reprieved twice and then pardoned. Opposite Town Hall stood a house that had been visited by Gen. U.S. Grant. In the shadow of the spire of the First Parish Meeting House was the town common, where Minutemen had assembled on the morning of April 19, 1775, to make ready to confront British soldiers marching out from Boston.

One hundred nine years later, on a ninety-acre farm, the Reverend Endicott Peabody realized his dream of establishing an Episcopal school for boys where the headmaster, as in English schools, would be a pastor. Founded in 1884 and named after the town, it offered parents the assurance that their sons would receive both religious training and secular teaching, along with physical conditioning through athletics.

Because Ted's education had been garnered at Cove Neck School when he was living at Oyster Bay, at schools in Washington when his father was in the government there, and at the military academy in Albany, he began the six-year program at Groton educationally behind other students of his age by two years. Never having been separated from both parents and his siblings, he felt severe pangs of homesickness, but soon dispelled the loneliness by playing football with his dormitory team. Three weeks later he proudly noted in a letter to home that he had been named captain.

Presently, reports reaching Sagamore Hill became a cause of parental concern that Ted had somehow turned into a bully. One of these came from a family friend whose son was also at Groton. Edward Sanford Martin, editor of the humorous weekly *Life*, informed TR that Ted had "licked all the boys in his form." When TR seemed alarmed, he hastened to add that Ted had done so in "amicable wrestling and boxing bouts." Now looking pleased, TR confessed that some of the responsibility for Ted's pugnaciousness was attributable to his father's instilling his son with "fighting proclivities."

After a teacher rebuked him for "scrapping" during study hours, the teacher returned to Ted's room to apologize for having been "unduly severe," Ted replied, "Oh, no matter. It will make me remember not to do it again."

While adjusting to school life and getting used to being away from home, Ted followed his famous father's campaign-trail activities in newspapers. Almost everywhere he traveled on behalf of President McKinley and himself, according to the reporters, he was greeted by huge, enthusiastic crowds. But there were a few notable exceptions. When he arrived in Cripple Creek, Colorado, backers of Democratic candidate William Jennings Bryan greeted him with a hail of rocks. Ted read that only a rush by a flying wedge of Rough Riders saved him from injury.

He also read with much amusement a satirical account written by the humorist Finley Peter Dunne of one appearance. According to Dunne's imaginary philosopher "Mr. Dooley," at one gathering "Gov'nor Rosenfelt bit his way through th' throng" and brought down "with a well-aimed shot th' chairman iv th' Dimmycratic commity."

On the Saturday before the election the vice-presidential candidate was in New York City for a final rally at Madison Square. A heavy rain was falling as he arrived on Madison Square, and as he made his way to the auditorium for his speech, ninety thousand people shouted, "Teddy, Teddy, Teddy." In a newspaper story about the event, Ted read his father's answer to a reporter who had asked if Roosevelt feared that the drenching might lead to a cold or a touch of rheumatism. TR exclaimed, "Rheumatism? A cold? Why, I never felt better in my life! There isn't a twinge in a single muscle. In fact, I believe the shower bath did me good. Tell me honestly, do you really think that such a demonstration under any conditions whatsoever could make a man sick? No, no! It's not that sort of thing that gives a man a cold. The atmosphere may be chilly, but your flesh keeps you warm when you get a welcome like that."

With the campaigning done, Ted awaited election day with confidence that when all the ballots were tallied, Father would be the next vice president of the United States. His faith was justified as the Republicans won their biggest victory since 1872, garnering a plurality of nearly a million votes and a 292-to-155 tally in the Electoral College.

With the rigors of campaigning finished, TR sought refreshment in a hunting trip in the wintry wilds of the West. From Keystone Ranch, Colorado, on January 14, 1901, he wrote a letter that began, "Blessed Ted." It demonstrated the narrative skill which made many of his books bestsellers and provided much of the income that supported his family.

The letter introduced Ted to "the hunter Goff, a fine, quiet, hardy fellow, who knows his business thoroughly." Starting soon after sunrise from the frontier town of Meeker, they made their way, "hunting as we went, across the high, exceedingly rugged hills, until sunset."

Curled up on his bed in his room in the Groton dormitory, Ted felt as if he were at his father's side "hunting cougar and lynx or, as they are called out here, 'lion' and 'cat.'"

The letter went on:

The first cat we put up gave the dogs a two hours' chase, and got away among some high cliffs. In the afternoon we put up another, and had a very good hour's run, the dogs baying until the glens rang again to the echoes as they worked hither and thither through the ravines. We walked our ponies up and down steep, rock-strewn, and tree-clad slopes, where it did not seem possible a horse could climb, and on the level places we got one or two smart gallops. At last the lynx went up a tree. Then I saw a really funny sight. Seven hounds had been doing the trailing, while a large brindled blood-hound and two half- breeds between collie and bull stayed behind Goff, running so close to his horse's heels that they continually bumped into them, which he accepted with philosophic compo-sure. Then the dogs proceeded literally *to climb the tree,* which was a many-forked pinion; one of the half-breeds, named Tony, got up certainly sixteen feet, until the lynx, which looked like a huge and exceedingly malevolent pussy-cat, made vicious dabs at him. I shot the lynx low, so as not to hurt his skin.

Describing hours spent with a friend and a pack of dogs, tracking a cougar that had killed a deer the night before, he continued, "Soon we saw the lion in a treetop, with two of the dogs so high up among the branches that he was striking at them. He was more afraid of us than the dogs, and as soon as he saw us he took a great flying leap and was off, the pack close behind. In a few hundred yards they had him up another tree. They could have killed him by themselves. But he bit and clawed four of them, and for fear that he might kill one I ran in and stabbed him behind the shoulder, thrusting the knife right into his heart. I have always wished to kill a cougar as I did this one, with dogs and the knife."

The tale was even more thrilling for Ted because the knife his father used was one that Ted had given him.

For the swearing-in of Theodore Roosevelt as vice president of the United States in a ceremony held on March 4, 1901, in the chamber of the U.S. Senate, Ted arrived in Washington, D.C., from Groton wearing trousers of one suit, the coat of another, and vest of a third. Shocked that his mother was not pleased, he said, "Now, Mother, you know you wrote me to come in my best clothes, and these are the best."

At an inaugural luncheon held at the White House he drank two glasses of champagne, thinking it was "fizzy water." Edith noted in a letter to her sister, "Happily, it took no effect whatever, which speaks volumes either for Ted's head or the President's champagne."

Following the festivities, Ted returned to Groton until spring vacation, to be spent at Sagamore Hill. When TR was invited by his successor in the governorship, Benjamin Odell, to attend a dinner in Albany with state Republican leaders, TR pointed out that if he attended he would have to "give up divers sprees we have planned together and which he [Ted] has four small cousins coming out to share."

When Ted returned to Groton, TR wrote from Oyster Bay on May 7, 1901, proving that he was keeping his pledge not to push Ted too hard:

It was the greatest fun seeing you, and I really had a satisfactory time with you, and came away feeling that you were doing well. I am entirely satisfied with your standing, both in your studies and in athletics. I want you to do well in sports, and I want even more to have you do well with your books; but I do not expect you to stand first in either, if so to stand would cause you overwork and hurt your health. I always believe in going hard at everything, whether it is Latin or mathematics, boxing or football, but at the same time I want to keep the sense of proportion. It is never worth while to absolutely exhaust one's self or to take big chances unless for an adequate object. I want you to keep in training the faculties which would make you, if the need arose, able to put your last ounce of pluck and strength into a contest. But I do not want you to squander these qualities. To have you play football as well as you do, and make a good name in boxing and wrestling, and be cox of your second crew, and stand second or third in the studies, is all right. I should rather be sorry to see you drop too near the middle of your class, because, as you cannot enter college until you are nineteen, and will therefore be a year later in entering life, I want you to be prepared in the best possible way, so as to make up for the delay [because of having been two years behind]. But I know that all you can do will do to keep substantially the position in class that you have kept so far, and I have entire trust in you, for you have always deserved it.

Looking forward to being freed from school for the summer, Ted glee-fully read in a letter dated May 31, 1901, "Have you made up your mind whether you would like to try shooting the third week in August or the last week in July?"

They planned a week's shooting in Long Island marshlands and fish-ing off the sloop *Showabase*. But for a moment the vacation seemed im-periled when TR's friend Paul Morton, president of the Santa Fe Rail-road, announced that he hoped to visit Roosevelt at Sagamore Hill at the same time as the outing. TR promptly informed the railway tycoon, "On Monday I start with two of my sons and four of their little cousins for a four days' shooting trip, and it would break their hearts if I aban-doned it."

Ted would write of the adventure, "It was a most courageous under-taking on Father's part, and the fact that we all returned uninjured speaks volumes of his discipline. Kermit was so small that, when he shot, Father had to support the gun. We wandered about the marshes and were bitten by mosquitoes. We sat patiently in eelgrass blinds and felt the thrill that comes when the first birds circle down half-seen in the gray of early dawn."

Occupying an office that he regarded as "a fifth wheel on a coach" and "not a stepping-stone to anything but oblivion," Vice President Theodore Roosevelt took up his pen late that summer, as Ted returned to Groton, to write his friend William Howard Taft, who was serving as governor-general of the Philippines. He confessed, "I am rather ashamed to say that I am enjoying the perfect ease of my life at present. I am just living out in the country, doing nothing but ride and row with Mrs. Roo-sevelt, and walk and play with the children; chop trees in the afternoon and read books by the fire in the evening."

At summer's end he set out on a speaking tour that included a meet-ing of the Vermont Fish and Game League on Isle La Motte in Lake Champlain. Not many miles away in Buffalo, New York, the president of the United States was concluding a two-day visit to the Pan American Ex-position. In an appearance at the Temple of Music he was to greet any-one from the public who might wish to shake his hand. As McKinley ar-rived to take his place amid a bower of palm trees, his secretary, George B. Courtelyou, pleaded with him to cancel the event. With a fatherly smile that had helped persuade American voters to grant him a second term as president, McKinley asked the worried aide, "Why should I? No one would want to hurt me."

Moments later, as an organist played a Bach cantata, the president smiled at a young man whose right hand was wrapped in a handkerchief. When the president extended his left hand, the man's seemingly injured hand swung up to press a pistol to McKinley's chest.

He fired it twice.

When the news reached Ted that a fanatical anarchist named Leon Czolgosz had shot the president, but that McKinley had survived and was expected to recover, he also learned that his father had raced from the political meeting at Lake Champlain to Buffalo. Three days later, the president's physician declared McKinley was out of danger and that the vice president could join his family on a planned vacation in the Adirondacks.

Following the crisis in newspapers at the Groton School, and confident that his father would not be sworn in as president of the United States, Ted returned to his studies. But late in the day on September 14 he learned that McKinley's condition had taken a sudden turn for the worse and he had died. News accounts also reported that Vice President Roosevelt had been notified of McKinley's impending death while climbing the highest peak in the Adirondacks. He had scrambled down Mount Marcy to again rush to Buffalo. Shortly after three in the afternoon of the fourteenth, in Buffalo's Wilcox Library, surrounded by members of McKinley's cabinet, guests, and reporters, Secretary of War Elihu Root turned to his friend Theodore Roosevelt and suggested that he take the oath of office without delay. It was administered by Judge John R. Hazel.

What all this meant to Ted was unclear until the headmaster came to his room to tell him that a telegram from his mother had been received with instructions that Ted was to depart as soon as possible for home in order to accompany her on a train to Washington. His father would precede them aboard the special train carrying President McKinley's body to the capital for the state funeral.

Upon Ted's arrival at Sagamore Hill, Edith gave him mourning bands for his hat and the left sleeve of his dark suit. As they waited to board a ferry at West Twenty-third Street to cross the Hudson River to the Pennsylvania Railroad depot on the New Jersey side, they found that a considerate stationmaster had set up barricades to keep reporters and photographers at bay. But one managed to approach Ted to ask if he was more pleased to have his father president or to have shot his first deer?

Peering through his thick glasses at the newspaperman with disbelief and contempt, Ted replied, "I have no time to answer such questions."

Reporters covering the funeral services at the White House observed the fourteen-year-old son of the new president in his somber suit with a black crepe bow on the left sleeve. They found him grave and courteous and noted for their readers that Ted presented a "strong and sturdy" figure" and a "modesty of demeanor and appreciation of the solemn occasion." Others thought he resembled his father, had a surprisingly firm handshake for a boy his age, and that he looked "seriously at the world through a pair of gold-rimmed spectacles."

The boy who had been the son of a famous author, the son of a member of the Civil Service Commission, son of the president of the New York Police Board, son of the assistant secretary of the navy, son of the hero of the Spanish-American War, son of the governor of New York, and son of the vice president of the United States, was suddenly the son of the *president.* The rude question posed by the reporter at the ferry slip, Ted realized, had signaled a dramatic change in his status. From now on, evidently, he would be fair game for journalists.

A longtime resident of Oyster Bay informed an inquiring reporter from the *New York Evening World* that young Teddy was "just as original as his dad and will be heard from someday." The president's namesake, the man continued, was "a persistent, energetic little chap" who never let up. "He works hard at his books and he works hard at his play, like his father, and when he rides, he goes like a cowboy chasing a Comanche."

Because he was a student at the Groton School, Ted found himself mercifully removed from the prying eyes of newspapermen and lenses of photographers in Washington who were fascinated by the flock of Roosevelt children ensconced in the White House. But he learned that he could not escape his role as the president's oldest son. When a classmate at Groton teased him by calling him "the first boy in the land," the taunt was answered with what one observer described as "a thrashing."

Relieved that distance removed him from the Washington limelight, he read with disbelief a story in the *New York Herald* that "not a single head" of his brothers and sisters "had been turned in the fierce light that beats upon the American throne." Knowing Kermit, Archibald, Quentin,

Ethel, and Alice, he could not imagine them not relishing the attention. Although their father had warned reporters to "lay off" his children, they proved irresistible. Stories of their antics constantly appeared in print. One told of a schoolteacher who'd asked Kermit what his father did for a living. Kermit replied, "Father? Oh, Father's *it*." Another reported President Roosevelt's rebuke of Quentin for walking on stilts in a flower garden, with Quentin retorting, "I don't see what good it does me for you to be president. I can't do anything here. I wish I was back home."

Then came the story of Archie's calico pony, named Algonquin. With Archie sick in bed with the measles, Quentin decided to cheer up his brother by taking Algonquin to his room. He did so by persuading the White House coachman, Charlie Lee, to help him get the pony upstairs by way of the elevator. And there was Sister, whom newspaper writers were calling "Princess Alice" and the "belle of the White House." A feature in Chicago's *Tribune* saw the eighteen-year-old "straight and slender but supple and graceful; athletic but not robust; likes to read, but is not studious; loves music, but dislikes the drudgery of practice; not domestic in her tastes but accepts gracefully the duties which of necessity fall to her."

Content to see the nation's attention concentrated on Alice and the younger children who had to live in the president's house in Washington, D.C., Ted happily resumed studies at the Groton School and looked forward to joining the family for Christmas at Sagamore Hill in the hope that somehow the reporters and photographers could be kept at a distance. He found his wish realized as guards posted at approaches to the hilltop residence, and sharp-eyed watchers at the train station and boat landings, shunted away uninvited visitors.

Once again at Groton and feeling shielded from the scrutiny of the press, he settled down for the long winter months of January and February 1902 while keeping up on the activities of his father, mother, and siblings through letters and newspapers. But in February when he came down with pneumonia, he found himself thrust into headlines. One in the *New York Times* noted with alarm: DOUBLE PNEUMONIA. During the following week, the entire country waited for bulletins. Americans held their collective breath as the president and Mrs. Roosevelt and Alice rushed up to Massachusetts to be at his side.

With an announcement from Groton that the crisis had passed, the *Times* declared that Ted was "safe" and that the president was returning to the capital. Edith followed a few days later, along with Alice and Ted. TR noted his arrival "bundled to his eyes with blankets."

Accepting the fact that all the attention paid to him, Alice, and the other children would be a part of their lives for so long as their father was president, and probably after he had left office, Ted understood that life at Sagamore Hill could never be the same. The evidence of this came in June as he arrived home for summer vacation and found the newspapers referring to the homestead as "the Summer White House."

For readers who were eager to know all about the Roosevelts a reporter for the *New York Evening Sun* provided an insider's glimpse of a family morning:

> Young voices chirped and called. A maid opened the front door. There was a rush of children across the porch, down the steps, and out onto the sloping lawn. There were somersaults and impromptu wrestling matches on the dewy grass, in the cool morning air; and shouts and howls and wails; then the quick stride of the President on the wooden floor of the piazza, and more shouts, a general rough-and-tumble, followed by a united rush back into the house.

A daily feature was tennis, with fourteen-year-old Ted testing his father's footwork by dropping the ball just over the net when TR was on the backline. Doubles games matched TR and Ethel against Ted and Archie.

On the subject of boys and athletics, in an article in the August 1890 issue of the *North American Review,* TR had written, "The years of late boyhood and early manhood—say from twelve or fourteen to twenty-eight or thirty, and often much later—are those in which athletic sports prove not only the most attractive, but also the most beneficial to the individual."

Accordingly, on October 4, 1903, with Ted joined at Groton by Kermit, he wrote what he called "a preaching letter" to Kermit on the subject of the boys' playing football. Concerned that they might devote most of their attention to athletics, "because I think it tends to take up too much time," he continued, "I would rather have a boy of mine stand high in his studies than high in athletics, but I could a great deal rather have him show true manliness of character than show either intellectual or physical prowess; and I believe you and Ted both bid fair to develop just such character."

Two days later, Ted received a response to a letter he had written, in which he had expressed disappointment at having been left off the second squad of Groton School's football team because of his size and age, adding that he might be reinstated if his parents granted permission. As TR considered the plea, he was mindful that Ted had already suffered a broken collarbone, but had bravely played on to the end of the game. He had complimented Ted for having minded the injury "so little."

What Ted did not know was that his father had written to Headmaster Peabody of his concern that Ted was getting beaten up. "In addition to Ted's collarbone," he had noted in the letter, "the dentist tells me that he has killed one front tooth in football, and that tooth will get black. Now I don't care a rap for either accident in itself; but Ted is only fourteen and I am afraid that if he goes on like this he will get battered out before he can play college."

With these worries in mind, TR replied to Ted's letter by "strongly" advocating that Ted accept the decision to keep him off the second squad and that Ted recognize "the chance" of being injured. "Now, I should not in the least object to your being laid up for a season if you were striving for something worth while," he continued. "But I am by no means sure that it *is* worth your while to run the risk of being laid up for the sake of playing in the second squad. I do not know that the risk is balanced by the reward. However, I have told the Rector that as you feel so strongly about it, I think that the chance of your damaging yourself in body is outweighed by the possibility of bitterness of spirit if you could not play. Understand me, I should think mighty little of you if you permitted chagrin to make you bitter on some point where it was evidently right for you to suffer the chagrin."

Giving Ted "the benefit of the doubt," he assented to Ted's playing, but warned that if the coaches "come to the conclusion that you ought not be in the second squad, why you must come off without grumbling."

Admitting that he was "delighted to have you play football," he could not resist a chance to play the teacher:

Did you ever read Pliny's letter to Trajan, in which he speaks of its being advisable to keep the Greeks absorbed in athletics, because it distracted their minds from all serious pursuits, including soldiering, and prevented their ever being dangerous to the Romans? I have no doubt that the British officers in the Boer War had their efficiency partly reduced because they had sacrificed their legitimate duties to an inordinate and ridiculous love of sports. A man must develop his physical prowess up to a certain point; but after he has reached that point there are other things that count more. In my regiment nine-tenths of the men were better horsemen than I was, and probably two-thirds of them were better shots than I was, while on the average they were certainly hardier and more enduring. Yet after I had had them a very short while they all knew, and I knew, too, that nobody else could command them as I could. I am glad you should play football; I am glad you should box; I am glad that you should ride and shoot and walk and row as well as you do. I should be very sorry if you did not do these things. But don't ever get into the frame of mind which regards these things as constituting the end to which all your energies must be devoted, or even the major portion of your energies.

When coaches decided that Ted was not ready for the second squad and placed him on the third, he accepted the verdict as his father had hoped. In a letter from the White House on October 11, 1903, TR admitted that he had feared that if Ted were allowed to play on the second squad, he would "get smashed up" in such a serious way that the injury would "prevent your playing later" on the Groton School's varsity team "or playing for your class team when you get to Harvard."

Writing that he considered it "a little silly to run any imminent risk of a serious smash simply to play on the second squad instead of the third," he explained, "I am judging for you as I would for myself. When I was young and rode across country I was light and tough, and if I did, as actually happened, break an arm or a rib no damage ensued and no scandal was caused. Now I am stiff and heavy, and any accident to me would cause immense talk, and I do not take the chance; simply because it is not worth while. On the other hand, if I should now go to war and have a brigade as I had my regiment before Santiago, I should take any chance that was necessary; because it would be worth while. In other words, I want to make the risk to a certain accident commensurate with the object gained."

The "smashing" that TR feared occurred to Ted a few weeks later, though the injury was slight, a sprained ankle. On November 28, 1903, President Theodore Roosevelt's letter to his laid-up namesake counseled, "If I were you I should certainly get the best ankle support possible. You do not want to find next fall that Webb beats you for end because your ankle gives out and his does not. If I were in your place, if it were necessary, I should put the ankle in plaster for the next three weeks, or for as long as the doctor thinks it needful, rather than run any risk of this."

Because Ted was at Groton, and recently joined at the school by Kermit, he was able to largely avoid the public spotlight (except when he came down with pneumonia). Furthermore, why should reporters care about the president's sons when they had a much better story to tell by following the activities of their sister Alice?

Beautiful, lively, "of age," and with her own money, she was free to choose her friends and to engage in a social life separate from the often dreary and boring official events on the White House calendar. Doting journalists were constantly giving accounts of her activities and giddily predicting her imminent engagement to a veteran of the Rough Riders, a diplomat, the son of a prince, or a European nobleman. Someone had even described the color of one of her evening gowns as "Alice Blue," prompting a songwriter to pen a tune, "In My Beautiful Alice Blue Gown." According to the newspapers, she also possessed a delightfully biting wit that spared no one. A story made the rounds that during a visit to the president by TR's friend Owen Wister, Alice had burst into the president's office three or four times. Frustrated by the interruptions, the famous author of the Western novel *The Virginian* asked, "Theodore, isn't there anything you can do to control Alice?"

"I can do one of two things," TR replied. "I can be president of the United States, or I can control Alice. I cannot possibly do both."

While being in Massachusetts put Ted largely out of reach of the press, he found he was not able to elude attention when he went home to Sagamore Hill for winter and spring vacations and in the summer. An activity such as a horseback ride to visit Uncle Barnwell at his home in Sayville on the South Shore, which used to be of no concern to anyone except those who made the trek, suddenly became a news story. Noting that the president, Ted, and cousins George and Phillip Roosevelt had returned from an overnight journey to pay a call on Uncle Barnwell, a reporter for the *New York Telegram* noted that the riders seemed "somewhat fatigued," but "enthusiastic over the trip."

A story in the *New York World* asked, "Now that the President has proved by actual experience that the trip from Oyster Bay to Sayville can be made on horseback, with which new discovery will he next thrill a waiting nation?"

Impatient with being paid so much attention, Ted complained to TR's old friend from his days as police commissioner, newspaperman Jacob Riis, "I wish my father would soon be done holding office. I am sick and tired of it."

An elderly resident of Oyster Bay who claimed to have known Ted since he was a babe in arms boasted to a newspaper reporter that as Theodore Roosevelt's oldest son was growing up, they'd had "many a talk" on numerous topics. In the course of one of these confabs, the old man continued as the journalist scribbled down notes, Ted had asked, "Don't you think that it handicaps a boy to be the son of a man like my father, and especially to have the same name? Don't you know there can never be another Theodore Roosevelt? I will always be honest and upright, and I hope someday to be a great soldier, but I will always be spoken of as Theodore Roosevelt's son."

5

Among the topics discussed between Ted and his father during Ted's respite from school at Christmas of 1903 was where Ted would go to college. Having made up for the educational deficiencies that were noted on his arrival at Groton and that had placed him scholastically behind other boys his age, Ted had done so well in classes that he would be graduating from the six-year school in four. Having always expected Ted to study at his own alma mater, Harvard, TR felt surprised and dismayed to hear Ted say that he had set his heart and mind on becoming a soldier by going to the U.S. Military Academy at West Point. Should he fail to qualify there, he would give the navy a try by applying to the Naval Academy at Annapolis, Maryland.

While nothing was settled before Ted returned to Groton, TR promised to assemble the application forms and other documents dealing with qualifications at both academies and send them to Ted. He did so on January 21, 1904, enclosing the materials with a remarkable letter in which he analyzed and contrasted the merits of military and civil life. Noting that he had given a great deal of thought to the matter, "and discussed it at great length with Mother," he wrote, "I feel on the one hand that I ought to give you my best advice and yet on the other hand I do not wish to constrain you against your wishes."

After warning "Dear Ted" that "this will be a long business letter," he wrote:

> If you have definitely made up your mind that you have an over-mastering desire to be in the Navy or the Army, and that such a career is one in which you will take a really heart-felt interest—far

more so than any other—and that your greatest chance for happiness and usefulness will lie in doing this one work to which you feel yourself especially drawn—why, under such circumstances, I have but little to say. But I am not satisfied that this is really your feeling. It seemed to me more as if you did not feel drawn in any other direction, and wondered what you were going to do in life or what kind of work you would turn your hand to; and wondered if you would make a success or not; and that you therefore inclined to turn to the Navy or Army chiefly because you would then have a definite and settled career in life, and could hope to go on steadily without any great risk of failure

The letter expressed "great confidence" and a belief that Ted possessed "the ability and, above all, the energy, the perseverence, and the common sense, to win out in civil life." But in the army and navy, he asserted, "the chance for a man to show great ability and rise above his fellows does not occur on the average more than once in a generation." As evidence he cited his "melancholy" experience "down in Santiago" of seeing "how fossilized and lacking in ambition, and generally useless, were most of the men of my age and over, who had served their lives in the Army. The Navy for the last few years has been better, but for twenty years after the Civil War there was less chance in the Navy than in the Army to practice, and do, work of real consequence. I have actually known lieutenants in both the Army and the Navy who were grandfathers—men who had seen their children married before they themselves attained the grade of captain. Of course the chance may come at any time when the man of West Point or Annapolis who will have stayed in the Army or Navy finds a great war on, and therefore has the opportunity to rise high."

Conceding that graduation from West Point or the Naval Academy would oblige Ted to serve only four years of duty, he granted that Ted would obtain "an excellent education and a grounding in discipline and, in some ways, a testing of your capacity greater than I think you can in an ordinary college." On the other hand, he went on, except for the profession of an engineer, Ted would "have had nothing like special training, and would have less independence of character" and "individual initiative" than he would gain if he went to a nonmilitary school.

"Supposing you entered [one of the academies] at seventeen," he posited, "with the intention of following this course [of leaving the service after four years duty]. The result would be that at twenty-five you would leave the Army or Navy without having gone through any law school or any special technical school of any kind, and would start your life work three or four years later than your schoolfellows of today, who go to work immediately after leaving college. Of course, under such circumstances, you might study law, for instance, during the four years after graduation; but my own feeling is that a man does good work chiefly when he is in something which he intends to make his permanent work, and in which he is deeply interested."

He advised Ted to "think over these matters very seriously," warning that it would be "a great misfortune for you to start into the Army or Navy as a career, and find that you had mistaken your desires and had gone in without really weighing the matter. You ought not to enter unless you genuinely feel drawn to the life as a life-work. If so, go in; but not otherwise."

Still with the subject of a West Point education in mind, the president wrote on February 19 to tell Ted that "you have too much in you for me to be glad to see you go into the Army." But of more interest to Ted was an account of a visit to the White House by Buffalo Bill Cody. TR reported that the frontier's most famous hunter's presence for luncheon had reminded TR of his campaign train stopping in a town in Kansas when he was running for vice president. Also in town was Buffalo Bill's Wild West Show. TR continued with pleasure, "He got upon the rear platform of my car and made a brief speech on my behalf, ending with the statement that 'a cyclone from the West had come'; no wonder the rats hunted their cellars."

In a March 5 letter that Kermit shared with Ted, their ever astonishing father gleefully reported, "I am wrestling with two Japanese wrestlers three times a week. I am not the age or the build one would think to be whirled lightly over an opponent's head and batted down on a mattress without damage. But they are so skillful that I have not been hurt at all. My throat is a little sore, because once when one of them had a stranglehold I also got hold of his windpipe and thought I could perhaps choke him off before he could choke me. However, he got ahead."

While noting in a letter to Ted dated April 9 that he was "very glad I have been doing this Japanese wrestling, but when I am through with it this time I am not sure I shall ever try it again while I am so busy with other work as I am now. Often by the time I get to five o'clock in the afternoon I will be feeling like a stewed owl, after an eight hours' grapple with Senators, Congressmen, etc."

The tussles with Congress and others that had marked the Roosevelt agenda through 1903 had centered on criticism of the administration's foreign policy, especially United States intervention in a rebellion in Columbia by insurgents seeking independence for the Isthmus of Panama. Envisioning an opportunity for the United States to complete a long-abandoned French project to carve out a canal linking the Atlantic and Pacific Oceans, he told a reluctant Congress, "Under such circumstances the government of the United States would have been guilty of folly and weakness, amounting in their sum to a crime against the nation, had it not acted otherwise than it did in the revolution of November 3 that last took place in Panama. This great enterprise of building the interoceanic canal cannot be held up to gratify the whims, or out of respect to the governmental impotence, or to the even more sinister and evil peculiarities, of people who, though they dwell afar off, yet against the wish of the actual dwellers on the Isthmus, assert an unreal supremacy over the territory."

He would later boast with great satisfaction that while Congress debated, the Panama Canal was built.

At the end of May, following a visit to Washington by Ted and Kermit, he wrote to Ted that despite having "a reasonable amount of work and rather more than a reasonable amount of worry" associated with living and working in the Executive Mansion, "I do not think that any two people ever got more enjoyment out of the White House than Mother and I. We love the house itself, without and within, for its associations, for its stillness, and its simplicity. We love the garden. And we like Washington."

When he wrote this letter, he had been president for more than two and a half years, but, in his words, "an accidental" one because he had come into office as the result of the assassination of McKinley. Whether the American people would deem him worthy to continue in office in the November 1904 election remained to be seen. With confidence that the people would do so, he asserted, "I am sure that the policies for which I stand are those in accordance with which this country must be governed, and up to which we must all live in public and private life, under penalty of grave disaster to the nation."

On the campaign trail he coined a motto for his kind of government, declaring, "We must treat each man on his worth and merits as a man. We must see that each is given a square deal, because he is entitled to no more and should receive no less."

As the results were tabulated, giving him 7.6 million votes and 5.1 million for his Democratic Party opponent, Alton P. Parker, he cabled Senator Henry Cabot Lodge, "Have swept the country by majorities which astound me."

Basking in the confidence of voters and looking ahead to being sworn in as president in his own right, he welcomed reporters to cover the White House Thanksgiving Day celebration. At one point in the festivities the smaller children were seen chasing a turkey around the grounds as their father looked on laughingly. Also watching the spectacle, a correspondent for the *Boston Herald* found nothing funny in it and wrote that he considered it cruelty to an animal. Infuriated by the story, the president accused the reporter of "deliberate fabrication" and ordered agencies of the government to drop the *Herald* from lists of publications that received press releases. On behalf of the children, he also demanded a retraction and a printed apology.

After the paper complied, the news embargo was lifted, but Theodore Roosevelt's love affair with the press, which had bloomed when he was New York City's crusading commissioner of police, quickly wilted. Reporters who had delighted in relating stories about the White House children found their jobs harder to do. This was particularly true regarding Ted and Kermit at the Groton School. But as the day neared when Ted was to matriculate at Harvard (his zeal for the rigors of West Point or the U.S. Naval Academy having been squelched), the president advised, "The thing to do is to go on just as you have evidently been doing, attract as little attention as possible, do not make a fuss about the newspapermen, camera creatures [press photographers], and idiots generally, letting it be seen that you do not like them and avoid them, but not letting them betray you into any excessive irritation."

By ignoring the press, he counseled, "I believe they will soon drop you."

Written to Ted at Harvard from the White House on October 2, 1905, after TR read in a newspaper that a group of reporters and photographers had waited for Ted to show up for football, the letter was as remarkable as the one he'd penned on the subject of the life Ted could expect to find in the military. He wrote:

I saw that you were not out on the football field on Saturday and was rather glad of it, as evidently those infernal idiots were eagerly waiting for you, but whenever you do go [out for the Harvard football team], you will have to make up your mind that they will make it exceedingly unpleasant for you once or twice, and you will just have to bear it; for you can never in the world afford to let them drive you away from anything you intend to do, whether it is football or anything else, and by going about your business quietly and pleasantly, doing just what you would do if they were not there, generally they will get tired of it, and the boys themselves will see that it is not your fault, and will feel, if anything, rather a sympathy for you. Meanwhile I want you to know that we are all thinking of you and sympathizing with you the whole time; and it is a great comfort to me to have such a confidence in you and know that though these creatures can cause you a little trouble and make you feel a little downcast, they can not drive you one way or the other, or make you alter the course you have set out for yourself. This is just an occasion to show the stuff there is in you. Do not let these newspaper creatures and their kindred idiots drive you one hair's breadth from the line you had marked out in football or anything else. Avoid any fuss, if possible.

After taking his father's advice, Ted read in another letter nine days later:

I was delighted to find from your last letters that you are evidently having a good time in spite of the newspaper and kodak creatures. I guess that nuisance is now pretty well abated. Every now and then they will do something horrid; but I think you can safely, from now on, ignore them entirely.

Noting that Ted had gone out for the position of end, TR expected Ted to "find it hard to compete with the other candidates, as they are mostly heavier than you."

The Harvard alumnus, Class of 1880, also offered advice on other aspects of life on the Cambridge campus:

In my day we looked with suspicion upon all freshmen societies, and the men who tried to get them up or were prominent in them rarely amounted to much in the class afterwards. . . . Exercise your own best judgment and form some idea of what the really best fellows in the class think on the subject. Do not make the mistake of thinking that the men who are merely undeveloped are really the best fellows, no matter how pleasant and agreeable they are or how popular. Popularity is a good thing, but it is not something for which to sacrifice studies or athletics or good standing in any way; and sometimes to seek it overmuch is to lose it. I do not mean this as applying to you, but as applying to certain men who still have a great vogue at first in class, and of whom people will naturally tend to think pretty well.

In all these things I can only advise you in a very general way. You are on the ground. You know the men and the general college sentiment. You have gone in with the serious purpose of doing decently and honorably; of standing well in your studies; of showing that in athletics you mean business up to the extent of your capacity, and of getting the respect and liking of your classmates so far as they can be legitimately obtained. As to the exact methods of carrying out these objects, I must trust you.

On a stormy June morning in 1944 on a French beach code-named Utah, Brig. Gen. Ted Roosevelt would adapt this fatherly advice to the purpose of leading men into battle. It would serve him and them very well.

Part 2: Brothers in Arms

Well, I am very proud of you—and of all my boys.

—Letter from Theodore Roosevelt to Maj. Theodore Roosevelt Jr.,
American Expeditionary Force, somewhere in France, August 22, 1917

6

Having just turned eighteen, weighing 130 pounds, and bearing the same name as the twenty-sixth president of the United States, the slightly bewildered-looking, bespectacled freshman passing through the Mc-Kean Gate into Harvard Yard in September 1905 found himself unable to elude the attentions of a flock of newspapermen and photographers. Most of the cameramen acted as if they knew him personally. They yelled, "Hey, Ted," "Ted, look this way," and "Let's see that big Roosevelt smile!"

Struggling to hold his temper in check, he remembered his father's prediction that if he did nothing to acknowledge their presence they would lose interest in him and drift away. For once Father proved wrong. The "gentlemen of the press" were ubiquitous and tenacious as they way-laid him on his way to classes, dogged him to the library, caught him on Sundays going to and from services at Holden Chapel, and set up camp outside his residence, Claverly Hall.

Displeased by the relentless attention being paid to Ted by the press, the president of the United States shot off a letter to the president of Harvard: "I am inclined to tell him [Ted], if he sees any man taking a photograph of him, to run up and smash the camera, but I do not like to do this if you would disapprove. I do not suppose you could interfere; I don't even suppose it would be possible to tell one or two of the influential college men to put an instant stop to the cameras, and to the news-papermen running around after Ted."

In a letter to the beleaguered object of what he deemed journalistic harassment, the father whom the Sagamore Hill bunnies lovingly called "Big Bear" inquired, "How is the little bear getting on with his troubles?"

Because the situation was "just one of the occasions that the big bear cannot help the little bear at all," he continued, the only thing Ted could do was study hard, get good grades, go out for football, and forge a happy and profitable college life. Soon, reports reaching the White House from friends at Harvard contained such satisfying descriptions of Ted as "very modest, very manly." Undaunted and trying hard to appear oblivious to a persistently clamoring press, he not only qualified for freshman football, but he became by all accounts a key player at end who usually wound up after a play, according to one observer, "with half the team crisscross above him." A *New York World* account of one game noted that the son of the hero of San Juan Hill was "a chip off the old block" who had worked "like a demon" to win.

After a contest with the Yale freshmen that ended with him nursing a broken nose, the newspapers reported that the Yalies had singled him out and "ganged up" on him. Ted dashed off a letter to tell his father the story was "a lie." The Yale team "played a clean, straight game." Harvard lost because Yale "beat us by simply and plainly outplaying us."

Just as enthusiastically as he threw himself into football, Ted plunged into the social life of the college, but at the expense of his studies. When required to translate a Latin epic poem in an examination for which he had not prepared, he wrote the translation in blank verse, with an explanatory note saying he had made certain changes in the original because of the meter. Out of amusement at the brazenness the professor graded him A.

Although interest in Ted by reporters and cameramen did not end during Ted's years at Harvard, its intensity diminished, allowing him to lead a relatively normal student life. Grades that had seemed stuck at the level of "gentleman's C" rose to B and then A, qualifying him for the dean's list. Having proved himself a capable end on the freshmen football team, he found himself playing varsity second-string. A delighted father offered him congratulations. In a letter written while on a hunting excursion in Louisiana he said, "I have been greatly interested in what I have seen in the papers. I don't suppose you have much chance to make the first eleven [because of Ted's slight build], but I shall be awfully interested to see how you do."

(NOTE: Ted's collegiate football career ended when a broken ankle was mistaken for a sprain and the injury was not treated properly, with the result that the ankle did not fully recover its strength.)

Ted's next letter from his father was written on October 22, 1907, as TR hurried back to Washington to deal with a stock market crash three days earlier. Momentarily setting aside his concerns about a financial panic, he joyfully reported a "successful trip." Its highlight had been a bear hunt. Noting that "it was not until the twelfth day of steady hunting that I got my bear," he described shooting it "in the most approved hunter's style, going up on it in a canebrake as it made a walking bay at the dogs." He added that he had also killed a deer, "more by luck than anything else, as it was a difficult shot."

During the following tense days, Ted anxiously read newspaper accounts of his father's efforts to stem the crisis as vital financial institutions went under and others appeared to be on the brink of collapse. Presently, after negotiations with financier J. P. Morgan and other Wall Street moguls, Morgan issued, in the president's name, a statement that confidently asserted, ". . . underlying conditions which make up our financial and industrial well being are essentially sound and honest."

When details of the deal that had been struck between the White House and the House of Morgan became known, Ted noted ruefully, his father was roundly excoriated for agreeing to "a scheme" in which Morgan's U.S. Steel Corporation was able to reap a financial windfall. TR later explained in his *Autobiography*, published in 1913, "It was necessary for me to decide on the instant." To stop the panic it was necessary to restore confidence. The only way to do so, he asserted, was through Morgan. The reaction on Wall Street was a rally. The president noted, "The result justified my judgment. The panic was stopped, public confidence in the solvency of the threatened institution being at once restored."

As President Roosevelt gratefully observed that, to his relief, day-to-day press attention was shifting away from Ted's activities at Harvard, he found no respite concerning Alice. He wrote to Ted, "Sister continues to lead the life of social excitement, which I think is all right for a girl to lead for a year or two, but I do not regard it as healthy from the standpoint of permanence. I wish she had some pronounced serious taste."

From within the ivy-covered walls of Harvard, Theodore Roosevelt Jr., Class of 1909, followed press coverage of Alice Lee Roosevelt's whirl of "social excitement" with little expectation that she would suddenly acquire the "pronounced serious taste" for which their father yearned. She was, after all, the girl whom Washington wags had recently named "Alice in Wonderland."

She was the same freewheeling big sister Ted had always known. She was able to flaunt propriety by smoking in public, placing bets at the racetrack, and driving a red runabout through Washington at breakneck speeds. Should she present herself at a White House dinner, such as the one on January 12, 1905, attended by Henry James, Henry Adams, sculptor Augustus Saint-Gaudens, and other luminaries, an eager press was interested in knowing only what Alice did, what Alice said, what Alice wore. With her good looks, stylish dresses, and cartwheel hats, she caught every eye, and all ears listened for her latest bon mot.

Bits of gossip made their way to Harvard linking Alice romantically to every bachelor in the capital. One of these stories even concerned a congressman from Ohio, Nicholas Longworth. Because he was fifteen years older than Alice, Ted discounted the story. He then learned that Alice was joining an official contingent of Americans headed by Secretary of War William Howard Taft on a journey to the Philippines and other places in the Far East. The entourage included a commission of senators and representatives and their wives. As Alice boarded the ship at San Francisco, a woman reporter for the *Call* informed the paper's readers that the president's daughter presented a "mobile face" with frank, fearless eyes, firm round chin, and "saucy little nose." But even more fascinating to dockside reporters than Alice's appearance was the presence of Nicholas Longworth.

As the Taft delegation proceeded across the Pacific, a story circulated that Alice had been invited to join the harem of the sultan of Sulu. An editorial in the *New York Press* opined that Alice ought to accept. The writer noted, "Here she has only metaphorical slaves; there a whole regiment of the real article will be at her feet" and that she would be the "jewel of one of the nicest little harems in the Pacific."

Speculation and poking fun concerning Alice's choice of husband came to an abrupt and astonishing end when she announced her acceptance of a proposal by the congressman that she become Mrs. Alice Roosevelt Longworth. The date for the nuptials, Ted was presently advised, would be February 16, 1906.

The ceremony would be held in the East Room of the White House.

The first and only wedding held in the White House prior to Alice's had been in 1886 when President Grover Cleveland married Frances Folsom. A twenty-one-year-old beauty who had been Cleveland's ward since the death of her father, she had been a child when Cleveland was Folsom's law partner in Buffalo, New York. The last daughter of a president married in the White House had been Nellie Grant, in 1874. But the press had never called her a princess.

Alice's springtime wedding would be the second involving Roosevelts in a less than year. On March 17, 1905, the president and the "First Family" had gathered in New York City for the marriage of Uncle Elliott Roosevelt's daughter, Eleanor, to a more distant cousin, Franklin Delano Roosevelt. As the newlyweds greeted the guests after the ceremony, TR had grasped the groom's hand and said, "Well, Franklin, there's nothing like keeping the name in the family."

Alice had been Eleanor's bridesmaid. Now Alice was to be the bride.

Looking forward to seeing Sister marry, Ted felt confident that with her as the center of attraction, he could go to the wedding without worrying about "idiot" reporters and the "kodak creatures" paying attention to him, nor to the rest of the bunnies.

In a stream of stories filed for the amusement of an affectionate public by the presidential press contingent, two of the Roosevelt youngsters had become famous as "the White House Gang." With Ted at Harvard, Kermit still at Groton, and Ethel attending the Cathedral School and at home only on weekends—and with Alice always traveling here and there—the "gang" consisted of Archie and Quentin. Newspaper accounts recorded the gang's antics. In the quietude of his Harvard room Ted read of games of hide-and-seek played throughout the White House. One story told of a guide escorting visitors on a tour on a rainy day; opening a door to one of the ceremonial rooms filled with historical furniture, the usher found "a little towheaded boy" walking on stilts. The grinning culprit, eight-year-old Quentin Roosevelt, explained that even though there was a little rain outside, there were always ways of getting exercise in the White House.

Asked once by a reporter what the president was doing at that moment, Quentin replied, "I see him occasionally, but I know nothing of his family life."

Three years older than Quentin, Archie was less robust but he possessed, as a woman reporter noted, "his father's genius for making and keeping friends." When it was announced that Archie had diphtheria, the American people worried as much about his recovery as they had when Ted had pneumonia. A story in the *New York Times* noted that "many anxious watchers in the night" got up in the morning to "eagerly" scan the newspaper wondering, "How's Archie?"

Although TR feared he would "not pull through," the crisis passed and Archie resumed his role as one of the White House gang. The poet Arthur Guiterman would write of the gang:

The White House knew untrammeled joys
That shamed its customs prim and starchy,

When cataracts of little boys
Came storming down the stairs with Archie.

Whether the boys would behave themselves at Sister's wedding remained to be seen. As did the manner in which Alice would handle the
event. She did not disappoint. First, she let it be known that there would
be no bridesmaids. The spotlight would be on her alone. After the exchange of vows, she surprised her stepmother by kissing Edith on the
cheek. At the reception protocol was abandoned. "If the secretary of state
ranked the chambermaid," remarked White House usher Ike Hoover,
"no one worried about it this day." When time came to cut the cake, Alice used a sword, grabbed from the hand of a startled military aide.

A week after attending the wedding, Ted found the college dean in
no mood to tolerate slacking. Noting that Ted had not been showing up
for classes, the dean wrote to TR: "You may know where your son Ted is.
We do not." The letter informed TR that Ted had been placed on academic probation. Big Bear roared at Ted in a letter:

> There is not leeway for the smallest shortcoming on your part. Un-
> der no circumstances and for no reason short of sickness which
> makes you unable to leave your room, should you cut a lesson or
> a theme or fail to study hard right along. If you cannot study at
> Claverly (and I bitterly regret that I ever engaged you a room there)
> hire a quiet room outside of college and I will pay for it. I need not
> say to you to pay no heed whatever to athletics, to the social life, or
> to anything else that will in the slightest degree interfere with your
> studies. It is no use being popular in the class if you are going to
> be dropped out of the class.

Evidently remembering the promise given to the doctor when ten-
year-old Ted suffered anxiety attacks because of his father's excessive expectations, TR expressed "unlimited confidence in your ability to pull
yourself together, not to get depressed." He finished the letter with
"Good luck, old boy! You'll come out all right. I know you have the stuff
in you, and I trust you entirely. Anyone might come a cropper like this;
now get up and retrieve it."

More amusing than troubling to Big Bear was a report from college
authorities that Ted had been arrested. He and friends had been to the

theater in Boston. Dashing across the Common to catch a trolley to Cambridge, Ted spied a man following them. Wheeling around, Ted confronted him and gave him "a little push." The man produced a policeman's badge. There had been a rash of night robberies by a gang of young men on the Common and when the detective spotted three running youths, he thought he'd found the culprits.

Although the policeman complained that Ted's "little push" had given him a broken nose and rib, no charges had been lodged, and Ted and his friends had been let go.

Chastened by the close call with the Boston police and the letter chastising him for having been placed on academic probation, Ted devoted the remainder of the term to studying and looking forward to summer vacation at Sagamore Hill. Upon arrival he discovered that Big Bear was not as quick to join in the usual athletic pastimes. Admitting to being out of condition as a result of too much eating, not exercising enough, and working in a "sedentary fashion," TR said he had become "both old and fat." He wrote to Henry Cabot Lodge in August of having "a real rest this summer" and realizing "that I have reached that time of life when too violent exercise does not rest a man when he has had an exhausting mental career."

What had not changed about Ted's father was the liveliness and quality of conversation at the dinner table. On the agenda were seemingly incessant squabbles of European powers, anti-Asianism among citizens on the West Coast who demanded restrictions on Japanese immigration, and a popular movement favoring United States intervention in Cuba against insurgents who threatened the interests of the American sugar trust.

"If I am forced to intervene," asserted the hero of San Juan Hill and famous fighter for *Cuba libre,* "it will be not until it is evident that no other course is left me. Just at the moment I am so angry with the infernal little Cuban republic that I would like to wipe its people off the face of the earth. All we have wanted from them is that they would behave themselves and be prosperous and happy so that we would not have to interfere. And now, lo and behold, they have started an utterly unjustifiable and pointless revolution and may get things into such a snarl that we have no alternative save to intervene—which will at once convince the suspicious idiots in South America that we do wish to intervene after all, and perhaps have some land hunger."

Domestic issues that were debated included the perennial question of tariff rates, interstate commerce regulations regarding railroads, and a Roosevelt plan to impose federal food and drug inspections. When Congress passed a pure food and drug law and TR signed it, he claimed that the measure, along with passage of a railroad rate bill, "mark a noteworthy advance in the policy of securing federal supervision and control of corporations."

Another frequent topic in the summer of 1906 was the forthcoming congressional elections, a subject that led invariably to talk about the political future of Theodore Roosevelt. When he'd attained the presidency in his own right in 1904, he had vowed not to seek reelection in 1908. The question now being asked by friend and foe alike was "Did he mean it?"

The query was unanswered when Ted returned to Harvard, and it remained so when TR announced plans to become the first sitting president to leave the country, in this case to see how the work was progressing on the Panama Canal. Accordingly, he and Edith boarded the USS *Louisiana* on November 8. The former assistant secretary of the navy who had fought to gain a world-class American fleet toured the ship and declared, "It gives me great pride in America to be aboard this great battleship and to see not only the material perfection of the ship herself in engines, guns, and all arrangements, but the fine quality of the officers and crew."

After surveying the progress of "the big ditch" being gouged across the Isthmus, he took great delight in operating one of the huge earth-moving shovels and declared, "The work is being done with a very high degree of efficiency and honesty." He was struck by "the character of American employees who are engaged not merely in superintending the work, but in doing all the jobs that need skill and intelligence."

Sailing toward home on November 20, he wrote so vividly to the son at Harvard who had once considered joining the navy that Ted felt as if he were also on the *Louisiana:*

This is the third day out from Panama. We have been steaming steadily in the teeth of the trade wind. It has blown pretty hard, and the ship has pitched a little, but not enough to make either Mother or me uncomfortable.

Panama was a great sight. In the first place it was strange and beautiful with its mass of luxuriant tropic jungle, with the treacherous tropic rivers trailing here and there through it; and it was lovely to see the orchids and brilliant butterflies and the strange birds and snakes and lizards, and finally the strange old Spanish towns and the queer thatch and bamboo huts of the ordinary natives. In the next place it is a tremendous sight to see the work of the canal going on.

Reading the letter and trying to imagine all that his father had seen, Ted could only hope that one day he might find himself having such an adventure and being capable of writing such a letter about it to a son of his own. But while he was a student at Harvard the closest he came to matching his robust father's expeditions was a vacation in the wilds of Minnesota.

7

Although Ted had entered Harvard expecting to graduate as a member of the class of 1909, he did so well in reversing his lackadaisical approach to his classes that he qualified to receive his bachelor of arts degree a year earlier. As he looked forward to donning the cap and gown in June 1908, he found himself waiting, along with the nation, to hear whether his father would stand by his pledge made after his 1904 victory not to seek reelection. Pressures on him to decide had been increasing. Republicans urged him to make up his mind soon, so that if he chose not to run, the party would have time to organize the nomination of a standard bearer.

As TR weighed the pros and cons of running again he electrified the country with a show of American power in the world by announcing that a "great white fleet" of American warships would unfurl the Stars and Stripes in the major ports of the world in a globe-circling cruise. As the sixteen white-painted battleships got under way from Hampton Roads, Virginia, they passed in review for the former assistant secretary of the navy who was now their commander-in-chief. Beaming with pride, TR asked, "Did you ever see such a fleet? Isn't it magnificent? Oughtn't we all feel proud?"

The fleet's odyssey proved a resounding success, and as the ships steamed into port again at Hampton Roads on February 22, 1909, the president was there to greet them. "Not until some American fleet returns victorious from a great sea battle," he declared solemnly, "will there be another such homecoming."

Eleven years earlier he had returned from Cuba wrapped in the glory of his crowded hour to bound down a ship's gangway at Montauk and into the political arena. Now, he was fifty years old. He kept his pledge not to run for president in 1908 and designated his trusted friend William Howard Taft as his preference for the Republican presidential nomination. Having decided to retire, he wrote to Ted that as ex-president, "instead of leading a perfectly silly and vacuous life around the clubs or in sporting fields," he was going to enjoy himself. "Every now and then," he noted, "solemn jacks come to me to tell me that our country must face the problem of 'what it will do with its ex-presidents.' I always answer them that there will be one ex-president about whom they need not give themselves the slightest concern, for he will do for himself without any outside assistance; and I add that they need waste no sympathy on me—that I have had the best time of any man of my age in all the world, that I have enjoyed myself in the White House more than I have ever known any president to enjoy himself, and that I am going to enjoy myself thoroly [sic] when I leave the White House, and what is more, continue just as long as I possibly can to do some kind of work that will count."

Part of that "work," he informed his startled family, the nation, and the world, would be undertaking a year-long safari into the dark depths of Africa to hunt big game and collect data and specimens for the Smithsonian Museum.

With Ted graduating from college, would he be interested in going along? Ordinarily, Ted would have gleefully accepted the invitation and begun packing gear. But he explained he was in love and could not bear the thought of being away from the young woman for one day, let alone an entire year.

The twenty-one-year old namesake of the soon-to-be ex-president of the United States and a nineteen-year-old, fair-haired beauty named Eleanor Alexander had met in October 1908 on the platform of the railroad station at New Haven, Connecticut. Both had been invited to a weekend party by a mutual friend, Mrs. Arthur M. Dodge, of Simsbury. That evening as the guests sat for dinner Ted took a chair beside Eleanor and promptly learned she had spent two summers riding and camping with her mother in Yellowstone Park. Ted pointed out that his father had been cofounder of the Boone and Crockett Club, which, in pressing for passage of the 1894 Park Protection Act, had been instrumental in the saving of Yellowstone from exploitation by timber interests. As Eleanor listened with fascination, Ted went on to relate that he knew "the western country" well. He asked her to tell him more of where she had been and what she had done out West. Conversation continued after dinner as they sat on the stairs while the other guests played parlor games. When he asked her to ride with him the next day during a "paper chase" [a fox hunt with a paper target substituted for the fox], she smiled and nodded yes.

"When the evening was over," Eleanor recalled in her 1959 autobiography, *Day Before Yesterday,* "I went to bed pleased with the world."

Awake early on a "crisp and cool" morning "bright with sunshine," she dressed in a new riding habit: whipcord breeches under a long coat that hooked securely so that her knees would not show when she dismounted. As she approached the polo pony she was to ride, she saw Ted admiring her habit and "flattered" herself that she was "appearing to advantage."

The scene that unfolded resembled a slapstick comedy. As Ted helped Eleanor into the saddle, the pony bucked, whirled, and bolted for the stable while Eleanor "hung on desperately." When the pony stopped short at the stable door, she nearly flew over his head. Looking at Ted and expecting to find him laughing, she saw a face "set like a rock," as if nothing unusual had happened. With the pony quieted by a groom, they set out to join the other riders as Ted tactfully suggested they go slowly. Eleanor remembered:

> I could not have done anything else. Any attempt at a trot or canter would have meant my doom. That wretched pony would not walk, he would only jog-trot sideways. His mouth was made of iron. My hat was shaken off and, final and inexcusable humiliation, my hair fell down below my waist and flapped in the breeze, scattering hairpins. Ted recovered my hat, and while I frantically stuffed my hair under it, trying my best to make it secure, he held my bridle. All the while he kept talking to me pleasantly on various subjects, but my misery kept me from answering him. Before we had gone a mile I realized that I could not possibly go on the chase but would rather have died than confess it to the rest of the party.

She blurted, "It's no use, Mr. Roosevelt. I just can't do it. What on earth am I to say?"

"Don't say anything," Ted replied. "You've a right to change your mind, haven't you? If you like, I'll tell the others you prefer not to go after all. Never make unnecessary explanations."

• • •

Daughter of Henry Addison Alexander, a Wall Street figure who considered Ted's father a traitor to his class, Eleanor had been born in 1889 at 59 East Seventy-third Street in New York. She was of Scottish heritage on her father's side. Her mother, Grace Green, had four ancestors on the *Mayflower*. (Eleanor would write that she "was astonished" to find out after Ted's death that Ted's mother claimed the same four ancestors on the Pilgrims' ship.) Her parents divorced when she was three, and she and her mother moved to California to live with her grandfather. They stayed two years and then lived for a time in Rome. After a move to Paris, her mother remarried her father and the family settled in a house on a little square off the Avenue du Bois de Boulogne for six years. In 1900 when Eleanor was twelve, her parents again divorced. Mother and daughter returned to New York, where Eleanor attended Miss Spencer's finishing school for young ladies, graduating in 1907.

Because of the social and economic status of her father and several uncles who were also prominent in the world of finance, Eleanor was welcome in the homes of New York and Connecticut high-society families, including the Dodges. Although Ted was a Harvard graduate with the pedigree of the Roosevelts, one of whom currently occupied the White House, he was living on his own and earning his living in a carpet factory. Determined to obtain employment without intervention by the president of the United States, and to live without an allowance, he had accepted an offer of a position from Robert P. Perkins, president of the Hartford Carpet Company. In its mill in Thompsonville, Connecticut, he earned seven dollars a week, five of which went for food, lodging, and laundry. He worked ten hours on weekdays and five on Saturday. But when newspapers learned that the son of Theodore Roosevelt was working as a common laborer, stories appeared speculating that the job was a publicity stunt. Once again the object of press fascination, he did his best to ignore the "idiot" reporters and "kodak creatures," but one day a photographer snapped him arriving at the mill smoking a cigarette. As a result, he was publicly scolded by several clergymen and women's organizations for setting "an evil example" to youth. He noted with amusement that no such criticism had been directed at Alice when she was seen puffing in public.

Although the work at the mill was hard, he showed an unexpected talent for the sorting of wool. Noting this ability in her memoir, Eleanor explained, "A company making carpets buys wool in quantity, and before buying raw wool it must be able to judge the quality accurately in order to show how much it will shrink and how much weight it will lose when washed. This is done by feel, smell, and taste and can make a difference between profit and loss. Ted seemed to have an innate ability for this (totally useless in later life), for he soon qualified as an expert and got a raise."

In spite of the rigors of the job, the attentions of journalists and photographers, and the disapprovals voiced about the president's son's employment and his poor example to the young of the country regarding smoking tobacco, Ted persevered with the tenacity and the singleness of purpose imbued in him in countless lectures by the Big Bear whose natural den was Sagamore Hill, but whose present address was the White House.

It was while there in December 1908 for sister Ethel's coming-out dance that Ted next encountered Eleanor Alexander. She wondered if Ted would remember her. Delighted to learn that he did, she found herself being teased by envious young women about dancing so often with him. He asked what train she was taking back to New York. She answered that she would be going via the Baltimore & Ohio. He said he would be on the same train and looked forward to keeping her company during the trip.

When he did not appear, she assumed he had changed his mind. But a day after she was back in New York she received a letter from him stating that he had walked the length of the B & O train twice looking for her. Only then did she realize that she had told him the wrong line. Her ticket was for the Pennsylvania Railroad.

Because Ted's work kept him in Connecticut six days a week, Eleanor found herself receiving almost daily letters, each with the greeting "Dear Miss Alexander," as good manners required. When one arrived that began "Dear Goldilocks," she tore it up and stopped replying to his letters. When she saw him at the Tuxedo Autumn Ball, she expressed her annoyance at his "being fresh." He begged forgiveness and she granted it.

On occasions when he'd saved enough from his wages for a round-trip ticket to New York, he traveled down on Saturday afternoon, reaching the city at eight in the evening. He returned via a 10:30 P.M. train on Sunday, sitting up in a day coach until he arrived at Thompsonville in time to report to the carpet mill at seven on Monday morning.

Having accepted that Theodore Roosevelt Jr.'s employment in a carpet factory was not a publicity stunt, the newspapers turned to specu-

lating on the subject of when, and whom, he would marry. Not knowing
about Eleanor, one opined that the junior Roosevelt's bride would be a
popular young actress, although Ted had met her only once. In another
paper he read that he was engaged to the daughter of a Chinese diplomat, whom he had not met. To avoid reporters' seeing him and Eleanor
together, and then hounding them, they went for long walks along Riverside Drive, often in the snow. They hoped they would not encounter
someone they knew who might inform the press. All of these meetings
were conducted without their observing the propriety of being accompanied by a chaperone. "Sometimes we had tea in a little inconspicuous
restaurant in spite of the disapproval of my mother, who said emphatically that this was not done," Eleanor recorded in her autobiography. "I
doubt if I ever did anything that made me feel quiet so daring as having
tea in a restaurant *alone with a man.*"

While Eleanor had found a warm welcome at the White House, and
been greeted by TR with "Dee-lighted to know you," Ted found little re-
ciprocation from members of Eleanor's family. "Mother, of course, knew
all about it from the start," Eleanor recorded. "She liked Ted but was inclined to be influenced by her Wall Street friends, to whom his father's
name was anathema, and was not at all sure she wanted me to marry
him."

Eleanor's step-great-grandmother, Mrs. Thornton R. Butler, always a
staunch supporter of the president, was thrilled by the prospect of
Eleanor marrying his son. She told Mrs. Alexander, "I must say *I* should
be extremely gratified."

The mother relented and announced that her daughter was engaged
to Theodore Roosevelt Jr. in February 1910. Accustomed to the news of
such events being confined to a discreet notice in the social columns of
the respectable newspapers, she was appalled to find reporters from the
"sensational" press swarming in the street in front of her house. Responsibility for this was attributed to Ted's father's "notoriety."

With the announcement made, everyone understood that there would
be no wedding until the former president returned from his adventure
in Africa.

8

Within three weeks after TR turned over the reins of government to William Howard Taft, TR and twenty-year-old Kermit, along with a small group of professional naturalists, had sailed from Hoboken, New Jersey. Observing the departure, Henry Cabot Lodge gazed at his friend waving from the bridge of the ship and later wrote to Roosevelt, "In all the striking incidents of your career, I never saw one which impressed me more. It was not merely the crowd but the feeling which was manifested which was so striking."

As the fifty-year-old ex-president and his energetic son trekked through East Africa, Lodge informed TR that the American people "follow it all with the absorbed interest of a boy who reads *Robinson Crusoe* for the first time."

Following his father's progress through news dispatches, Ted was amused to learn that natives had given Big Bear the name "Bwana Makuba" (Great Master). When sporadic letters arrived, he read with delight that Big Bear was having "a bully time." Kermit was "as hardy as a bull moose" and the admiration of the party's professional hunters. The favorite of native gun-bearers, Kermit was able to "outrun, when after a wounded beast, or outlast, in a day's or week's tramp, any man, black or white, in the outfit." Kermit was "cool and daring" but on occasion "a little too reckless and keeps my heart in my throat."

In taking part in one of the largest safaris ever fitted out in East Africa, Kermit was at his father's side and in the company of the Smithsonian scientists, 15 native soldiers *(askaris)*, 260 porters, and a handful of white hunters. By the end of the expedition TR and Kermit would tally 512 animals, including 17 lions, 11 elephants, 20 rhinos, 8 hippos, 9 giraffes, 47 gazelles, 20 zebras, and other creatures Ted had never heard of: the dik-dik, aardwolf, klipspringer, and bongo. All of these, TR explained, were killed for food and collected as specimens that had been requested by the museum.

When the safari ended at Khartoum, TR and Kermit were joined by Edith and Ethel. They proceeded to Egypt and on to Europe for a grand tour that was described by one writer as "rich months, with emperors and kings, presidents and cheering thousands." When in Rome, he turned down an audience with Pope Pius X after the pope demanded that he not agree to see a group of American Methodists, one of whom had offended His Holiness by calling him "the whore of Babylon." TR then snubbed the Methodists.

Warmly received in Paris, he spoke at the Sorbonne on the "Duties of Citizenship."

In the address he voiced a philosophy which had characterized his life and that he hoped would be followed by his sons:

It is not the critic who counts, not the man who points out how the strong man stumbled or whether the doer of deeds could have done better. The credit belongs to the man who is actually in the arena; whose face is marred by dust and sweat and blood; who errs and comes up short again . . . who knows the great enthusiasms, the great devotions, and spends himself in a worthy cause; who at least knows in the end the triumph of high achievement; and who, at worst, if he fails, at least fails while doing greatly, so that his place shall never be with those cold and timid souls who know neither victory nor defeat.

Visiting the country of his ancestors, he marveled at the tulips of Holland's annual flower show. Moving northward to Stockholm, Sweden, he donned a suit of white tie and tails to accept the Nobel Peace Prize, a ceremony belatedly held in recognition of his mediation of a treaty of peace that had ended the Russo-Japanese War of 1905.

His acceptance speech called for limitation of naval armaments by the European powers, and formation of a "League of Peace," that would be backed by force if necessary. "The ruler or statesman who should bring about such a combination," he predicted, "would have earned his place in history for all time and his title to the gratitude of mankind."

He would not live to see the refusal of the U.S. Senate to ratify American membership in the League of Nations following the First World War, but his vision would be partially realized in the creation of the United

Nations after World War II at the instigation of a lifelong admirer and political emulator of "Cousin Teddy," President Franklin D. Roosevelt.

Going on from Sweden to Germany, the former president paid a call on a ruler who was busily building battleships. Kaiser Wilhelm was so impressed by his illustrious guest, and with himself, that he gave TR a photograph that was taken as they met. The inscription read, "When we shake hands we shake the whole world."

TR's penultimate stop en route home was England, where family members joined him. He arrived in time to be designated by President Taft to represent the United States at the funeral of King Edward VII. A week and a half later he was given a rare honor for an American (not to be matched until 1945 by Gen. Dwight D. Eisenhower) of giving an address at London's historic Guildhall. Ted noted as he read press coverage of the event that the man who had helped end Spanish sovereignty in Cuba, and who had recently been a visitor to British-dominated Egypt, lectured the government of the new king, George V. He told the astonished assembled dignitaries in their regal robes, "Now, either you have the right to be in Egypt or you have not; either it is or it is not your duty to establish and keep order."

If they were not prepared to rise to their responsibilities, he said, they should get out. He hoped that in the interest of civilization, and with "fealty to your own great traditions," that they would rise to them.

After delivering the Romanes lecture at Oxford University, he must have felt a little like Ted when the archbishop of York declared, "In the way of grading which we have at Oxford, we agreed to mark the lecture 'Beta Minus,' but the lecturer 'Alpha Minus.' While we felt that the lecture [on the subject "Biological Analogies to History"] "was not a very great contribution to science, we were sure that the lecturer was a very great man."

On June 18, 1910, with Ted and Eleanor aboard the revenue cutter *Manhattan* in New York harbor, "the great man" returned home to a tumultuous welcome. As the steamer *Kaiserin Auguste Viktoria* sailed into the harbor, she was saluted by the battleship *South Carolina* and a flotilla of destroyers and yachts. Eleanor watched every craft in the harbor "decked with banners and blowing whistles" as TR's ship docked at the Battery to the roaring of "great crowds and a "tumultuous cheering," followed by speeches, and a parade of horse-drawn carriages, marchers, and five hundred Rough Riders who had come to New York from all over the country.

After the parade the family gathered for lunch at 433 Fifth Avenue, a house built by Eleanor's great-grandfather. Following the meal, they took a ferry and train to Oyster Bay.

Two days later, at the Fifth Avenue Presbyterian Church, Ted and Eleanor were married.

Their honeymoon took them by way of Philadelphia and Chicago to San Francisco, where Ted was to work in the San Francisco office of the Hartford Carpet Company. Hoping to dodge the press, they traveled under fake names, but the ruse proved futile.

"We thought the newsmen would get tired and go away, but they didn't," wrote Eleanor. Describing one failed attempt to dodge an army of reporters by leaving their hotel by means of a freight elevator and service door, Eleanor admitted, "By this time I would have been enjoying the excitement of having to escape like international spies if it hadn't been for Ted's anxiety and distress over the situation."

In San Francisco Ted agreed to grant an interview to John Francis Neylan, the political reporter of the *Bulletin*, acting on behalf of the swarm of journalists clamoring for a story. Ted told Neylan that the publicity he had been getting as the president's son was both embarrassing and damaging to his business career. He was not in politics, he protested, and all he wanted was to stand on his own two feet.

Eleanor wrote sympathetically in her autobiography, "The disadvantages of being a great man's son far outweighed the advantages. Ted's truly remarkable career was to be cloaked inevitably and perpetually by the shadow of his father's fame. At twenty-five he was compared to his father at fifty and found wanting. He was always accused of imitating his father in speech, walk, and smile. If he had taken this seriously and tried to alter himself he would have been unbearably self-conscious."

In a discussion of Ted's dilemma with Charles Evans Hughes, the associate justice of the U.S. Supreme Court counseled Eleanor, "People will always say Ted is copying his father unless he does nothing but sit on the piazza and do crossword puzzles. Then the same people would attack him for being so different."

Resigned to their situation, Ted and Eleanor hoped for seclusion by settling into a rented small gray frame house with a little garden at 1942 Pacific Avenue. The back windows afforded a view of the Golden Gate. Eleanor installed window boxes and filled them with heliotrope and pink geraniums. The garden was planted with roses, dahlias, various annuals, and some spring-flowering bulbs. Their furniture, shipped from New

York, consisted of wedding presents and items Eleanor and her mother had been collecting for years. Ted and Eleanor considered the little house as "a dream of perfection."

In January 1911 Ted wrote to his parents that Eleanor was pregnant, with the baby due in August. TR replied excitedly, "Mother and I are almost as delighted as darling Eleanor and you. Both of you are now even more in our thoughts than ever; and our hearts well over with tenderness for Eleanor. . . . Home, wife, children—they are what really count in life. I have heartily enjoyed many things; the Presidency, my success as a soldier, a writer, a big game hunter and explorer; but all of them out together are not for one moment to be weighed in the balance when compared to the joy I have known with your mother and all of you; and, as a merely secondary thing, this house and the life here yield me constant pleasure. Really, the prospect of grandchildren was all that was lacking to make perfect mother's happiness and mine."

When TR wrote to Ted, the big house on the hilltop overlooking Oyster Bay was uncommonly quiet. Alice was married, but still the vivacious gadfly, she basked in the spotlight as both wife of a congressman and daughter of a former president. Kermit was back at Harvard as a sophomore, although the experiences of his African and European hiatus left him feeling much older. Ethel was at home. Archie was away at school in Arizona. Enrolled at Groton, Quentin had amazed the faculty and his parents by suddenly ascending nearly to the top of his class.

In response to this news TR wrote to him, "To think of one of our family standing as high as that! It's almost paralyzing."

The first of the next generation of Roosevelts was named Grace Green, after Eleanor's mother. "In those days no one thought of going to a hospital and turning a family event into an operation," Eleanor wrote. "Before she arrived Ted used to come home to lunch almost every day so that I would not be lonely. He was enchanted by the baby and used to hurry home from the office to hold her in his lap for half an hour before her bedtime. He had a knack with tiny babies. Gracie, according to the fashion of the day, wore dresses about a yard long. When he picked her up he would first wind his right hand in the skirt, then slip his left under her head and shoulders. All our babies seemed to feel safe in his arms and loved to have him hold them."

There would be four children: Grace, Theodore Roosevelt III, Cornelius, and Quentin. But only Grace was born in California. Accepting a position with the banking firm of Bertron Griscom Company, Ted left the carpet business in 1912 in the expectation that in returning to New York he could earn sufficient money to allow him both to support his family and to invest enough to ensure a reliable income that would permit him to eventually follow in his father's formidable footsteps on a political path.

Getting started as a bond salesman proved harder than Ted had anticipated. He often found himself thwarted by a customer's animosity toward his father. Calling upon one prospective client, he was told, "I never expected to see the son of your father here. Kindly make your call brief."

The situation was exacerbated by the fact that in 1912 Theodore Roosevelt was again a candidate for president. Dismayed and disillusioned by the White House performance of his handpicked successor, President Taft, and unable to wrest the Republican nomination from him, TR carried the banner of the Progressive (Bull Moose) Party. As a third-party candidate he would run against Taft and the Democratic standard-bearer, Woodrow Wilson. Acknowledging that "the great bulk of my wealthy and educated friends regard me as a dangerous crank," the old warrior marched again into battle. He asserted that he wanted to find a remedy for evils that, if left unremedied, would in the end do away not only with wealth and education, but with pretty much all of civilization. "It is a fight that must be made, and it is worth making, and the event lies on the knees of the gods."

For the now grown-up and mostly independent bunnies of Sagamore Hill (except fifteen-year-old Quentin, whom TR called "that cheerful pagan") the tumult of Big Bear running for office was a familiar phenomenon. But for the mother of little Grace Roosevelt as they set foot in the house in the summer of 1912 the scene she encountered was a shock. Roosevelt family chronicler Hermann Hagedorn noted that for TR and Edith, "having their first grandchild in the house for months on end was an experience that made a presidential candidacy seem so secondary as to be in the nature of an impertinent periodic interruption."

Eleanor wrote in her autobiography:

It was the first time I had been there when the entire family was at home. Before twenty-four hours passed I realized that nothing in my bringing up as an only child had in any way prepared me for the frenzied activity into which I was plunged. Something was going on every minute of the day. The house was full of people. Conferences went on all day. The telephone never stopped ringing. In the evenings my father-in-law received the newspapermen. At first I thought everyone would be tired when the day was over and would go to bed early, but I soon found out that nothing of the kind could be expected. The Roosevelt family enjoyed life too much to waste time sleeping. Every night they stayed downstairs until nearly midnight; then, talking at the top of their voices, they trooped up the wide uncarpeted stairs and went to their rooms. For a brief moment all was still, but just as I was going off to sleep for the second time they remembered things they had forgotten to tell one another and ran shouting through the halls. I tried going to bed with cotton in my ears, but it never did any good.

Edith Roosevelt wrote to her sister-in-law about how thrilled TR was with his granddaughter, whom he called Gracie. "He runs in half a dozen times a day," said Edith, "and picks her up in his arms."

While Grace's mother endured the noisy days engulfed by her husband's family, Ted was in the city. She remembered in her book that Ted regarded waking hours as working hours and usually took time off only to get hard physical exercise in the shortest possible time, such as by playing squash. His chief pleasure and relaxation was an evening at home, a dozen books on the floor around his easy chair. Two of the reasons for Ted's intensity of effort, Eleanor believed, were his "strong feeling that he must prove worthy of his father, whom he adored, and a deep love of country."

Ted stood foursquare behind his father's run for the presidency, as did everyone in the family. They had weathered other campaigns, and no matter how this contest came out, they would be fine. But their confidence was shaken on October 12 with horrifying news that as TR was leaving the Hotel Gilpatrick in Milwaukee, Wisconsin, to address a campaign rally, a man wielding a pistol had lurched out of a crowd of well-wishers on the sidewalk and fired a shot into TR's chest. The terrifying report was quickly followed by word that he not been killed, or even seriously wounded, but had actually delivered his speech.

Ted was not surprised to learn that his father began by saying to the audience, "I shall ask you to be as quiet as possible. I don't know whether you fully understand that I have just been shot; but it takes more than that to kill a Bull Moose." Nor was he surprised that the speech went on for an hour and a half, with TR repeatedly brushing aside appeals that he stop and get himself to a hospital. His survival was attributed to his good physical condition and to the fact that the text of his speech had been tucked into an inside pocket and blunted the impact of the bullet.

Expressions of admiration for this latest demonstration of courage by the hero of San Juan Hill by the American people did not translate into sufficient votes to enter the Roosevelt name in the annals of American history as the first president to serve a third term. "We have fought the good fight, we have kept the faith," he said to an old friend a few days after losing to Wilson, "and we have nothing to regret."

Seven months later he announced from Sagamore Hill that he was in receipt of an invitation from the governments of Brazil, Argentina, and Chile to visit those countries for the purpose of delivering a series of lectures. Anticipating a chance for yet another adventure, he accepted. "I have to go," he said. "It's my last chance to be a boy."

Because Ted was married and a father, there was no request that Ted accompany him. Eager for another adventure in exploring, and already working in Brazil for the Anglo-Brazilian Iron Company, Kermit had no impediment to going except an engagement to Belle Willard, the daughter of the owner of Washington's Willard Hotel, which was postponed.

On October 4, 1913, Ted, Eleanor, and fourteen-month-old Grace were on the dock as TR and Edith sailed for Rio de Janeiro. Ted would not see them until May 19, 1914, when TR returned looking thinner and older. He used a walking stick, made necessary by an injury to his right leg from which he had almost died in the jungle. In the seven months he was gone he had kept his lecture schedule and set off to explore and map fifteen hundred miles of Brazil's River of Doubt. It was immediately renamed Rio Teodoro in his honor. Barely off the gangway, he found himself in a mob of reporters with a host of questions, not so much about his explorations, but whether he might be thinking of running again for president in 1916.

9

Five weeks after Theodore Roosevelt returned to Sagamore Hill from having realized his last chance to be a boy again, on the morning of June 28, 1914, in Sarajevo, capital of Serbia, someone hurled a bomb at a car carrying Archduke Franz Ferdinand, the heir to the Hapsburg empire. The bomb bounced off the side of the royal vehicle and exploded against a following auto, injuring two officers. Continuing to city hall, the archduke was greeted by the mayor and teasingly asked the embarrassed official, "So you welcome your guests with bombs?"

Later that day as Ferdinand and his wife were driven through the city again, on their way to a reception at the governor's residence, nineteen-year-old Gavrilo Princip, a Bosnian Serb who had had a role in the failed attempt at assassination by bombing, took advantage of the slowing of the car to step toward it with a pistol in hand. He fired two shots. One struck the archduke, who bled to death as he was being rushed to a hospital. The other killed his wife.

Over the next month nations of Europe, which had so recently welcomed Theodore Roosevelt and heard his plea for creation of a world organization to assure global peace, went to war. As the conflict erupted, President Woodrow Wilson declared United States neutral. TR agreed with the policy in an article in the August 22 issue of the magazine *The Outlook*. He wrote, "Only the clearest and most urgent national duty" would ever justify deviating from a policy of neutrality and noninterference. While believing that he had a duty to publicly support the president and to offer to work with him "hand in hand" during the crisis, he let it be known to family and friends that he stood on the side of England and France. He feared a German "iron heel" on Europe.

He privately scorned the man who had defeated him in 1912 as "a college president with an astute and shifty mind, a hypocritical ability to deceive people, unscrupulousness in handling [political] machine leaders, and no real knowledge or wisdom concerning internal and international affairs as the head of a nation." But Wilson was president and Theodore Roosevelt was a retired politician just back from a grueling and nearly fatal jungle expedition.

His partner in that harrowing adventure was now married to Belle Willard, whom TR called "a perfect trump." Ethel was married and mother of a boy, Richard. Archie and Quentin were home from school for the summer. And Ted and Eleanor were parents again. A boy, born in June, he was named Theodore Roosevelt III, but known to all as "Teddy."

They now lived in Philadelphia, where Ted had accepted a partnership in the investment banking firm of Montgomery, Clothier and Tyler. Ted's new job was a step toward going into public life with an independent income. To attain this goal, Eleanor explained in her memoir, "we considered his earnings as principal, not income. He put every cent back into the firm, then borrowed from the firm for our living expenses." By 1915 Ted's share of the company's profits amounted to more than $150,000. That Christmas his gift to Eleanor was a pair of magnificent emerald-and-diamond earrings.

Regarding the hostilities in Europe, the Roosevelts of Philadelphia were convinced that the plain duty of the United States was to join the Allies. "All of us shouted for war," Eleanor recalled. "We felt it was a case of right versus wrong and that it was cowardly to be neutral."

As a clamor rose and swelled across the United States in favor of the United States giving aid to the Allies, many people urged Theodore Roosevelt's return to the White House in 1916 in order to pilot the American ship of state through the turbulent waters at home and the storm of war in Europe. Sixteen-year-old Quentin Roosevelt opined, "The trouble with Father's situation is that he is expected to pull everybody's chestnuts out of the fire."

But Wilson was president and the ex-president residing at Sagamore Hill was on record as supporting Wilson's policy of neutrality. However, this did not keep his eldest son and his wife from making their views known. The forum Ted and Eleanor chose for doing so was a "Preparedness Parade" in New York from Madison Square, up Fifth Avenue, to Fifty-ninth Street. Encouraged by Ted to organize "a battalion of women" to take part, Eleanor recruited twelve hundred, many of whom had never marched before. In the greatest parade in the city at the time, scores of thousands began marching at nine in the morning. Behind the banner INDEPENDENT PATRIOTIC WOMEN OF AMERICA, carried by Mrs. J. Borden Harriman, chosen as bearer because she was tall and strong enough to keep it aloft, the contingent proceeded up the avenue just after dusk. They wore white dresses and carried lanterns. Walking behind a band, Eleanor had a broad blue ribbon with MARSHAL in gold letters across her chest.

In *Day Before Yesterday* she provided this account of her participation:

I have never seen so many people. They jammed the sidewalks, hung out of windows, looked down from roofs. We reached the Public Library, where people were crowded on the wide steps, sitting on the balustrade, and even perched on the stone lions. Directly opposite was the Union League, which had its own private grandstand filled with men we knew [including Ted]. I felt rather self-conscious at this point and was going along with my chin up, looking neither to the right nor to the left as the band played "Columbia, the Gem of the Ocean," when Ted ran out from the sidewalk and grabbed me by the arm.

"For heaven's sake, stop!" he shouted. "You've lost your battalion."

I looked back over what seemed miles and miles of empty asphalt with little white figures in the distance. The police had halted the parade at Thirty-fourth Street to let the crosstown traffic through, and from there Daisy Harriman and I had marched alone. Just the two of us. Men in the Union League Club's stand were doubled up with laughter. There was nothing to do but stand still, overcome with embarrassment, until the parade caught up with us. It was five years before I saw anything funny about it.

Brooding about the events in Europe as he sat with Edith on the piazza at Sagamore Hill, the president who had mediated an ending to the Russo-Japanese War in 1905 saw little likelihood that President Wilson's hope that the European conflict could be settled through American good offices. He bristled at what he deemed an appalling lack of steps to mobilize an army and navy for possible United States entry into the war to save England and Europe from German domination. He feared an inevitable alliance between triumphant Germany and an imperialist Japan that would be aimed at driving the United States out of the Pacific.

He was not alone in lamenting American unpreparedness. By 1916, in the words of the Roosevelt biographer William Henry Harbaugh, "*preparedness* and *Roosevelt* were virtually synonymous. Yet most Americans in the autumn of 1916 were not responding to a clarion call to arms." When they went to the polls in the presidential election of 1916 they gave Wilson a second term because, as his campaign slogan had asserted, "He kept us out of war."

Frustrated and disgusted, the noncandidate resident of Sagamore Hill left his home on November 3, 1916, for Manhattan to speak at Cooper Union. On the platform where Abraham Lincoln had made a speech that was credited with winning him the presidential nomination in 1860, TR abandoned his prepared address. He had on his mind the innocent people aboard the ocean liner *Lusitania*, sunk in 1915 by German torpedoes, and the soldiers being slaughtered in Europe while Woodrow Wilson lounged at his summer home in Shadow Lawn, New Jersey:

> There should be shadows now at Shadow Lawn; the shadows of the men, women, and children who have risen from the ooze of the ocean bottom and from the graves of foreign lands; the shadows of the helpless whom Mr. Wilson did not dare protect lest he might have to face danger; the shadows of babies gasping pitifully as they sank under the waves; the shadows of women outraged and slain by bandits. . . . Those are the shadows proper for Shadow Lawn; the shadows of deeds that were never done; the shadow of lofty words that were followed by no action; the shadows of the tortured dead.

He spoke with the wolf rising in his heart and echoes of the guns of San Juan Hill in his memory as he condemned the president of the United States for the gravest sin of all, failing to uphold the national honor. In letter to a friend in February he had written contemptuously of the president, "I don't think he is capable of understanding the emotion of patriotism, or the emotion of real pride in one's country."

As ever, Theodore Roosevelt stood ready to back up his words with his body. In February of 1917 he appealed to Wilson "for leave to raise a division," but the former professor turned down the ex-colonel of the

Rough Riders. Wilson told his Cabinet, "War means autocracy." But when the weight of public opinion shifted in favor of Roosevelt's view that neutrality had failed and that the United States must go to war to preserve European civilization and freedom itself, he reluctantly sent a message to Congress seeking a declaration of war against Germany and her allies. Accepting that "the right is more precious than peace," he confided to Frank Cobb, editor of the *New York World*, "To fight you must be brutal and ruthless, and the spirit of the ruthlessness will enter into the very fiber of our national life, infecting Congress, the courts, the policeman on the beat, the man in the street."

With war declared, the man on the street, women, and children heartily joined in singing a song written by George M. Cohan, telling the war-ravaged people "over there" not to despair because "the Yanks" were coming and would not come back till the war was won.

On May 18, 1917, TR sent a telegram to Wilson asking to be allowed to immediately "raise two divisions" for service at the front. The president declined. While conceding he was probably "too old" for battle and that he might "crack," TR felt that he embodied the promise of the Cohan song. He felt that if he were given a commission the news would "arouse the belief that America was coming." If he did crack "over there," the president could use him to "rouse more enthusiasm here and take some more men over."

Although he was unable to lead men into battle himself, he had four sons who could go forth to war. Indeed, Ted, Archie, and Quentin had been preparing for such an opportunity at a summer "citizens' training camp" at Plattsburg, New York. After the sinking of the *Lusitania* in May 1915, the idea of establishing an unofficial army training camp for young business and professional men had been discussed by Ted and fourteen other men at a meeting of about fifty friends and acquaintances. All were eager to sign up. At a second meeting of about a hundred volunteers a committee of three, including Ted, was authorized to prepare a plan of action. They approached the army officer who had been the professional organizer and trainer of the Rough Riders at San Antonio, Leonard Wood. A colonel in 1898, he was now a major general and the commander of the army's Department of the East. Wood agreed to set up a camp, which would initially take twenty-five men. If they qualified they would be commissioned in the army reserve.

Response to the announcement that the first camp would open in August 1915 resulted in a thousand applicants. All were enrolled, and the second camp had almost as many. The men were lawyers, artists, farmers, bankers, journalists, and businessmen of every kind. Among those at the first camp were Robert Bacon, the U.S. ambassador to France; John Purroy Mitchell, the mayor of New York; George Wharton Pepper, later a U.S. senator from Pennsylvania; New York City police commissioner Arthur Woods; and Dudley Field Malon, collector of customs of the Port of New York. Ted, Archie, and Quentin attended from the beginning. Ted and Archie finished the course in 1916 with reserve commissions of major and first lieutenant. Quentin decided to go into army aviation and went to flight-training school at Mineola, Long Island.

Twelve days after the declaration of war, Quentin became best man when Archie married his fiancée, Grace Lockwood, in a spur-of-the-moment ceremony in Boston after he and Ted received orders placing them on active duty and sending them to Plattsburg to plan for training draftees. Restless and eager to get into the war as soon as possible, Ted appealed to TR for help.

The result was a letter to an old friend and comrade-in-arms in Cuba, Gen. John J. Pershing, commanding the American Expeditionary Forces. Dated May 17, 1917, the letter said in part:

> I write you now to request that my two sons, Theodore Roosevelt, Jr., aged 27, and Archibald B. Roosevelt, age 23, both of Harvard, be allowed to enlist as privates with you, to go over with the first troops. The former is a Major and the latter a Captain in the Officers' Reserve Corps. They are at Plattsburg for their third summer.
>
> My own belief is that competent men of their rank and standing can gain very little from a third summer at Plattsburg, and that they should be utilized as officers, even if only as Second Lieutenants. But they are keenly desirous to see service; and if they serve under you at the front and are not killed, they will be far better able to instruct the draft army next fall or next winter, or whenever they are sent home, than they will be after spending the summer at Plattsburg.

The letter contained two errors. Ted was thirty and TR had promoted Archie one grade. But the letter achieved its purpose. Pershing agreed to let them join the first contingent of the AEF in their officers' ranks.

To be certain that they were not left behind, Ted enlisted the help of Eleanor by asking her to contact a friend of her family, Gen. J. Franklin

Bell. Commandant of Governor's Island in New York harbor, he was in charge of troop embarkations. Exclaiming, "I like that spirit," he promised Eleanor that he would see that Ted "gets off on the first ship leaving after he gets his orders." Eleanor was so relieved and happy for Ted that she burst out laughing. So did Bell and his aide, Capt. George C. Marshall.

On June 20, 1917, Ted and Eleanor's seventh wedding anniversary, she was dockside to wave good-bye to Ted and Archie, with their officers' rankings intact, as the war-converted liner *Chicago* sailed for France.

10

When Gen. Joseph-Jacques-Césaire Joffre took time from a visit to the United States to pay a call at Sagamore Hill, the French army hero told the former leader of the Rough Riders that if Roosevelt had been allowed to come to Paris and march down the Champs-Élysées, "if only with a fife and drum corps, the effect on French morale would have been electric."

But it was Theodore junior and Archie who went in his stead. Soon, perhaps, Quentin would join them as an aviator. On the day Ted and Archie sailed, he had his commission and was awaiting orders to sail. Only Kermit remained at home, in training at Plattsburg.

Unlike his brothers, Kermit had not spent much time at the camp. Nor did he seem to have their natural bent for the military life. Always more interested in intellectual matters than in the physicality exhibited by his siblings, he was more comfortable holding a book than a gun. But he was his father's son and so, he wrote to TR about the war, "As long as it's going on I want to be the first in it." Though married with an infant son, the man who had shared adventures in Africa and Brazil with his father wrote to him, "I wish you were in this war so that I could go off with you again and try for the malevolent hyenas with the courage of simba."

With his brothers already "in it," he implored TR to see what he could do to speed up the process. Seizing upon the happenstance of a visit to Sagamore Hill by the British publisher Lord Northcliffe, TR wondered if the press baron might use his friendship with Britain's secretary of war, Lord Derby, to get Kermit a commission in His Majesty's forces. Northcliffe, sure that there would be no difficulty about it, said he would see what he could do.

Presently, TR wrote exultantly to Ted in France that Kermit had been offered "a staff position with the British General in Mesopotamia and he'll be sailing immediately," and that Quentin "hopes to sail in ten days."

At the age of twenty Quentin had completed two years at Harvard studying mechanical engineering. He took his flight training at an airdrome in Mineola, Long Island. Because he had poor vision he had passed the eyesight test by getting a copy of the eye chart and memorizing it. With no barracks facilities available at Mineola he had slept at Sagamore Hill, rising early in the morning and donning a long oil-spattered coat, riding breeches, boots, and a black silk stocking over his head to keep his hair in place. The stocking dangled down his back like a pigtail. To his comrades in flight training his aviation skills left much to be desired, but he loved to fly and to come in low above Sagamore Hill to "buzz" the house as TR waved at him in delight. To his comrades he was good natured and reliable, though often impetuous and headstrong.

When TR learned that Quentin would "go over with the first ten fliers to the French Aviation School," he griped to Archie, "Everybody works but Father!"

A note sent to Ted in France reporting on Quentin's imminent departure and Kermit's posting to the British general in Mesopotamia ended with "Your loving father, THE SLACKER *MALGRE LUI.*"

Soon after Theodore Roosevelt Jr. and brother Archibald first set foot on French soil at Bordeaux, Ted noted in a letter home that the "poor people" who greeted them "were bitterly disappointed when they found out that the handful of untrained men" coming ashore were not "simply the first contingent of an enormous army which would follow without interruption." To the average Frenchmen, who had always been accustomed to their well-trained men flocking to the colors immediately when called, George M. Cohan's musical promise of a flood of Yanks coming "over there" had been taken to mean they would be there quickly and in the thousands. Instead, the Americans who came were few and obviously unready.

Upon arriving in France, General Pershing informed the disappointed French government that the Americans would need many months of preparation before going into battle. To get them started the general, who had been nicknamed "Black Jack" for having commanded the Negro 10th Cavalry on the southwest frontier, established a system of training schools for the new arrivals.

Reporting to Pershing in Paris, the Roosevelts got their assignments. Archie was posted to the 16th Infantry. Ted was ordered to the town of Demange-aux-Eaux to help arrange for the billeting and further training of troops. In July, with the rank of major, he joined the 26th Infantry of the 1st Division. When TR learned of this, he wrote to Archie, "I am surprised and immensely pleased at Ted's having been assigned to duty as a major in the line." Regarding Archie's duties with the 16th Infantry, he expressed pleasure and pride that Archie was serving with a unit that had been in "the San Juan fight" and to "the immediate left of our dismounted cavalry" as he led the Rough Riders to the top of Kettle Hill.

Despite this indirect connection to TR's crowded hour in Cuba, Archie wished to be reunited with Ted in the 26th. TR thought it was a bad idea that one brother would be under the command of another, even in a training situation. The patriarch of Sagamore Hill was also unhappy to learn from Eleanor that he would soon have a daughter-in-law serving in France. She was determined "to do some sort of war work in order to be on the same side of the Atlantic as Ted" and had volunteered herself to the National War Work Council for the task of setting up YMCA canteens for American soldiers in France. Although TR had declared "emphatically that no women in the family were to follow their husbands," Eleanor felt that "in this case I had to disregard his wishes."

Realizing it would be "a terrible wrench" to leave the children, she thought Ted might need her more. Gracie was five, Teddy three, and Cornelius a year and a half. They were left with her mother. Had they been ten years older, Eleanor wrote in her memoir, she would not have gone. In sailing to France she disobeyed Ted, who had expressed misgivings about her going. But when she cabled him that she would sail on the *Espagne* on July 24, 1917, and noted her expected arrival date and the address of an aunt with whom she would be staying in Paris, he sent a wire to be handed to her when she arrived:

SIMPLY DELIGHTED YOU ARE HERE FELT SURE YOU WOULD COME ALL ALONG.

Barely settled into the large house at the corner of the Avenue du Bois de Boulogne and the Rue de Villejust, Eleanor received a second wire:

SEND AT ONCE TWELVE BARRELS SOFT DRINKS TEN POUNDS PIPE TOBACCO PHONOGRAPH RECORDS COM-

PLETE BASEBALL OUTFIT TWELVE PAIRS BOXING GLOVES
TWELVE SOCCER BALLS SIX BASKETBALLS EIGHT FIFES
EIGHT DRUMS AND STICKS GOOD HORSE SADDLE AND BRI-
DLE MUCH LOVE TED

The message had come *sans origine*, leaving Eleanor with no idea as
to where Ted was located so that she could deliver the requested items,
assuming she could find them in a city she had not seen since her mother
had taken her back to New York at the age of ten. Having gotten most
of the requested items, and learning the area where Ted's outfit was located, she made a friend of a man in charge of supplies at the YMCA
and persuaded him to allow her to send the items "on a Y truck that was
going in the general direction of Demange-aux-Eaux." With the truck
on its way, YMCA officials who heard what she had done issued an order
not to repeat the deed, advising her that "the YMCA was there to serve
the American Expeditionary Forces, not merely the 1st Battalion, 26th
Infantry."

In a further effort to provide sports equipment for his trainees to use
in their time off Ted supposed that the nearby city of Bar-de-Luc would
certainly have a store similar to New York City's famed Abercrombie and
Fitch. In search of such an establishment he stopped an elderly couple
and, in his halting French (learned on the ship that carried him to
France), asked for directions to a "*maison de sport.*" The old man offered
a suggestion, but his wife provided Ted another address. He discovered
it was a thriving brothel.

On an expedition with Archie and three privates from camp to improve the quality of food, Ted found a nearby chicken farm. Paying for
fourteen birds with his own money, he proceeded to expertly wring their
necks. Ted explained to the astonished enlisted men that he'd learned
how to kill and pluck chickens from a cook in the White House who had
been serving meals to presidents and their families since the days of Lincoln. In an attempt to both entertain and enlighten the minds of men
under his command Archie lent them books, each with a bookplate
pasted in the front noting that it came from the library of President
Theodore Roosevelt.

On August 9, 1917, TR responded to a letter from Ted about his assignment: "Your letter has come, and I am delighted, all the more because of my surprise, for I had no idea that you could make a *regular* regiment in a line position, and I knew, and cordially sympathized with, your

desire to be in the line. You have the fighting tradition! It is a great thing you have done; I am very greatly pleased."

On August 22 he wrote to Eleanor, "Well, I am *very* proud of you— and of all my boys. And my only personal consolation is that I was in the only war I had a chance at, even tho [*sic*] it was only a small one." After receiving a letter from Eleanor the next day he again wrote approvingly to her of her work with the YMCA. He called her "you lovely competent person."

He continued, "Everybody works but Father! I spend my time refusing innumerable requests from Tom-fools who think speeches *would* count, and making the very speeches which as a matter of fact *don't* count. Large masses of men still feel vaguely that somehow I can say something which will avoid all criticism of the government and yet make the government instantly remedy everything that is wrong; whereas in reality nothing now counts except the actual doing of the work; and that I am allowed to have no part in."

Condemned by presidential decree to sit out "the great war" in Europe, he kept busy by writing and occasionally speaking. He told Ted of receiving "various offers which are good from the financial side, but my interest of course now lies entirely in the work of you four boys, for my work is of no real consequence—what I did was done in the Spanish War and the decade following; and now I am overjoyed that you four have your chance, whatever the cost."

All "the boys" were now "in it." Kermit was in Mesopotamia. Quentin was in France and posted as a supply officer at the American flying school at Issoudun, near Bourges. And Archie and Ted were close to the front, training men for action that was bound to become their war.

While gaining the loyalty and respect of enlisted men proved easy, the reserve-army sons of the former president and renowned hero of America's last foreign war found only skepticism among regular army officers. From captain up they saw "the Roosevelt boys" as amateurs who had gotten their rank only because of the political influence of their father. As a result Ted and Archie found themselves in the same predicament as had the newly minted Lt. Col. Theodore Roosevelt when he'd arrived at Camp Wood near San Antonio in 1898, "all duded up" in a uniform custom-made by Brooks Brothers.

But as the training continued, these doubters found themselves witnesses as Ted was awarded two commendations for exemplary performance from the inspector general, AEF. Regular army officers found themselves passed over on December 11, 1917, when Brig. Gen. B. B. Buck, commanding the 2d Brigade of the 1st Division, offered to make Ted brigade adjutant. Ted declined the staff post, stating that he preferred "to remain with troops."

On January 28, 1918, Brig. Gen. George B. Duncan recommended Ted for promotion to lieutenant colonel and transfer to the18th Infantry. He wrote, "For six months I have had under observation the work of Maj. Theodore Roosevelt Jr. He commanded a battalion in my regiment, the 26th Infantry, directly under me. I consider Major Roosevelt an officer of unusual ability. He is most conscientious in the performance of every duty, never falters, has been an excellent commander of men, and is to-day probably the best battalion commander in the 1st Division—I know he is superior to any on the 1st Brigade."

In a telegram to General Pershing, dated March 26, 1918, from Maj. Gen. J. G. Harbord, deputy chief of staff, AEF, Ted would again be proposed for higher rank on the recommendation of Maj. Gen. Robert L. Bullard, commanding the 1st Division. Promotion would be advised again on May 31, 1918. All of these would be rejected at the General Staff Headquarters, primarily because it was felt that Ted "had not been long enough in the service."

Meanwhile, Pershing made it clear to the French that he could not commit Americans to battle until they were ready. If all went according to plan, that would be in the summer of 1918. He expected that by that time he would be in command of a million men who would be ready to fight and win. Such a force taking to the field would tilt the military balance of power away from the Germans and toward the Allies. From his headquarters in Paris he set up the infrastructure required to keep his promise. A line of communications system linked ports where "doughboys" arrived and then cockily marched off ships as bands played "Over There" and a host of patriotic tunes turned out by the songsmiths of New York's Tin Pan Alley. Training was in special camps and at forward bases. Pershing brushed aside as "technicalities" warnings that some of the procedures he established had no authorization from Congress.

On September 1, 1917, he received a report of the first American casualties. Four men were killed in an air raid on a British base hospital. The next day two American engineers died when German artillery shells exploded as the men were repairing a railway track well behind the battle line at Gouzeaucourt.

A few days later, Eleanor found herself in Pershing's formidable presence at a dinner party in his home on the left bank of the Seine. She reported "getting along beautifully" and "thoroughly enjoying myself when suddenly a thought struck the general."

Turning to her with "his face set like the Day of Judgment," Black Jack barked, "How do you happen to be here anyhow? No wives are allowed to come overseas. Where are your children? Your place is with them, not here. I think you ought to be sent home."

Eleanor felt "as if the Angel Gabriel had blown his horn at her." Everyone stopped talking to listen. She was startled and murmured something about having come over before restrictions against wives being overseas had been imposed. She explained that she wanted to be near Ted and had left her children with her mother. "It took more nerve than I had to wrangle with the Commander in Chief of the American Expeditionary Forces," she remembered. "He seemed to disapprove of me completely, and I went home feeling as if I had been spanked."

She wrote Ted about it "to the last detail."

Soon after, in order to be closer to training camps and nearer the front, Pershing shifted his headquarters from Paris to Chaumont. Less than a month later, he assessed the readiness of the 1st Division. This involved observing a demonstration of how Maj. Theodore Roosevelt Jr. would direct his men in an attack on a German entrenchment. Finding a "lack of competence," he exploded with an anger that was assuaged only by the intervention of the same captain who had joined in Eleanor Roosevelt's delighted laughter when General Bell, back in May, agreed to speed up Ted's departure for France. George C. Marshall patiently explained the difficulties in training men who were green. Pershing's frustration shifted from Major Roosevelt to "some general officers who have neither the experience, the energy, nor the aggressive spirit to prepare their units or to handle them under battle conditions as they exist today."

Ted took advantage of the general's presence, and of the fact that Pershing was a friend of his father, to bring up the subject of Pershing's rebuke of Eleanor at the dinner party. "My goodness, sir," he said, "but you're in bad with my wife."

When Eleanor met Pershing again in Paris after his inspection tour of the camps, Black Jack took both her hands in his and said, "I'm afraid I must have hurt your feelings that night at dinner, but really I didn't mean to. Can we be friends again?"

• • •

To Ted from Sagamore Hill came a letter that TR had written on September 13, Ted's thirtieth birthday. It began, "Many happy returns of the day!" He expressed a hope that Ted was spending it with Eleanor. For the most part a chatty letter about family and friends, it told of his entertaining a number of officers from a National Guard division in training at Mineola. He noted that not until Ted was an old man would Ted be "able quite to understand the satisfaction I feel because each of my sons is doing and has done better that I was doing and had done at his age—and I had done well. And of course this is preeminently true of you. I don't mean that any of you will be President; as regards the extraordinary prizes the element of luck is *the* determining factor; but getting in the class of those who have to their credit worthy, and even distinguished, achievement—that's what I mean."

At the end of September, Ted was on a brief leave in Paris, "tanned and looking as if he were made of steel." He and Eleanor spent the first day driving around the city, buying things he needed and visiting YMCA headquarters, where Eleanor "showed Ted off to everybody." The two days "passed like a flash."

On November 29, a proud TR reported to Ted, "I have just had two very nice letters from General Pershing and Colonel Harbord, both speaking of you in high terms; the latter speaking of your having got your men to a 'razor edge' of efficiency. Indeed there is a curiously marked agreement of everybody as to how well you are doing—and Archie's belief in and devotion to you are quite touching."

Another cause for TR's paternal satisfaction and pride was a letter concerning Quentin. Sent to Sagamore Hill by New York policeman Crain A. Gardiner, it had been written by Gardiner's son. A sergeant who was a mechanic at Quentin's air base at Issoudun, he wrote, "We have a real man commanding us now, just like his father I guess, one of Colonel Roosevelt's sons. We have had him only a short while but would do more for him than all the time we knew the other man [who had been the previous commander]."

During these early days of United States involvement in the war, as Quentin Roosevelt and other young Americans climbed into airplanes that looked as fragile as kites, none of them expected that they would be pictured by a fascinated world as a romantic breed of dashing, heroic figures who made warfare in the skies above France a kind of gentlemanly, if deadly, sport. One of these daring aviators who would ignite the world's imagination when Quentin was in charge of supplies at Issoudun was the base's engineering officer. Before long, Lt. Eddie Rickenbacker would be famously known to Americans by a new word in the dictionary of warfare—*ace*. Having expected Theodore Roosevelt's youngest son to "have the airs and superciliousness of a spoiled boy," Rickenbacker found Quentin to be "absolutely square in everything he said or did" and one of the most popular fellows in the group. "We loved him," Rickenbacker recalled, "for his own natural self."

Just before Christmas Quentin came down with pneumonia. Eleanor rushed from Paris to Issoudun and found him in bed in a long, narrow barracks inadequately heated by a stove at one end. Granted three weeks' leave by the doctor, he went to Paris with Eleanor with the intention of proceeding to a period of recuperation in the sun and warmth of the Riviera. Discovering nothing but snow and rain at the resort, he returned to Paris and spent Christmas with Eleanor and her French relatives and friends. It was the first Christmas that Theodore Roosevelt would spend at Sagamore Hill not surrounded by his beloved brood of bunnies.

11

In January 1918 a war correspondent for the *New York Tribune,* Heywood Broun, who had been enrolled for the Harvard Class of 1910, but dropped out after two years, went looking for a subject for a feature article on New Yorkers among the growing numbers of Yanks who were "over there." He found Maj. Ted Roosevelt, Class of 1908. Ted immediately remembered Broun as a large, untidy-looking, and somewhat indolent freshman who, instead of going out for football, had chosen basketball, only to have his athletic career aborted by a knee injury. His goal in life, Ted recalled, was to be a playwright. He'd gone into journalism by starting at the bottom with the *Morning Telegraph.* After Broun began covering the war for the *Tribune,* Ted heard a funny story concerning the first time General Pershing laid eyes on the correspondent. Gazing at the unkempt figure, the spit-and-polish commander-in-chief of the AEF blurted, "What in blazes happened to you? Did you fall down?"

Reporting to *Tribune* readers on his inspection of Ted's division, Broun described Major Roosevelt as "alert and efficient" in an article that dealt at some length with Ted's having overcome "initial prejudice against him among regular officers." After reading Broun's references to the extremely cold weather being endured by the Americans, TR wrote to Ted, "The accounts of the arctic weather in France have of course given us constant anxiety about you and Archie."

Considerably more worrisome to Ted, Archie, and Quentin than the French weather was disturbing word from their mother in the first week of February that Big Bear had been rushed to the hospital (Roosevelt Hospital, endowed by a cousin). TR suffered from abscesses in his ear and on the leg he had injured on the Brazil expedition. For a time, after an operation to relieve pain in his ear, it was feared he might die. As the crisis passed, Quentin got a letter expressing his father's impatience "over there being any anxiety" in his sons about him. "It's about you and the other boys that we have to think," he wrote, "and not about utterly unimportant troubles of their elderly civilian kinsfolk!"

TR rallied and recovered in time to hail the birth of another grandchild, Archibald B. Roosevelt Jr. Archie learned he had a son by reading the news in the *Paris Herald.* An exultant letter soon followed from TR that said, "Well, think of little Archie being born with his father just promoted to a Captaincy and in the trenches."

On January 18, 1918, the 1st Division had entered the front line in the Ansauville area of the St. Michel Salient. The move was intended to give the green troops experience in holding a line. No offensive action was anticipated. But when the Germans learned of their presence, they raided an American listening post. Two Americans were killed, two wounded, and one captured. In an ambush of an American patrol in "No-Man's-Land" Germans killed four more, wounded two, and captured two. On February 5, a lieutenant named Thompson became the first American aviator to defeat a German in aerial combat. Excitement over his victory was dimmed with news that on the same day a German submarine sank the British troopship *Tuscania,* killing 166 American soldiers en route to the war and 44 British sailors. Later in the month, American volunteers joined a French raiding party on German trenches at Chevregny, south of German-held Laon. In the half-hour attack the raiders captured 25 Germans. Compared to the fighting in the previous three years of the war, noted a correspondent of the *New York Times,* the action did not amount to much, but because February 25 marked the first day that Americans had ventured into a battle, the reporter proposed, the date "will always be remembered in the history of the war."

Two days before the doughboys joined in the raid at Chevregny, Britain's minister of munitions, Winston Churchill, was touring the Ypres Salient. Contemplating the battles of the past three years, he wrote his wife a letter that could have been penned by another romanticizer of war, Theodore Roosevelt. "Death seems as commonplace and as little alarming as the undertaker," said Churchill. "Quite a natural ordinary event, which may happen at any moment, as it happened to all these scores of thousands who lie together in this vast cemetery, ennobled and rendered forever glorious by their memory."

One of the dead in the cemetery was an American friend of Churchill, Henry Butters of San Francisco. To get into the war well before the

United States formally entered it, Butters had managed to join the Royal Artillery by claiming to be British born. At the time of Churchill's visit to the bloody soil of France, troops from the United States were pouring into French ports and marching to camps near the front. On February 26 near Réchicourt the chief of staff of the 42d Division, Col. Douglas MacArthur, observed a French raid on German trenches and became so caught up in the fury and the excitement that he rushed in to take part. By helping capture several Germans he received the Croix de Guerre. A year earlier, when it was suggested by Secretary of War Newton Baker that a division be formed with men from many different states, MacArthur had said, "Fine, that will stretch over the whole country like a rainbow." The offhand remark was immortalized as the 42d's nickname, the Rainbow Division. Americans at home embraced the name with the same enthusiasm and pride that they had shown in 1898 in rallying behind Roosevelt's Rough Riders.

In early March Theodore Roosevelt's third son was felled by an exploding German artillery shell. A chunk of hot, flying shrapnel shattered Archie's kneecap. Another sliver of steel simultaneously broke his left arm and cut the main nerve. But it was the knee injury that proved of gravest concern. Doctors feared it would require amputation of the leg. Should they prove able to save it, they advised Archie, he could be a lifetime cripple. (The leg was saved and Archie recovered so well that he was able to command combat troops in the Pacific in World War II, and be wounded again.)

When informed of Archie's wounds, Ted sent a telegram to Eleanor in the hope that she could go to him at the hospital in Toul. But YMCA officials stood on regulations that would not allow civilian relatives visits to army hospitals near the front. Although deeply disappointed, Eleanor learned a few days later that Archie would soon be moved to a hospital in Paris.

News of Archie having been wounded reached the Roosevelts at Sagamore Hill in bits and pieces on March 13. First, a reporter appeared at the door to inform them that the French had awarded Archie the Croix de Guerre, but that he had not been seriously hurt. This was also the report telegraphed to Sagamore Hill by the War Department. Only when Ted cabled did they learn the extent of Archie's wounds.

TR wrote to the French political leader Georges Clemenceau about Archie's medal, "I am prouder of his having received it than of my having been President."

When the family learned that Archie would recover, his sister Ethel, who understood her competitive brothers very well, remarked to their father that unwounded and undecorated Ted was probably a "very sad and envious bunny." She posited that Ted could stand Archie's having either the wound or the medal, but not both.

To make matters worse for Ted, he also learned that Kermit had gotten a decoration for valor. In command of a light-armored motor battery at Tikrit, Iraq, during a January offensive on the city of Baghdad by the British against Germany's Near East allies, the Turks, Kermit had come upon a group of Turkish soldiers in a house. They were wounded and scared, but still armed and very dangerous. Barging into the building without thinking to draw his revolver and wielding only his officer's swagger stick, he demanded their immediate surrender. The startled Turks tossed aside their guns and threw up their arms. For this daring, if foolhardy, exploit Kermit was awarded the British Army Cross.

As active operations by the British in Mesopotamia drew to a victorious close toward spring of 1918, Kermit longed for a transfer from the British Army to the American, with a post in France. In hopes of achieving this he turned to his father for assistance. A letter from TR to Gen. William March, chief of staff, inquired if such a move were possible. March said it was and issued orders transferring Kermit to the U.S. Army as captain of artillery. TR wrote to Ted, "I am exceedingly glad that he [Kermit] should now be in American uniform."

All the Roosevelt boys would now be in France.

With a series of artillery bombardments on March 9, 1918, Germans launched a massive offensive across the Western Front. One of their targets the next day was an infantry post in the Parroy Forest that was manned by troops of the Rainbow Division. Nineteen of them died in a dugout. A corporal in the division, a poet named Joyce Kilmer, provided a verse to be read at the mass funeral. Death had come flying through the air, it said,

And stopped his flight at the dugout stair,
Touched his prey—
And left them there—
Clay to clay.
He hid their bodies stealthily

In the soil of the land they sought to free,
And fled away.

The German offensive began with the goal of driving British troops from the Somme and the French from the Aisne and then moving on to Paris. Two days after the nineteen Americans who had been killed in the Parroy Forest were buried, the German bombardment started with a rain of half a million shells containing mustard gas and phosgene.

"Apparently, the great German offensive has begun on an enormous scale on the British front," TR wrote to recuperating Archie. "It is a bitter thought to me that it is only our folly during the last three years, and especially during the last eighteen months, that has prevented us from having at this moment in France a couple of million fighting troops, fully equipped with guns, airplanes, and everything else; in which there could be no German offensive, no hideous loss of life, and peace on our own terms."

TR confided to a friend at Sagamore Hill that he often awoke "in the middle of the night, wondering if the boys are all right, and thinking how I could tell their mother if anything happened." He told another visitor, "I feel as though I were a hundred years old, and had *never* been young." A letter to Ted was brimming with frustration. "It is very difficult for me to hold myself within any bounds at all," he complained, "when over here the people responsible for our shortcomings not merely lie about them or complacently excuse them but actually boast about being unprepared and hold up the fact as something meritorious."

All his sons had been in it from the beginning, but only Quentin had yet to see fighting. Ted and Archie were not a bit reluctant to tell him that he was, in their view, a slacker unworthy of the Roosevelt name. The situation was not Quentin's fault. He was a trained aviator, eager to take to the skies in battle with "the Huns," but he was left grounded because of a shortage of serviceable aircraft. While his brothers in the infantry did not grasp this fact, his father did. On April 21, 1918, TR wrote:

Dearest Quentin: We are all at sea as to where you are and what you are doing; and in this crisis the possibilities are such that we know not what conditions may have become when our letters reach you. I think that [Americans] really are somewhat aroused by that fact that we [the United States forces] are of so little weight in the terrible battle now going on; and, accordingly, one year after the event, the [Wilson] Administration is endeavoring in earnest to speed up matters. . . . For example, a layman like myself is utterly unable to make out what our airplane situation is. We all know that you have no American bombing planes (I am doubtless using the wrong terms), but we cannot tell you how soon you will have them, and in what proportion you will get them from the French or be utilized by the French fliers. Therefore I have no idea whether there is any possibility of your getting to the front; I have no idea what you are doing—whether you are fighting, or raging because you can't get to the fighting line

He wrote to Ted, "Mother bears herself, as she always does in every crisis, with as fine gallantry as any heroine of history. After all, I don't wonder that her sons have turned out as you four have turned out."

A letter to Archie in the hospital in Paris declared, "I can't say how proud we are of you. Our pride even outweighs our anxiety. You and your brothers, by what you have done during the last year, have more than justified our lives. . . . Whenever I say what our people *ought* to have done, I think of what you *have* done; and I hold my head high."

Noting that he had received "dozens of newspaper clippings and scores of letters about your wounds and the cross," he continued, "I really think that our people generally felt a genuine pride in your 'proving your truth by your endeavor,' and thoroughly understand my pride in you; and a good many felt that, inasmuch as you were going to recover, they were rather glad that one of *my sons* had the dangerous honor of being among the first to be wounded in battle."

Again writing to Ted, the proud father observed, "What has befallen you I have no idea, but of one thing I am sure, my first-born son, that, no matter what the conditions, you have borne yourself with the utmost courage, coolness, and efficiency."

He had this on no less authority than his old friend and comrade-in-arms, Leonard Wood. Just back from an inspection trip to the front, the general reported that Ted's battalion had earned a reputation that surpassed all others in the army. Less than a month after Wood's visit to Sagamore Hill, British general G. T. M. "Tom" Bridges came to lunch and told TR that the 1st Division was the only American force fully up to battle requirements. And Brig. Gen. George B. Duncan wrote that he'd "never known a harder-working, more conscientious leader" than Maj. Ted Roosevelt.

A stream of letters went to Ted from Sagamore Hill:

You have made good in really extraordinary fashion and I, who have done nothing in this war, walk with my head high because of the honor you four have won.

The only thing I take a real interest in is the war, and I loathe being unable to *do* anything.

I would rather have you four stand at Armageddon even than stand there myself. You, personally, are now in the position of the greatest danger; but when the trumpets sound for Armageddon only those win the undying honor and glory who stand where the danger is sorest.

In May, as Eleanor divided her days between YMCA canteen work and visits to the hospital to see how Archie's recovery was coming along, Quentin arrived in Paris on a five-day leave. He found her preparing for Ted's arrival, also on leave. Quentin informed TR by letter that she was "making up a regular trousseau" for the event. "It's really amusing, too amusing. She feels that she must have everything that is absolutely the prettiest and nicest for those wonderful seven days when Ted is here, so she has bought a whole flock of new dresses and new shoes and new everythings."

Quentin was the only unmarried son of Theodore Roosevelt. But he did have a fiancée. Flora Payne Whitney was the twenty-year-old daughter of Harry Payne Whitney and Gertrude Vanderbilt Whitney. Her mother's father was Cornelius Vanderbilt II, president of the New York Central Railroad. Her uncle, Arthur Gwynne Vanderbilt, had died in the sinking of the *Lusitania.* Speaking of her one evening with Eleanor, in springtime Paris, about what Flora would do if he got "bumped off" in the war, he said she'd be sad for a while. But knowing "just how I would want her to act," she would accept life as "such a wonderful thing, that she must live, and if she must drink the cup, then drink it in thankfulness for what we have already had, and then she must live on again. Life is glorious."

At the end of May the Germans launched their third offensive against the French lines. It started on the Aisne and threatened to succeed. On the thirtieth they reached the river Marne near Château-Thierry. The next day they were forty miles from Paris. Eleanor heard the guns clearly, and at night she saw flashes "like summer lightning in the north."

Four thousand German guns had opened fire along a twenty-four-mile front. By the end of the twenty-eighth they'd gouged a forty-mile-wide gap in the Allied lines. The wedge they drove into it was fifteen miles deep. Only the Americans at Cantigny on the Somme had been able to hold, and then go on the attack. A full brigade, nearly 4,000 men, led by twelve French tanks and given cover by French planes and artillery, launched the first sustained American attack of the war. With the village of Cantigny taken, they held it against seven counterattacks over seventy-two hours and suffered 200 killed. The same number were incapacitated by gas attacks.

Among the victims of the gassing was Ted. Despite this, with the town secured and German counterattacks repulsed and knowing that Paris was threatened with being overrun, he barged into the tent of Lt. Col. George C. Marshall at 1st Division Headquarters. He woke him out of a sound sleep at three in the morning to demand a pass to Paris in order to see that Eleanor was safe. Marshall blared, "For heaven's sake, Roosevelt, go and get some rest. You've been gassed and look like hell. Your wife will be all right. She must have friends in Paris who will look after her. Go away and get some sleep!"

"That's as it may be," Ted replied, "but I've got to be sure. She's the only wife I've got."

On Sunday, June second, Eleanor had the day off. As she sat at her desk at home, writing letters, the door opened and Ted walked in. She had never seen anyone look so ghastly, His face was scorched and inflamed, the whites of his eyes an angry red.

Between racking coughs Ted demanded, "Why are you still here? Don't you know the Germans are advancing on Paris? You must leave at once."

Recalling the moment in her memoir, Eleanor wrote, "To relieve Ted's mind we called up a friend in the provost marshal's office who assured Ted he would see I got away if the Germans came. Ted had a hot bath and a change of clothes, a smart new uniform and boots which I had ready for him. It was a lovely summer night, and for the first time in two weeks there was no air raid. Quentin appeared, overjoyed to see Ted."

After dinner they visited Archie at the hospital.

"When we got home," Eleanor's remembrance continued, "Ted told me he had not been able to lie down since being gassed, as he choked in that position. I propped him in pillows, and he was able to sleep between spasms of coughing. I would have given anything to keep him with me, and begged him to stay and have medical treatment. All he had to do was to report himself ill, but he laughed at me. 'Now that I know you're all right I'm as fit as a fiddle.' He left early the next morning."

Three weeks later, Ted was cited for "high courage and leadership." The citation read, "At Cantigny, although gassed in the lungs and gassed in the eyes to blindness [he] refused to be evacuated [and] retained command of his battalion through heavy bombardment."

For these actions he was awarded the Silver Star and put on a par with Archie when the French gave him the Croix de Guerre. But at the time the medals were presented, Ted was concerned about Archie's continued recovery. The wounded left arm required another operation. The severed nerve was so shrunken that there was a gap of some inches between the two ends. The surgery was intended to place them in a position in which they would grow together, but it would be eight months before Archie would know if he would recover completely.

This unsettling prospect was offset somewhat a few days later with news from Quentin that he'd been in his first dogfight and shot down an enemy plane.

Orders to Lt. Quentin Roosevelt to report for combat duty with the 1st Pursuit Group of the 95th Aero Squadron, nicknamed the "Kicking Mule Squadron," had been issued in mid-June.

The news thrilled the old man at Sagamore Hill. He wrote to a relative, "Now he, too, is where he may pay with his body for his heart's desire."

After motorcycling from Issoudun to Paris to see Eleanor and his brothers, Quentin reported at the 95th's base at Orly Airfield, outside Paris, knowing that the men he'd commanded at his former post had promised that if he got shot down and captured they would come rescue him. That he might fly into misadventure would not come as surprise to them. He was regarded as a daredevil. Like his father during the dash up that famous hill in Cuba, he would go all out for glory, no matter the risk. Almost immediately upon reporting to Orly Airfield, he was in the air for a half-hour ride to get used to "my plane" and the sector in which he would flying.

He wrote to Flora, "Then later on I went out on a patrol just up along the lines, to, as they put it, get used to being shot at by the [Germans]. It is really exciting at first when you see the stuff bursting in great black puffs round you, but you get used to it after fifteen minutes."

His first meeting with the enemy in the sky occurred on July 6, 1918. He was flying a pursuit plane in a squad of escorts for a photographic reconnaissance plane. Although he shot down no enemy craft, he found himself so thrilled with the action, as he would write home to his mother, "that you forget everything except getting the other fellow and trying to dodge the tracers when they start streaming past you."

Five days later, he engaged three German planes in an aerial skirmish that ended with an unknown German aviator's plane spiraling down to earth in flames, its fuselage riddled with bullets from his machine guns, while the other two broke off the fight and zoomed away.

When TR read of the event in press dispatches, he dashed off an exultant note to Ted.

"The last of the lion's brood," exclaimed the veteran African explorer and big game hunter, "has been blooded."

The warrior of 1898 wrote to daughter Ethel, "Whatever now befalls Quentin he has now had his crowded hour, and his day of honor and triumph."

What TR did not know was that Quentin's "crowded hour" had been more like a circus in the clouds. Returning from the escort mission, he had become separated from his group and swept up by a gust of wind into a shelf of clouds north of Château-Thierry. Descending into the clear, he spotted three planes and believed they were part of his squadron. They were Germans. Since he was so near, he decided he "might as well take a crack at one of them." Pulling up a little nearer, he squeezed the trigger of his machine gun.

"My tracers were shooting all around him," he said in a letter to Flora, "but I guess he was so surprised that for a bit he couldn't think what to do."

Eager to relate his first "kill" to Archie, he mounted his motorcycle and headed to Paris, barged in on his sister-in-law at Eleanor's YMCA office, and demanded that she accompany him to the hospital. Eleanor suggested that they celebrate his victory and give Archie a treat by taking him wild strawberries and Normandy cream from the Café de la Régence. The dessert was carried in a china dish tied up with paper and string. Unfortunately, as Eleanor and Quentin were walking along the Avenue de l'Opéra, the string broke. Archie's treat crashed to the pavement to ooze strawberries and cream in all directions. Whether they told Archie about the mishap was not recorded in Eleanor's book.

That evening Quentin and Eleanor dined at Ciro's and went to the Grand Guignol. In the morning Quentin got on his motorcycle and returned to duty.

Eleanor, Archie, Ted, Kermit, and the Roosevelts of Sagamore Hill would not see him again. On July 14, 1918, as the French were celebrating Bastille Day, Quentin was in his plane in pursuit of a flight of the red-nosed Fokkers favored by Germany's famous Flying Circus. Because its dashing leader, Rittmeister Manfred von Richtofen, romanticized the world over as the "Red Baron," had been killed seven weeks earlier, the Germans were now commanded by a svelte and cocky ace by the name of Hermann Göring. Over Chamery, far behind enemy lines, one of the Germans opened fire on Quentin's plane and shot it down.

German aviators saw that the body of the handsome twenty-year-old American flier was retrieved from the plane's wreckage and buried with full military honors, including a battery of infantry standing at attention.

The devastating word of Quentin's death was announced by the German government. It was passed to Ted and his brothers through U.S. Army channels and to the rest of the Roosevelts, and the world, in news reports. Confirming to the world that Quentin Roosevelt had valiantly and bravely made repeated attacks on seven German planes, a German news agency reported, "This culminated in a duel between him and a German noncommissioned officer, who, after a short fight, succeeded in getting good aim at his brave but inexperienced opponent." Quentin was dead before his plane hit the ground, shot twice in the back of the head. His belongings, noted the Berlin news agency, would be returned to his parents through neutral parties.

"Mother," TR wrote to Kermit, "will carry the wound to her grave."

He expressed a hope to his three surviving sons that whichever of them first became the father of a boy, he would name the boy Quentin.

To Bob Ferguson, an old Rough Rider comrade, the brokenhearted but proud hero of the Cuban war wrote, "It is bitter that the young should die." But there were "things worse than death, for nothing under Heaven would I have had my sons act otherwise than as they acted. They have done pretty well, haven't they? Quentin killed, dying as a war hawk should . . . over the enemy's lines; Archie crippled, and given the French cross for gallantry; Ted gassed once . . . and cited for 'conspicuous gallantry'; Kermit with the British military cross, and now under Pershing."

12

About a month after Quentin was killed, the spot where his plane crashed was in control of the Allies. Three Americans went in search of the grave. They found it near the wreckage of his plane. It had been marked by German pilots with the smashed plane's propeller. *Roosevelt* was scratched into the paint. The three men included a classmate of Quentin's at Groton, Bill Preston; a Colonel McCoy, a former aide to President Roosevelt; and the Roman Catholic chaplain of New York's "Fighting 69th" Infantry Regiment, Father Francis P. Duffy. Preston wrote to Flora that they had placed a makeshift cross on the grave and that Father Duffy held a service.

Five days after Quentin's death, Eleanor was sitting upstairs in her home reading when a maid threw open the door and announced excitedly, "*Major Roosevelt* is here!"

Eleanor dashed downstairs and saw Ted being lifted out of an automobile in front of the house. With a little wave and a smile as he was carried in, Ted said, "I got wounded this morning, and here I am!"

Pinned to his uniform was a tag: GUNSHOT WOUND SEVERE.

He had been shot through the leg by a machine gun at Ploisy near Soissons, he explained, adding nonchalantly, "If only I could have got hold of a horse, I could have gone through the day at least. The fighting was so hot there were no ambulances around or they'd have taken me to a field hospital, but I came out in a field artillery limber and got away from them."

He'd ridden for several hours in the sidecar of a motorcycle, dodging through traffic and over shell-pitted roads until he ran across an old friend, a colonel, who had a car.

Eleanor insisted that he go to a hospital. Gingerly settling into an easy chair, Ted put up his feet and declared, "I want a bath. Then I want dinner: black bean soup, broiled live lobster, steamed clams, wild duck and hominy, rare roast beef and browned potatoes, and buckwheat cakes with maple syrup. If you're out of all that, I'll settle for whatever you have in the house. But start with a quart of Champagne."

At that moment the door opened and in walked their brother-in-law, Lt. Col. Richard Derby (Ethel's husband). Chief surgeon with the 2d Division, he was in Paris suffering from "Flanders flu." Examining Ted's right leg, he found two holes. A machine-gun bullet had gone in above the knee and exited at the back of the leg. "It's in a bad place," said Derby. "That part of the leg is a bottleneck, with all the important tendons, nerves, and veins going through it." Explaining that the wound was full of dirt and small pieces of uniform cloth, he warned, "If it's not opened and thoroughly cleaned out right away it will get infected and you may lose the leg. We're going to the hospital now."

Ted begged, "At least let me have my dinner."

Overruled by Derby, he was taken to the hospital where Archie was convalescing. In the Rue Piccini across the Avenue du Bois, it was run by Col. Joseph Blake primarily for Americans in Paris. Soon after Ted was admitted, Blake operated on the leg. With the surgery over, an assisting doctor announced, "When this has healed he'll be as good as new." Although the main nerve had escaped injury, Ted would be left with no feeling in his heel for life.

Two days later he was officially listed "sick in quarters" and discharged to recover in Eleanor's house. She requested a month off from her YMCA duties to tend to him. Presently, the 1st Division was withdrawn from the front for a period of rest after taking part in the battle at Soissons. Its casualties had been so extensive that they included all the field officers. Ted's 1st Battalion had come off the line under command of a second lieutenant. When Gen. Charles P. Summerall was asked if the division was capable of making another attack after such losses, he replied, "When the 1st Division has only two men left they will be echeloned in depth and attacking toward Berlin."

To Ted on 1st Division Headquarters letterhead dated August 18, 1918, Summerall wrote:

Your services in this Division have been conspicuous for efficiency, energy, and leadership. It would be difficult to convey to you my appreciation of the manner in which you led your battalion in the Soissons fight, and of the great assistance rendered by you in moving boldly ahead of the line, thereby greatly facilitating the general movement that followed on July 19. The Corps Commander was present when the report was received of your enterprise in gaining ground under the most difficult circumstances, and he shared with me the relief and confidence that your conduct inspired. I think no one who has been a member of this Division occupies a higher place than you in the esteem of your comrades, and you will receive a warm welcome whenever it shall be our good fortune to return to us.

Eleanor sent a copy of the letter to TR. He wrote to Ted on September 13 that Summerall's letter was the finest tribute he'd ever known a division commander pay to the commander of a battalion. "You have made *the* great success of all our family," wrote the proud father, "for you have had the biggest and most responsible job, particularly delicate as you were a [Reserve] Major [in charge of] Regulars, and you have won really remarkable testimony to your success." But for now Ted's division was out of action and half a dozen of its men were in Paris to see their wounded major. Wearing white silk pajamas that Eleanor had bought for him, with his initials embroidered in blue on the breast pocket, Ted greeted them in their bedroom and led them in toasts to "the regiment" and "the dead of the regiment."

When the condition of the wound improved, the leg was fitted with a wire splint and Ted was allowed to get about on crutches. He eagerly joined Eleanor and Archie (with his arm in a cast) for drives around the city, explorations of antique shops, scouring bookstalls on the West Bank, and going to the theater. At the end of July 1918, Kermit turned up on his way to artillery school at Saumur. With him was his wife, Belle, who had managed to get to France by way of Spain, where her father was the American ambassador.

Painfully mindful that Quentin was gone, with no end of the war in sight, and acutely aware that they might not all survive, they accepted each day, in Eleanor's words, "with the feverish high spirits felt only in the shadow of death."

One Sunday the three brothers, Eleanor, and Belle lunched at a restaurant near Eleanor's house. Toward the end of the meal Kermit looked at Belle and declared that she looked pale and needed some good red wine. Belle said she was fine and did not want any. Kermit insisted. He picked up a bottle of wine, held her at the back of her neck, and laughed as he tried to make her drink from the bottle.

Felling embarrassed, Eleanor objected to being made conspicuous.

Grinning at Archie, Ted said, "Let's show them what being conspicuous *is*." He burst into "Hail, Hail, the Gang's All Here." Kermit joined in, then Archie. At that point, Ted got to his feet with his crutches and Archie and Kermit leapt up beside him. Pointing to the door with his plaster-encased arm, Archie shouted, "*En avant, mes braves*." As they trooped out into the street with their blushing women and several French soldiers with mending wounds following them, they waved and beckoned to startled onlookers to join the parade. Soon everyone was singing the popular French song "Madelon." A man with a fruit push-cart yelled, "*Vive l'Amérique*." Kermit bellowed, "*Vive la France*."

In September, Archie was sent home. TR found him "in far better shape" than expected. He wrote to Kermit, "Of our four hawks one has come home, broken-winged, but his soul as high as ever. Never did our falcons fly with such daring speed at such formidable fury."

Later in the month, a fragment of shell was found to be working out through Archie's knee. The metal was successfully removed surgically and Archie and his family settled into civilian life in an apartment in Manhattan. As he was doing so, Ted was growing increasingly restless with convalescing and having to rely on crutches. He griped to Eleanor about "sitting around" while others were fighting the war. His leg was partially paralyzed, requiring a regimen of exercises and daily massages.

When permission came from doctors for him to return to duty, it was not to go back to the 26th Infantry. His orders sent him to Langres as an instructor in the Army Line School and to study at the General Staff College. He left Eleanor behind in Paris on September 13, 1918—his thirty-first birthday. Three days later he learned he had been promoted to lieutenant colonel. It was the rank held by his father in 1898 when TR presented himself as the second in command of the volunteer cavalrymen, already known as Roosevelt's Rough Riders, at Camp Wood near San Antonio.

Like his father, who had feared that during the months of training men in Texas, the war in Cuba would end before he could get into it, Ted began his duties as an instructor and student dreading his war would end before he was declared fit to again lead troops in battle. His anxiety grew in October with the capitulation of Germany's ally Bulgaria. This first break in the enemy solidarity opened the possibility that Germany would sue for peace long before his leg was well enough for him to return to the front.

Desperate to be in on the finish, he seized an opportunity to do so when the commander of the 1st Division telephoned to Langres to ask him how the healing of his leg was progressing. If Ted's condition permitted, said Gen. Frank Parker, Ted's old regiment was in need of a commanding officer. If Ted could come at once, the job was his. Omitting the fact that he was certified for limited duty only, and that he had to walk with a cane, Ted replied that his leg was entirely well. Concerned that this lie would be exposed, he hurriedly packed his gear and left Langres. For the eleven days needed for orders to catch up with him he was technically absent without leave.

Placed in command of the 26th Infantry Regiment in the last weeks of the Meuse-Argonne offensive, he became the first reserve officer to command a regular army regiment in action. Soon after he took charge, Kermit finished the artillery course at Saumur. He got orders to report to the field artillery of the 1st Divsion, putting the brothers together in the final days of the war. In a continuation of an offensive launched on November 1 at the Meuse, Ted's 26th Infantry marched all night on the fifth to attack Mouzon. Fighting raged all the next day. At 5:00 P.M. an order came to withdraw and march thirty kilometers in rain to Sedan.

In the 504 days in which Ted Roosevelt had been on active duty in the U.S. Army, he'd painfully learned that if anything could go wrong it would, and that there was a phenomenon called "fog of battle." But nothing in his experience equaled November 6, 1918, for confusion. In the heady atmosphere of victory the advancing Americans found themselves in a situation of near chaos. Conflicting orders had units marching into one another and others unsure where they were. The situation grew so ludicrous, Ted learned later, that Douglas MacArthur, commanding an infantry brigade near Sedan and dressed in a uniform befitting his unique style, had actually been mistaken for a German officer by American sentries. They had taken him prisoner at gunpoint. In the case of Ted's 26th Infantry, in late afternoon on the eighth bewildering orders came from corps headquarters telling the 1st Division to retire from Sedan and turn over its gains to the Rainbow Division.

A sergeant in the 26th would later complain, "We could have taken Sedan easy. We were going strong until we got to Omicourt, where we met the French at a crossroad. A French general told Colonel Roosevelt to halt the regiment and let the [French] through. The colonel said his orders were to advance. The general said if we did we would get caught in the barrage he was going to put down. The colonel got mad and said nothing would keep him from carrying out his orders. Just then a runner came with new orders and we had to let the frogs go by."

The high command had made a political decision to give the French the honor of being first to enter Sedan.

Ted again led his wet and weary troops on a night march to a bivouac area at La Besace. Locating Gen. Francis C. Marshall, commander of the 2d Brigade, 1st Division, he hobbled with a cane into Marshall's tent and announced that he was looking for hot food for his men, but that he needed to rest for a moment. Looking worn and hungry, and with a happy smile that General Marshall would describe as "contagious" and "proud," Ted explained that because his automobile had broken down, "I'm afraid I will have to ask you for a horse. I doubt if I can walk back to camp."

The next morning in the Forest of Campiègne a German military delegation climbed into a blue railway carriage of the Compagnie Internationale des Wagon Lits to meet with French Army representatives of the Allied governments. Their purpose was to negotiate the end of the war. The Germans proposed a cease-fire while the talks proceeded in the hope that they could get better surrender terms. The head of the Allied delegation, Marshal Ferdinand Foch, answered, "No. I represent here the Allied governments, who have settled their conditions. Hostilities cannot cease before signing of the armistice." Until then, the fighting would go on, and more soldiers would needlessly die and suffer wounds.

When the Germans capitulated to the Allied terms at 5:10 A.M. on November 11, 1918, Foch sent a message to all Allied commanders to cease all hostilities on "the entire front at 11:00 A.M. French time" on that date.

Lieutenant Colonel Ted Roosevelt's troops fought on to that very minute.

His wife in Paris had "one idea; to reach Ted and tell him that as he was no longer in danger I would go home to the children."

Determined not to leave France without saying good-bye to him, she managed to borrow an army car and driver to take her as close to Ted's division at Bois de la Folie as possible. They arrived at the town of Bantheville on armistice day. The driver parked the car and went looking for Lieutenant Colonel Roosevelt. He found him almost immediately, saluted, and with a grin announced, "Sir, Mrs. Roosevelt is waiting for you just down the road."

Slogging through mud with the help of his cane, Ted found her and demanded. "How in the name of patience did you get here? Now I'm willing to believe the war is over."

Of that moment Eleanor wrote in her autobiography, "Yes, the war was over. The world had been made safe for democracy and we could all go home and live happily ever after. At least we would never have to fight another war, nor our children. People would have too much sense to fight wars. No doubt was in our minds."

She and Ted sat together in the car, silent with happiness. After a while Ted introduced her to his battalion commanders—Maj. Barnwell Rhett Legge, Maj. Rice Youell, and Maj. Lyman Frazier. They all joined hands in a circle, with everyone talking at the same time about going home. When time came for Eleanor to leave, she found her car stuck in the mud. The trio of majors insisted upon the privilege of extricating it. The division commander, Gen. Frank Parker, learned that Eleanor was visiting and would be heading back to Paris. He said that he had business there and invited her to accompany him. He then insisted that Ted also go along.

Having been given an extra day together, they had no idea when they would see one another again. Although she learned that it would be at least a month before she could get onto a ship to New York, Ted had orders to go with the 1st Division to Germany as part of the Army of Occupation. They spent a day shopping for items Ted needed, and parted on November 13.

Before going to Germany Ted reported to General Staff Headquarters at Chaumont. He ran into a prewar acquaintance who had been assigned to a staff job.

After he'd chatted with Ted about "the good old days" for a few minutes, the friend's mood turned serious. With hushed voice he confided that Ted had been recommended several times for promotion and cited two or three times for France's Legion of Honor.

The staff officer continued, "Now, I don't want you to feel we think you don't deserve these, old man. You've made a good record—I think I may say very good. But I'm sorry–really sorry–that none of them could have gone through."

Although there is no record of Ted's reaction to what he was hearing, it is not unreasonable to speculate that he thought about his father having been denied the Congressional Medal of Honor. Recommendations that he receive the medal from TR's superior officers in the Spanish-American War had been refused because Secretary of the Army Alger felt that TR's postwar criticisms had embarrassed him and the army. In a letter to TR he'd written, "You have been a most gallant officer and in the battle before Santiago showed superbly." But he'd declined to endorse TR for the nation's highest military medal.

Now, here was a staff officer who had never been in battle saying Ted must not receive the Legion of Honor because, as the staff officer explained, "People might say that you were promoted or decorated because you're the son of your father, and might criticize us. We can't have that sort of thing, now, can we? I'm sure you will understand our position and will agree."

13

As Americans welcomed Armistice Day, the senior Theodore Roosevelt found himself back in Roosevelt Hospital. He was there to be treated for anemia, vertigo (caused by his old ear infection), leg troubles left over from his last chance to be a boy, and general signs of physical exhaustion. In the previous six weeks he had been on a whirlwind speaking tour. On October 1 at Alliance, Nebraska, he had demanded a total American victory so that no nation would ever dare to "look cross-eyed at us." In Billings, Montana, on the fifth and back at Oyster Bay the next day he promoted the fourth Liberty Loan bond sale. The thirteenth found him addressing the Liederkranz Associates about the war bonds and declaring the United States must accept nothing less than Germany and her allies' "unconditional surrender." On the sixteenth, the Council of Jewish Women, meeting at Temple Emanu-El on Fifth Avenue, heard him push the Liberty Loan, and on the eighteenth the Newport Naval Brigade heard his opinion that after the surrender the peace conference should be held in Berlin. Republicans attending a party rally at Carnegie Hall on October 28, hoping he would announce his candidacy for president in 1920, were heartened by his attack on President Wilson's conduct of the war.

November had begun with an address to the Boys Victory Mobilization meeting in the interest of the United War Work Campaign. On the third of the month, again at Carnegie Hall, his venue was a benefit for the Circle for Negro War Relief. He spoke effusively in praise of the military service of blacks in the war, while reminding his listeners that black soldiers had been part of his crowded hour in the dash to the top of Kettle Hill in 1898.

To his delight and relief, on the seventh, Republicans swept to victory in congressional elections in what he considered a repudiation of Wilson's war policies, and therefore vindication of his own relentless criticism of it. To one of the doctors attending him in the hospital he said of Wilson, "I would like to be left alone in this room with our great and good president for about fifteen minutes, and then I would be cheerfully hung."

Informed that he would have to remain hospitalized for some time, he kept busy with correspondence, drafting magazine and newspaper articles, and greeting well-wishers who came to call. None of those appearing in his room in mid-December was as welcome Ted's wife.

She'd gone directly from the ship to the hospital. TR beamed with pride as she told him and Edith, who had moved into the hospital in a room next to TR's, about Ted's new post with the Army of Occupation in Germany. Her reunion with her in-laws was kept short, however. TR and Edith appreciated that Eleanor was eager to be with three children she hadn't seen in a year and a half.

Grace was now seven, Teddy was four and a half, and Cornelius was three. Only he had difficulty adjusting to having her around. Despite having been thoroughly prepared to meet his parent by Eleanor's mother, and having greeted Eleanor warmly, Cornelius, nicknamed Sonny, watched suspiciously as she took off her hat. He asked Mrs. Alexander, "Why did that lady take off her hat in our house? How long is she staying?"

Eleanor found that Sonny always began his bedtime prayer with "Our Father who art in France." He had once asked Mrs. Alexander if his father would bring back any of the Germans he'd killed so that they could be stuffed.

Grace lost little time in expressing to her mother her hope that Eleanor would make her brothers behave without Grace's help. Sounding very much like Aunt Alice when Alice had to deal with young brothers, Grace exclaimed, "I am so tired of being an example."

Within a week of the reunion of the wife and children of Theodore Roosevelt Jr., the master of Sagamore Hill was informed by doctors at Roosevelt Hospital that they could do no more for his condition. They discharged him from the hospital. Offered a wheelchair, he refused to use it. Shrugging off the assisting hand of a doctor, he snapped, "Don't do that. I am not sick, and it will give the wrong impression." Unaided, he walked through a group of reporters and into the backseat of a car on Christmas Day.

He got off a letter to Ted that said it would be "a couple of months before I am in any kind of shape." But it didn't matter, he added, because "this happens to be the very time when I do not care to speak or to take an active part in politics." He wrote of Eleanor returning home "pretty and dainty and happy, but dreadfully homesick for you. Of course, I was enthralled with everything she had to tell. Well, next Xmas I hope we shall have the whole family, for three generations gathered at Sagamore Hill."

He also corresponded with old friends. One was Rudyard Kipling. To the author who had used his pen to glorify war and compose a poem about what it takes for a boy to become a man, he proudly wrote of two of his own sons, "Ted moved Heaven and earth to get to the front and to get Kermit to the front, and just three weeks before the end [of the war] they went back to the first division, Ted as Lieutenant Colonel commanding his regiment, still limping, but able to hold his job, and Kermit as Captain of Artillery in the same division."

Ted wrote to his mother, "I know Father will be glad that all of his family that are in physical shape were in the front lines fighting when the bell rang and the curtain went down on the play."

Proposals had been made and ideas proffered concerning a monument for the Roosevelt son who had been killed in action, but TR turned them down. One remembrance did please him. The airfield at Mineola where Quentin had learned to fly was renamed Roosevelt Field. He was also gratified to have gotten a cable saying that France had named a destroyer after Quentin. His grave near the spot where his plane came down, he was told, had become a place of pilgrimage for the French and Quentin's comrades. Archie had brought home Quentin's trunk. Eleanor and Kermit had joined Archie in going through its contents: his pistol, a compass, and another aeronautical instrument that they knew nothing about, letters Quentin had received from his parents, and his uniform and a "jaunt cap."

On the day of New Year's Eve came an envelope from Paris containing France's official commemoration in the form of a citation for his sacrifice on behalf of French freedom.

January 1, 1919, was for TR a day of sitting on a sofa in the old nursery looking out a south-facing window. On the third a rheumatic specialist from Roosevelt Hospital came to look him over. The next day, Edith wrote Kermit that his father was "having a horrid painful time."

TR stated on the fifth that he felt a little better. That day he was visited by the British poet Alfred Noyes. The young woman Quentin would

have married also dropped by. After Flora left, TR dictated a letter to
Kermit, then spent eleven hours honing proofs of a *Metropolitan Magazine* article and an editorial for the *Kansas City Star* newspaper. Its subject was the League of Nations. The man who had once called for a world
organization to keep the peace had chosen to denounce the proposed
body and oppose United States participation.

That evening as Edith sat nearby, playing solitaire, he said to her, "I
wonder if you will ever know how much I love Sagamore Hill."

When he complained to Edith of "a terribly odd feeling," as if his heart
and breathing were about to shut down, Edith woke the nurse and later
summoned a doctor. The physician gave him a shot of morphine and
TR's valet, James Amos, put him to bed around midnight. As the servant
settled into a chair to sleep, a table lamp was burning. TR said, "James,
please turn out that light."

They were his last words. He died in his sleep of a coronary-artery em-
bolism.

Archie cabled Ted and Kermit at their camp near Coblenz: "The old
lion is dead."

The message reached Ted in the early evening while Kermit was not
in camp. Ted found him later that night in his tent sipping wine. Kermit later wrote to their mother:

> We sat up the rest of the night and talked. Father somehow was
> very near, and as if he would never be far. I don't feel sorry for
> him; he wouldn't want it, that would be the last thing. There never
> was anyone like him, and there won't be. You're the only person
> I feel sorry for; for now you must walk in sad loneliness, for he
> who has lost a father, has lost all; but it isn't for long; man's life
> is but a span, as has been said throughout the centuries; for you
> it's probably even a shorter run than for me, but for none of us
> is it very long; and then we shall all be joined together on the
> other side of the last great adventure; and Quentin too will be
> waiting over there, with his smile. . . . It is foolish to think of one-
> self, but you will know how the bottom has dropped out for me;
> at first it was complete, but comes the realization that father could
> never really die, and that even though I can't bother him about
> every little decision, when a really vital one comes he will be there
> as unfailing as ever.

One of Theodore Roosevelt Sr.'s visitors on January 3, 1919, had been Eleanor. In the course of their conversation she had said, "You know, Father, Ted has always worried for fear he would not be worthy of you."

TR replied, "Worthy of me? Darling, I'm so very proud of him. He has won high honor not only for his children but, like the Chinese, he has ennobled his ancestors. I walk with my head higher because of him."

Part 3: Footsteps

A timid youth would have lived wretchedly as the son of Roosevelt.

—*Henry F. Pringle, "Chore Boy of the GOP,"*
in his book Big Frogs, *1928*

14

Six weeks after Theodore Roosevelt's death his namesake received an order signed by General Pershing at AEF General Headquarters. Ted was to come to Paris for the purpose of conferring with nineteen other reserve and National Guard officers of field rank. The agenda of the February 15 meeting was to be "betterment of conditions and development of contentment" in the U.S. Army in France during the slow process of demobilization. The "commission" met on the appointed date and proposed a system of entertainments, athletic competitions, and educational opportunities for troops at European universities.

During the conference Ted invited the officers to join him for dinner at his expense at the Allied Officers' Club in Paris on February 19. His purpose was to discuss with them the forming of an organization of veterans of the war that would maintain in them as civilians the "patriotism and common sense" that had motivated them during the war. The dinner ended with formation of a temporary committee with Ted as chairman, Bennett C. Clark the vice-chairman, and Eric Fisher Wood as its secretary. It was also decided that a caucus be held in Paris in mid-March at which the interests of enlisted men would be the topic. Ted's dinner guests then agreed that Ted should arrange a transfer back to the States to begin organizing the proposed fraternity of AEF veterans throughout the nation.

With all of this enthusiastically but "unofficially" approved by Pershing, Ted prepared to go home. At the same time, his mother was in France in order to see the grave of her youngest son. Edith traveled to Chamery on February 18 with her sister, Emily Carow, who came from her home in Italy. Edith laid flowers on Quentin's grave, knelt, and re-

cited the Lord's Prayer. Before leaving for home she endowed a fountain in Quentin's memory in the town and arranged for a stone marker
with an engraved phrase from the poem "Adonais" by Shelley:

HE HAS OUTSOARED THE SHADOW OF OUR NIGHT

A few days after Ted departed for the United States to carry out his
mandate to generate nationwide support for the proposed veterans' organization, the Paris caucus opened with more than six hundred delegates, both officers and enlisted men. Because their meeting was not an
official function of the U.S. Army, the men had to pay their own expenses. This was not a problem for the officers, but getting men from
the ranks to attend was. Because the enlisted men were still on duty, their
attendance was not authorized under army regulations. The problem was
surmounted in various ways. Some officers brought enlisted men as or-
derlies. One sergeant came in the guise of a courier with "important documents." Another claimed that he had orders to go to Paris to purchase
poison to control rats in his camp. A number of men feigned illnesses
so peculiar that only medical experts in Paris could treat them.

Recalling the inventiveness exhibited by officers and enlisted men that
spring in France, George S. Wheat wrote, "In some divisions the officer
delegates took up collections to defray the expense of enlisted delegates.
In numerous instances enlisted men refused such assistance and took
up their own collections. An enlisted man said that the 'buddies' in his
regiment had deliberately lost money to him in gambling games. So by
various means nearly two hundred enlisted delegates were in Paris by late
afternoon on March 14."

Immediately after the gavel fell to open the caucus, a resolution was
adopted to suspend all recognition of rank during meetings. During the
three-day congregation it was agreed that the organization would be
open to all soldiers, sailors, marines, and army nurses who served between April 6, 1917, and November 11, 1918. There would no distinc-
tions between army and navy, officers and enlisted ranks, nor those who
had served at the front and those behind the lines.

They next chose an executive committee and charged it with the responsibility of coordinating its work with the committee that would result from Ted's efforts in the States. The two committees would then be
merged during a national convention to be held on November 11, 1919,
the first anniversary of the Armistice.

The delegates gave themselves a name: the American Legion.

Surrounded by a throng of reporters on his arrival in New York, Ted astonished them by announcing that he would resign from his banking firm, sever all his business connections, including several corporate directorships, and go into politics at the first opportunity. To ensure that his connection with the American Legion would not be interpreted as part of his political plans, he declared that he would not accept any prominent position in the Legion's permanent organization.

To work with him in building support for the Legion in the United States he enlisted his brother-in-law Dick Derby; the former commander of the Fighting 69th, Gen. William "Wild Bill" Donovan; Cornelius W. Wickersham; H. B. Beers; Franklin D'Olier, Henry Fairfield Osborn Jr.; J. Leslie Kincaid; and Eric Fisher Wood. The men were described by George Wheat in *The Story of the American Legion* as "cheerful, competent optimists."

The committee set out to arrange a national Legion caucus with the intention of having its first meeting in St. Louis in May, to be followed by a national convention in November. At the time of this announcement there were temporary Legion "posts" in all the forty-eight states, Alaska, Hawaii, and the District of Columbia. In order to make their organizing task easier they sought support in Congress for a national charter of incorporation. It was issued on September 16, 1919. By then the American Legion had 5,670 posts throughout the United States and in Europe.

When the May caucus opened on May 8, the delegates declared their desire that Ted be their chairman. In noting this unanimous support, and that Ted refused the position, the *New York Evening Mail* reported on May 11, 1919, that the most amazing incident of the gathering so far "undoubtedly has been the refusal of Lieut. Col. Theodore Roosevelt to accept the chairmanship of the organization pending the national convention in November."

The item continued:

He remained adamant, and in doing so put an end to the criticism which maintained that the foundation of the American Legion was mostly a scheme designed to further his political ambitions.

As a matter of fact Colonel Roosevelt emerged from yesterday's extraordinary proceedings a national figure in his own right. There are plenty of delegates from states not usually Rooseveltian who are willing to credit him with the genius of real leadership.

There was no mistaking his hold on the gathering he called to order. It seemed an almost superhuman feat for a young man to refuse the honor tendered to him in such a manner. Delegate after delegate rose and called on him to reconsider his refusal to be nominated. But he never wavered.

The article pictured "a curious mixture of sensitiveness and iron purpose" as Ted paced from side to side on the stage while delegates shouted a phrase that on many similar occasions had been voiced about Ted's father: "We want Teddy."

As the din subsided from time to time, Ted advanced to the podium to try to proceed with caucus business, only to have the clamor resume. When he at last made the delegates see that he meant what he had said, he managed to move the meeting forward. On May 10, 1919, the delegates approved a preamble to the Legion's constitution in which Ted had a hand in writing:

For God and Country we associate ourselves together for the following purposes:

To uphold and defend the Constitution of the United States of America; to maintain law and order; to foster and perpetuate a one hundred percent Americanism; to preserve the memories and incidents of our association in the Great War; to inculcate a sense of individual obligation to the community, state, and nation; to combat the autocracy of both the classes and the masses; to make right the master of might; to promote peace and goodwill on earth; to safeguard and transmit to posterity the principles of justice, freedom, and democracy; to consecrate and sanctify our comradeship by our devotion to mutual helpfulness.

Commenting on Ted's refusal to accept the chairmanship, the reporter from the *Evening Examiner* wrote, "The man who could turn so much popularity aside for the sake of principle is destined to go far, in the opinion of the delegates here. They see not only in what he did the proof of character which is the foundation of statesmanship, but also the proof of intellectual qualities which in one naturally modest are not prone to reveal themselves cheaply. To anyone who witnessed those dra-

matic scenes, when hard-muscled men who have gone through all the
cynicism of war gave vent to an almost boyish hero-worship for so young
a man, the conclusion is irresistible that he will go, barring accidents, as
far as his ambition beckons him."

Republicans in New York City who were pondering picking him as
their candidate for president of the city board of aldermen learned that
he had running for a different office in mind. In 1880 his father
launched a political career by seeking election to the New York Assembly. TR had been sent to Albany from a district in Manhattan. Ted announced his intention to seek the Republican nomination in the 2d Assembly District in Long Island's Nassau County.

Until then he followed the preparations for the November Legion
convention, at which he would not be the presiding officer. He also began writing a war memoir. In 1899 his father had produced a book on
his war, *The Rough Riders.* Ted's title was *Average Americans.* But the writing was suspended in mid-June for a trip to Cambridge, Massachusetts,
in order to accept an honorary degree from his alma mater. On June 19,
along with nine other Harvard graduates who had served in the war, he
was given an honorary master of arts.

Yet neither an academic accolade, working on his book, speaking engagements, plans for the November convention of the American Legion,
or being given the Republican nomination in the Assembly race meant
as much to Ted in the summer of 1919 as Eleanor's news that she was
pregnant. She told him he could expect their fourth "blessed event" to
occur in January.

He also learned that fatherhood was in the immediate future for his
brothers. Kermit and Belle's baby was due in July. Archie would become
a father for a second time in November. Because he had left for France
soon after his marriage to Grace Lockwood on April 14, 1917, he had
not been with her for the birth of Archibald Roosevelt Jr. The three
brothers, who had been highly competitive siblings, were now prospective fathers mindful of their father's expressed wish that whichever of
them was first to father a son would name him after their dead brother
Quentin. Because Eleanor was not going to have their baby until January,
Ted resigned himself to the likelihood that it would be Kermit or Archie
who would savor the distinction of giving Quentin a namesake.

Although pregnant, Eleanor eagerly accompanied Ted as he began
his campaign for the Assembly. That he would win was never a question
in her mind. Everywhere they went in the district they found enthusias-

tic crowds. Listening to Ted speak and observing his very animated manner, the people heard echoes of his father's voice and discerned physical reminders of "the Colonel." But they also welcomed a young man who had a claim on them in his own right. He was not just the son of the great and beloved Teddy Roosevelt. He was "Ted" Roosevelt and a genuine hero of the Great War with battle scars and a trove of commendations attesting valor.

Consequently, when the voters of the 2d Assembly District cast their ballots on the fourth of November, they elected him with the largest majority ever given to a candidate.

One vote Ted did not get was his wife's. To Eleanor and Ted's delight the child they had not expected until January was an early arrival—on Election Day. Eleanor dressed the baby in the "double gowns" clothing that had been put on a child who had been born in October 1858 and grew up to be Ted's father. Ted claimed that it was "pure willpower" on Eleanor's part that she'd given birth two months early to a boy who would realize TR's wish that Quentin be honored by the christening of his next grandson Quentin Roosevelt II.

One week after the birth, on the first anniversary of the end of the Great War, the first American Legion convention was called to order in Minneapolis. The delegates chose as their first "national commander" one of the men whom Ted had named to the organizing committee of the St. Louis caucus, his friend Franklin D'Olier of Pennsylvania. The convention set an agenda for action that included addressing problems of confusion at the War Risk Bureau. It had been established by the federal government to administer the War Risk Insurance Act of 1917. Asserting that the bureau's record was replete with "broken promises and betrayed trust," the American Legion created its own division to help all veterans secure rightful benefits, unsnarl Liberty Bond tangles, receive unpaid discharge bonuses, and help to secure vocational training for vets. The ultimate goal was to persuade Congress to consolidate the work of the Risk Bureau, the Board of Vocational Training, and the Public Health Service into one veterans bureau, and to build hospitals especially for war veterans. The result within two years was passage of laws to construct such hospitals and to create the United States Veterans Bureau.

The convention also approved a resolution calling for creation of a parallel organization consisting of female relatives of Legion members or female relatives of men who if alive would have be eligible for Legion membership.

On the first of January 1920 in the Assembly Chamber of the State Capitol in Albany, New York, Theodore Roosevelt Jr. raised his right hand for the oath of office that his father had sworn on January 1, 1881. Like TR, he felt lonely and nervous. Like his father, he turned for a kind of companionship after a day's work to newspapermen covering the State House. Many of them had known his father. As they did with TR, they offered Ted counsel and advice and, as with TR, they liked the young freshman legislator. But there was a difference between them. TR had been a brash figure who dressed like "a dude" and spoke with "a wealth of mouth." Ted was "modest and unassuming," but still easily envisioned walking up the stairs in the State House one day, following in his father's formidable footsteps, and into the Executive Chamber as the governor of New York.

In the senior Theodore Roosevelt's day as freshman legislator, issues with which he was called upon to grapple were rooted in the politics of a rural Republican upstate versus the Democratic metropolitan downstate, dominated by the City of New York. Debates then dealt with the issue of how much self-rule to allow the city. Among these contentious matters was whether the state should force the private firm that ran New York City's transit system to reduce the fare from ten to five cents. Another question was what to do about rampant corruption in the New York City government, especially in its police department. And there was the perennially vexing dilemma of poverty, vast expanses of slum tenements, festering disease, and crime.

To the alarm of most members of the New York Legislature, as Theodore Roosevelt Jr. joined the Assembly, some voters of New York City had decided to have a voice in these matters by electing five Socialists to the Assembly. Fearing that these "radicals" were the spearhead in Albany for the "Bolshevism" that had been imposed on Russia by a revolutionary "Soviet" government, the Republican leadership of the legislature moved to prevent the Socialists from taking their legitimate seats.

The veteran reporters who had covered Ted's father's two terms in the legislature as TR consistently rose to speak on behalf of the people he deemed dispossessed, the downtrodden, and those who held controversial views on the role of government, waited to hear what TR's son had to say on the attempt to bar the Socialists. He chose to address the issue in his maiden speech. He said, "We abhor the doctrines of the Socialist Party. Many of us personally and through our families have suffered greatly from its actions and the actions of pacifists, for to them is attributed in large degree the unpreparedness of this country when war broke. Our actions, however, must have no reference to any except two things, justice and discretionary application. We must not let justifiable dislike force us to commit a crime against representative government."

Acknowledging that the Assembly was "sole judge of the qualifications of its members," with "the right to expel anyone and its decision is final," he called for the Socialists to be seated while the Assembly investigated evidence that their presence in the legislature would prove to be subversive. He cautioned "self-control, because the greater the power, the more dangerous the abuse."

When Ted finished, the speaker of the Assembly, Thaddeus Sweet, took the floor to quote Ted's father on the subject of "anti-Americanism." A member of the Assembly spied two of the Socialists actually seated in the chamber and thundered, "These two men who sit here with a smile and smirk on their faces are just as much representatives of the Russian Soviet government as if they were Lenin and Trotsky themselves. They are little Lenins, little Trotskys, in our midst."

After the Assembly voted to expel the five, an editorial in the *New York Times* said, "It was an American vote altogether, a patriotic and conservative vote. An immense majority of the American people will approve and sanction the Assembly's action."

Ted had joined a small minority voting against expulsion. For this stand, noted Eleanor, he was "extremely unpopular not only in his own district, but throughout the state." He received so many abusive letters that "we thought his political career might be over before it began."

In the next election the five Socialists would be reelected and take their seats without protest. Republicans were so confident that Ted would also be sent back to Albany in the next election that they asked him to take time from his campaign to travel West to speak on behalf of the Republican presidential slate. As he boarded a train to hit the hustings for the ticket of Warren G. Harding and Calvin Coolidge, he said to Eleanor, "By the way, since I shan't have any time for my own campaign, you'll have to fill my speaking dates."

Eleanor exclaimed, "Ted, I can't possibly do that. I never heard of such a thing."

With a smile he replied, "You know most of the people—after all, they're home folks, and you won't mind after you get started. I shall probably lose if you don't."

She made twenty-six speeches, or, as she charmingly noted in her autobiography, "the same speech with twenty-six variations." During all of them she was accompanied by her mother and a German shepherd dog named Caesar. He had been presented to her in France by General Parker. The dog lay at her feet on the speaker's platform until she was introduced, then went forward with her and settled on the floor again as she spoke. After a newspaper made note that "Mrs. Roosevelt Jr." was usually accompanied by "her dog" and "her mother," Mrs. Alexander told Eleanor that if she did not rate above the dog there was not much use in her being there.

Ted campaigned enthusiastically for Harding after having expressed a preference that the Republicans nominate TR's former comrade in arms in Cuba, Leonard Wood. When the GOP chose the senator from Ohio, Ted met with him and came out of the conference with a ringing endorsement in circumstances similar to those under which TR in 1896 had changed his mind about backing Speaker of the House Thomas Reed and thrown his support to another Ohioan, William McKinley. By doing so and in campaigning for McKinley in the West, TR was rewarded with the job of assistant secretary of the navy.

For Ted's support and his tireless barnstorming the triumphant Harding offered Ted the same position. In accepting the post he was not only stepping into his father's shoes, but following in the footsteps of his cousin, Franklin Delano Roosevelt. Five years older than Ted, he had idolized TR and had emulated him by studying at Harvard (after the Groton School) and reading law at Columbia University. He had been elected to the New York legislature from the district of his home, Hyde Park, although to the Senate, and as a Democrat. In 1913 he became the second Roosevelt to hold the office of assistant secretary of the navy, appointed by Woodrow Wilson. Like his cousin Ted, he'd married a girl named Eleanor, who happened to be TR's niece, and received TR's compliment on keeping the Roosevelt name in the family. Most recently (1920), he had again emulated TR by running for vice president on a slate topped by James Cox.

During the campaign the Republican National Committee decided it would be helpful, and fun, to have Ted trail his cousin as a "one-man truth squad" as Franklin toured the West. Ted made an issue of the family connection. He gleefully invoked cattle-raising imagery for audiences of sunburnt ranchers and cowhands, calling Franklin "a maverick" who "does not have the brand of our family."

The Cox-Roosevelt ticket lost in a landslide to Harding and Coolidge. Franklin declared stoically, "I am not really much surprised at the result because I have felt all along that we are in the middle of a kind of tidal flow of discontent and destructive criticism, as a result of the tremendous efforts of the war."

Political observers and journalists wondered if one day there might be a contest for the presidency between the Democrat Roosevelt from Hyde Park and the Republican Roosevelt of Sagamore Hill. But excitement over the likelihood of such a rivalry was cruelly dashed in the summer of 1921 when news came from Franklin Roosevelt's summer retreat home at Campobello Island in Canada that he had been stricken with poliomyelitis and left crippled in both legs.

With two active young politicians named Roosevelt it was inevitable that someone would mistake one for the other. In Franklin's case a man at a campaign rally in the 1920 presidential race shouted, "I voted for your father Teddy. You're just like the old Rough Rider!"

After a speech by Ted in 1922 to the Elks' national convention in Atlantic City, a man in the audience praised Ted's remarks and noted that it revealed the true courage and wisdom of a great man, Franklin Delano Roosevelt. After realizing his error, he sent Ted a letter of apology.

Although Franklin had left the Navy Department in 1920 to run for vice president, his seven-year term as President Wilson's assistant secretary of the navy had left those who worked with him wondering if Ted could measure up to his cousin's record—or to that of his father's brief but tempestuous and historic tenure under McKinley.

Ted's superior was Secretary of the Navy Edwin Denby. But Ted and everyone familiar with the history of the navy understood that responsibility for day-by-day running of the department lay with the assistant secretary. Under his immediate direction were the naval stations and shipyards and all the ships at sea. He would also implement the operating budget and be the one who would testify before congressional oversight committees.

Because the United States had committed itself in the peace treaty that formally ended the war to reducing the size of the fleet, the assistant secretary was also in charge of disposing of the navy's surplus war materials. He would also play a major role in the Conference for the Limitation of Armaments, scheduled to open in Washington in November 1921.

The task of organizing and supervising moving the Roosevelt family to the capital fell to Eleanor. Her main problem was finding a house they could afford that was large enough for four children. Grace was ten years old, Teddy seven, Cornelius six, and Quentin two. Eleanor found "a big ugly" house on Twenty-first Street that contained "rather queer" fur-

nishings. In the foyer was a hideously ornate chandelier. It was the figure of a girl in a white blouse and blue skirt with a red bandana. Sweeping back from under her skirt were deer antlers tipped with red, white,
and blue electric lights. The girl held a beer mug. In another room
Eleanor found a life-size portrait of a monk shaving. A second painting
was of a man being given a drink by a nun in a snowstorm. All these items
and more affronts to good taste were relegated to the attic.

Eleanor also had charge of entertaining. Dinner parties were usually
small groups of intimate friends and almost always included Alice and
Nick Longworth. She could be counted on to enliven conversations. He
was an excellent amateur violinist. Both were so passionate about playing poker that they brought their own poker table. The stakes were always high. In one of these games the players were the Longworths, Ted,
Shipping Board chairman Albert Lasker, Secretary of War John Weeks,
and Treasury Secretary Charles Mellon. At the end of the evening Mellon laid forty cents on the table and with a forlorn sigh said, "That's all
I have left."

Because most of their friends were either in the Harding cabinet or
in other government posts, Eleanor was interested in seeing how important work was done during dinners and after, as the women chatted
over coffee and the men had brandy and cigars. A frequent topic was
the forthcoming Conference for the Limitation of Armaments.

Scheduled for November in Washington, its aims were reduction of
naval armaments and settlement of affairs in the Far East. President
Harding had invited representatives of the British Empire, France, Italy,
Japan, Belgium, China, the Netherlands, and Portugal. The conference
began dramatically with a declaration by the U.S. delegate, Secretary of
State Charles Evans Hughes, that the United States was prepared to make
drastic cuts in its naval force. The announcement caused a sensation not
only for its boldness, but because there had been no hint that such a plan
existed. To maintain secrecy until he could unveil it, Hughes had asked
Navy Secretary Denby to appoint a three-member study committee. It
consisted of Ted, the chief of naval operations, and a member of the Navy
General Board. The committee submitted several plans before one was
accepted. Two days before the conference Hughes told Ted he wanted
fifty copies for distribution to the delegates after he'd presented it publicly. Ted did not even tell Eleanor what he had been working on. He
told her only "Be sure not to miss the opening day."

Appointed chairman of the conference's Subcommittee of Naval Experts, he noted in his diary on November 29, 1921, "The good part about all these negotiations is that, though they are so vitally important, we are all of us having a good time. Hughes in enjoying his work to the full, and no one is losing his sense of proportion. There are no ponderously wise individuals in the American delegation. It is good to be alive and to be in the thick of things."

It was also a good feeling to know that he was contributing to the possible realization of TR's appeal in Europe in 1910 for world disarmament. There was also irony to consider. When TR became assistant secretary of the navy in 1897 his goal was to give the United States a navy whose might would be unchallenged by any nation in the world. Now his son was in that very job and working on plans to dismantle the fleet. For that purpose Hughes asked him to draw up a proposed treaty of naval disarmaments. On the evening of December 29, 1921, Ted wrote to George Harvey, the U.S. ambassador in London, that he'd completed a rough draft.

"I would like it as short as possible and written in everyday English," he wrote. "If Noah Webster gives a meaning to a word, I don't want to have to say that in diplomacy it means something else."

The history of warfare had never recorded a proposal of such magnitude to limit the implements of war. The treaty entered into by the United States, Britain, France, Italy, and Japan established the tonnage ratio of 5-5-3 for the navies of the U.S., Britain, and Japan respectively. The American fleet would be equal to the British and second to no other navy. By terms of the treaty a number of American ships would have to be scrapped. The task of achieving this fell to Assistant Secretary of the Navy Theodore Roosevelt.

Immediately after the conference, a wave of pacifism threatened to scuttle the remaining ships. As a large segment of the public favored cutting the navy's strength even more deeply, a determined effort was made in the House of Representatives to reduce naval personnel from 86,000 to 67,000. While the debate raged for two weeks, Ted was on Capitol Hill daily, providing facts and figures to those congressmen who were fighting to prevent the cuts. When they prevailed and the bill was defeated in April 1922, Ted took his first vacation in over a year by going on a week-long fishing outing in Pennsylvania.

Eleanor remained at home to care for the children. As his wife she had cheerfully emulated her mother-in-law in accepting that she had married a Theodore Roosevelt, and that Ted was his father's son in every way: a war hero, a politician, assistant secretary of the navy, and a man whose ambition might carry him to what TR's political mentor Henry Cabot Lodge once called "a higher kingdom." That is, if Ted shared his father's desire to be president.

As TR had invested the care and keeping of house, home, and children to Edith, Ted had relied upon Eleanor to take care of their domestic affairs. But on July 19, 1921, he'd surprised her by giving her a handwritten letter. It said:

> I have decided to give you all my money. You have handled all our money affairs as far as spending is concerned ever since we were married. If I died, or if there was another war and I was lost, it would make it much simpler for you to have it all in your own right. You are the one primarily responsible for the most important undertaking we have, the children. It will therefore make me more comfortable to have our affairs arranged in this manner.
>
> I therefore give you all moneys, stocks, and securities that stand in my name at Montgomery & Co. and will notify them to this effect.

This meant that Eleanor had to assume all responsibility for investments, about which she admitted she knew "next to nothing." Her only experience in buying stock had been in 1920. She'd purchased a thousand shares of Sinclair Oil.

Ted had known Harry Sinclair before the war. His banking firm had helped finance the formation of the Sinclair Oil Company, and Ted had served as a director of the company until he shed all his business connections to devote himself to politics. Although no longer associated with Sinclair Oil in 1919, he'd asked Harry Sinclair for a job for brother Archie. Disabled in the war, he had a wife and children to support. The executive job entailed the company's foreign aspects and required Archie to make frequent trips to the oil-rich Near East.

At the time Eleanor bought her stock in Sinclair Oil, it had been considered a good buy. But in December 1921, when she discussed the financial duties Ted had given her with close friend Walter Janney, an ex-partner of Ted's, he advised her to dispose of the oil shares and buy bonds, which would pay an income that the stock did not. She did so at a loss, but the money was helpful in paying a tax bill. While Ted was fishing in Pennsylvania she had cause to be glad that she'd taken Janney's advice.

The chain of events that, ultimately, made Eleanor glad she'd lost money on her investment had begun in 1909 with a decision by Congress to guarantee that oil-powered ships of the U.S. Navy would never run out of fuel. By law three naval oil reserves were ordained. No. 1 was at Elk Hills, California. No. 2 was at Buena Vista, also in California. The third was Teapot Dome, near Casper, Wyoming. The area was named for an outcrop of rock that looked like a teapot. At all of these locations, it was soon noted by petroleum engineers, the amount of oil in the ground was susceptible to being drained away by any oil wells that might be drilled on nearby land not owned by the federal government. After a private well was sunk near the Elk Hills reserve and produced a gusher, Congress acted again by bestowing upon the secretary of the navy the power to do whatever he deemed necessary to protect the oil in the reserves. There were two choices. He could arrange to drill government wells at the edges of the reserves to assure that drainage went to naval use. Or he could lease the reserves to oil companies and let them pump out the oil for sale, so long as sufficient amounts were stored for the navy. President Taft's secretary of the navy chose the former policy. It remained in effect throughout Taft's term and during the war.

When President Harding appointed Albert B. Fall, a friend of oil companies, to be the secretary of the interior, Fall had no control over the oil reserves. But that changed on the eve of the disarmament conference. Some navy officers were anxious about a growing Japanese naval power in the Pacific and doubted the proposed arms-limitation treaty would work. To be ready for war with Japan they demanded immediate creation of fuel-storage facilities stocked with oil from the three reserves. Harding prepared an executive order transferring the reserves from navy control to the Interior Department. He sent the proposed document to Navy Secretary Denby, who passed it to Assistant Secretary Roosevelt for review.

Ted felt that the transfer would not be in the best interest of the navy. He argued that the Interior Department's mission was development of the nation's natural resources, but the oil in the reserves was there for the navy in case of real necessity. Secretary Denby replied that Ted's objection had come too late. But Ted managed to tack on an amendment that "no general policy as to drilling or reserving lands located in a naval reserve shall be changed or adopted except upon consultation and in cooperation with the secretary or acting secretary of the navy."

Free to release the reserve lands to the Interior Department, Secretary Denby did so, but without notifying his assistant secretary. Secretary Fall promptly granted drilling rights at Teapot Dome to the Mammoth Oil Company, owned by Harry Sinclair. This was done secretly without competitive bidding. Reserve No. 1 at Elk Hills went to the Pan American Company owned by Edward F. Doheny.

Ted learned of all this as he was returning from his fishing outing. A newspaper report provided details of the Sinclair deal. The paper also noted that the result was a leap in value of Sinclair Oil stock by ten points. Recalling that Eleanor had bought Sinclair Oil stock, he arrived home as upset as Eleanor had ever seen him.

Although he'd not known about the Sinclair deal, he explained to her, he feared that because they owned Sinclair stock the public would think the worst. "My political career is over and done with," he went on. "People will think my price is ten thousand dollars. I can never explain it."

As soon as Eleanor could get a word in she told him, "I sold that stock last December. We actually lost money on those stocks."

Unfortunately, that was not to be the end of the matter. "Teapot Dome" would return to haunt them two years later.

15

The Washington armament conference, which had opened on November 12, 1921, came to an end on February 6, 1922, with nine treaties having been drafted and signed. Contained in the agreements were pledges by the participating nations to observe a ten-year "holiday," during which no new capital warships would be built. The United States also agreed to reduce its fleet by disposing of ships whose combined displacement amounted to 845,000 tons.

The question to be answered was how to achieve this: by towing them out to sea and sinking them, or selling them as surplus to private firms that would render them into scrap? The proponents of scuttling expressed fears that unscrupulous scrap-metal companies might attempt to sell components to navies of countries that might become enemies, particularly Japan. Those in favor of scrapping, led by Assistant Secretary of the Navy Roosevelt, carried the debate by pointing out that sinking would cost the government money. Scrapping would add millions to the treasury. Supervision of implementation of the agreements also required a survey of all naval shipyards to sort out the closing of shipbuilding operations while maintaining elements needed for repairs and maintenance of ships that remained in service.

Reductions in the size of the fleet meant that fewer sailors would be needed both in the enlisted ranks and as officers. With this painful reality in mind, in the spring of 1922 the son of a previous assistant navy secretary, who, in 1897, had worked to build the fleet, was invited to speak to the U.S. Naval Academy at Annapolis, Maryland. As Ted addressed midshipmen who were to receive their commissions at the conclusion of the graduation ceremony on June 2, he could not forget that had it not been for his father's opposition to his going to West Point or into the navy by enrolling at Annapolis, he once might have been one of the "middies" arrayed before him in their crisp white summer uniforms.

As a souvenir of his visit he was given a copy of the graduating class's yearbook. Titled *The Lucky Bag*, it seemed to be a typical college yearbook, filled with formal photographs of the graduates, candid pictures of the men at ease, and action-filled snapshots of navy sports teams. The book went onto a shelf in his home library, only to be taken down two weeks later in a swirl of controversy when newspapers reported that it contained a slur against a Jewish midshipman by the name of L. Kaplan. While examining the patently offensive remark, written by the editor of the yearbook, J. L. Olmstead, Ted recalled that as president of the New York City police board in 1896 his father had shattered a police department bias against Jews by personally recruiting a young man named Otto Raphael. American Jews had fought and been wounded and killed in the Great War. Now here was a Jew who had qualified to become a student at the Naval Academy, and earned a place in the class of 1922, being insulted because of his faith.

Outraged that such a deplorable incident could have occurred in the navy, Ted nevertheless understood how and why it had happened. Since the end of the war the nation had been caught up in a frenzy of suspicion of people who were "different." Targets were the Negro, the Catholic, and the Jew. Even the New York State Assembly had been tainted in the matter of the seating of five Socialists. Part of this wave of hatred was attributable to a fear that "Bolshevism" would be brought to the United States by radical immigrants from Europe. The xenophobia had been inflamed by automobile maker Henry Ford. Through his newspaper, the *Dearborn Independent,* the man who had put Americans into cheap, reliable automobiles warned of the "International Jew." Ford discerned the "menace" as the cause of all the nation's problems, from high rents, a shortage of labor, the loosening of morals, women smoking cigarettes while dancing wildly to the corrupting new music called jazz, and even the timeless American sin of drunkenness. The result of this calumny was landlords refusing to accept Jewish tenants, and discrimination against Jews in employment and education. Even Ted's alma mater, Harvard College, had considered limiting the number of Jewish students. Now the disgrace had reached the Naval Academy.

Furious, Ted phoned the commandant of the Academy on June 14. He ordered a report on the incident. Should a reprimand of Olmstead be warranted, it must be given without delay. The editor was rebuked the next day.

With the embarrassing incident of anti-Semitism at the Naval Academy off the pages of newspapers, Ted returned his full attention to putting the navy in compliance with the provisions of the disarmament agreements. He also looked forward to escaping oppressive heat of summer in Washington, D.C., during a vacation amid the shady trees and cool lawns of Sagamore Hill, and then campaigning for Republicans in the 1922 congressional elections. Before departing for New York, he and Eleanor noted that a Senate investigation committee, headed by Thomas J. Walsh, a Montana Democrat, would be examining the oil-reserve leases to determine if they'd involved corruption or a conspiracy.

Back in the capital in November, Ted shared President Harding's disappointment that the election left the GOP with a reduced majority in House and Senate. The losses were attributed to a marked economic slowdown. Worried that the setback at the polls also stemmed from a loss of public confidence in the administration, Harding announced that early in 1923 he intended to go on a nationwide speaking tour to bolster support.

Soon after the election the president found faith in his government suffering a further erosion because of a mess in the Veterans Bureau. The agency that the fledgling American Legion had labored to bring into existence after the war was headed by a man whom Harding had met while visiting Hawaii. His name was Charles R. Forbes, himself a veteran of the Great War. Immediately after his appointment to the Veterans Bureau, he'd departed on a nationwide junket in order to "select" hospital sites, even though the locations had already been decided. Contracts were awarded without examination of the details, including the prices of items to be bought. Among items purchased were enough wax to polish floors for more than a century. The Bureau paid $.98 a gallon when the product could be purchased in stores for $.04 a gallon. The total cost to the Veterans Bureau was $70,000. Towels that could have been had for under $.04 apiece were bought for $.19 each. More than seventy-five thousand were acquired. In disposing of surplus items the record was just as shocking. More than eighty thousand bed sheets that had cost the government $1.37 each were let go for $.27 a piece, even as twenty-five thousand new sheets were being bought for $1.03 each.

Revelations of this situation in the press forced Harding to fire Forbes and replace him with a man of unimpeachable reputation, Brig. Gen.

Frank T. Hines. Forbes would eventually be convicted of fraud and sentenced to the federal prison at Leavenworth, Kansas. Rather than face questioning by Congress, the attorney for the Veterans Bureau, Charles C. Cramer, committed suicide. Another figure closely associated with Harding, Jesse Smith, who was one of a group of cronies from Harding's home state known to the press as "the Ohio Gang," also killed himself. He did so on the night of May 19, 1923, in a Washington apartment he'd shared with Attorney General Harry Daugherty.

To the Roosevelts in their house on Twenty-first Street in the months following the 1922 election, the Walsh committee's probe of the oil-reserves matter seemed to be going nowhere in its search for wrongdoing. Nor had the committee settled the question of whether the decision to grant leases had been sound policy. How all this might eventually be resolved was of little importance or relevance to Ted because he had done his best to protect the navy's interests with his amendment, and he certainly had done nothing unethical or legally questionable.

With work progressing well concerning implementation of the disarmament treaties, and decisions being required almost daily regarding the future role of naval shipyards, the assistant secretary of the navy found himself drawn into an intraservice debate on the future nature of naval warfare. The top brass of both the navy and army were split on the issue of the role of the airplane. Proponents of aviation contended that the bomber would be the decisive weapon in the next war. They argued that the pride of the navy—battleships—would prove to be as vulnerable to being sunk by planes as sitting ducks were to being blasted by a shotgun.

The chief proponent of this view was an outspoken army officer who had enlisted as a private in the Spanish-American War. Within a year, William Lendrum Mitchell, known to all as Billy, had been commissioned an officer in the army signal corps. A 1909 graduate of the Army Staff College, he had been chief of air service in the Great War for several units, including the U.S. 1st Corps and the First and Second Armies. Ted had heard about him from Quentin, always in the most glowing terms. He was promoted to brigadier general after the war and since 1920 he had been serving as assistant chief of the army air service. Lately, he had been proposing that he be provided several ships earmarked for scrapping so that he could use them to prove his thesis that capital ships could be easily sent to the bottom of the ocean by the air service bombers. On the basis of objections by dubious admirals the idea was rejected. In a statement issued on May 27, 1923, Ted adhered to a position taken by the Navy General Board expressing confidence that its battleships would not only survive aerial attacks, they would repel them. But this faith in the traditional warship did not mean the U.S. Navy was anchored in the past. Although the department opposed Mitchell's idea for a separate air service, it was not against development of an air wing of the fleet. If air power was to be the future, the navy wanted it carried "on the back of the fleet." To test the viability of the idea the department converted a coaling ship, the *Jupiter*, into an "aircraft carrier" and named it the *Langley*. Authorization was also given for plans to be drawn for the conversion of two battle-cruiser hulls into 33,000-ton carriers to be christened the *Lexington* and *Saratoga*. They were to operate in the Pacific. Looking ahead and considering the possibility (many admirals believed the likelihood) of war between the United States and Japan for naval dominance in the Pacific, the department developed Plan Orange. The carriers would be at the heart of a Pacific "battle force." This foresight, and some luck, resulted in the two carriers' becoming crucial in keeping the U.S. Navy in action following the destruction of many of the ships of the "battleship-and-cruiser" fleet in the Japanese sneak attack on Pearl Harbor on December 7, 1941.

The Congress also funded the building of eight badly needed heavy cruisers and provided money for three "V-class" submarines, which became prototypes of those that would operate successfully in World War II. A proposed symbol of this fledgling underwater fleet, a design incorporating two dolphins, was submitted to Ted and quickly approved.

In pondering the issues raised by Mitchell and other exponents of the need for the United States to look to the skies in future conflicts, Ted appreciated that had his youngest brother been alive to debate the issue at the dinner table, Quentin would have come down on Mitchell's side. So, too, might their father. Not only had TR been the first president of the United States to go up in an airplane and pronounced the experience "Bully!" as assistant secretary of the navy, he had witnessed a test of a prototype of the aircraft carrier. The demonstration failed when the plane crashed. But TR came away with an open mind on the subject of the possible role of aviation in naval operations of the future. No doubt he would have been "dee-lighted" to know that his son would play an important early role in the development of the flattops that would one day evolve into a nuclear-powered carrier named the *Theodore Roosevelt*.

Four years after TR's death, as a lovely spring turned to early summer in the city in which he had served as a civil service commissioner, assistant secretary of the navy, vice president, and twenty-sixth president, the gossip among politically astute circles in Washington, D.C., was that TR's able young namesake at the Department of the Navy had set his sights on claiming the chair his father had occupied for two years in the governor's mansion in Albany.

Those who envisioned a Roosevelt candidacy pointed out that Ted had chosen to pattern his life and career on his father's. Both went to war and came back heroes. Both ran for the state Assembly and won. Each accepted appointment to the office of assistant secretary of the navy. Surely, Ted's next step would be a run for the governorship.

If elected, would Theodore Roosevelt Jr. next imagine himself following his father into the White House?

The prospect that Ted could receive the Republican nomination was challenged by one Republican leader. W. H. Anderson asserted that Ted's candidacy would never gain the approval of the New York Anti-Saloon League.

The basis of the prohibitionist group's opposition was a vote Assemblyman Roosevelt had cast in 1920 to allow sale of beer with 2.75 percent alcohol content. Although TR had not been an imbiber of hard liquor, his grown-up sons saw nothing wrong with moderate drinking. Ted therefore regarded the Eighteenth Amendment to the U.S. Constitution outlawing the manufacture and sale of spirits "an iniquitous law." Nevertheless, believing that it and its enforcing law, the Volstead Act, were the will of the American people and must be obeyed, he had told Eleanor to gather up their small supply of prewar liquor and "pour it down the drain."

Eleanor's "Scottish thrift" would not let her do it. Despite Washington, D.C., being "dry," except on the property of foreign embassies, she retained the bottles. On occasions at which the guests in their home were known to be "wets" she offered them drinks.

Should Ted somehow be nominated by the Republicans to run for governor in 1924, his opponent would be the Democrat incumbent, Alfred E. Smith. A "wet," he was Roman Catholic. Born on the Lower East Side of New York on December 30, 1878, he had attended St. James Elementary School for eight years. He'd dropped out after his father died, leaving him in charge of a trucking business. His first political job had been an appointment as a process server and clerk in the office of the commissioner of jurors from 1895 to 1903. He first sought election to the New York Assembly with the support of Tammany Hall in 1903 and won. After seven reelections he was Democratic leader. When Democrats gained control of the Assembly in 1913 he was chosen speaker.

Deciding to leave the legislature in 1915, he ran for and was elected New York county sheriff. Two years later he was elected president of New York City's board of aldermen. When he made a bid for the governorship in 1918 he won narrowly. Seeking reelection in 1920, he found himself buried in the nationwide Republican landslide that engulfed the vice-presidential hopes of Franklin D. Roosevelt. Smith tried for the governorship again in 1922 and succeeded. That he would seek the office again in 1924 was not in doubt.

Whether he would find himself opposed by Theodore Roosevelt Jr. remained to be seen.

How well Republican state candidates did in 1924 would depend to a great extent on how voters felt nationwide about the record of President Harding. To take the country's temperature the president kept his promise to tour the nation. The "voyage of understanding" began on June 23, 1923. It was disrupted on July 27 in Seattle, Washington, when he was stricken by what his doctor diagnosed as indigestion caused by crabmeat. When he reached San Francisco on July 19, he seemed better. Then he was found to have pneumonia. Once again he rebounded. But at 7:35 P.M., August 2, 1923, as Mrs. Harding was reading to him in bed, he died of what his physicians speculated was a blood clot that went from his lungs to his brain.

To Mrs. Theodore Roosevelt Jr. he had been "a kindly" man who had chosen "the best cabinet in a decade," which included Charles Evan Hughes, her card-playing friend Andrew W. Mellon, John W. Weeks, and a man who had worked miracles in postwar relief in Europe, Herbert Hoover. Eleanor soon learned that Harding had also surrounded himself with schemers who "took full advantage of his never being able to say no to them."

A week after Harding's death, Ted wrote to Edith Roosevelt at Sagamore Hill and spoke of Harding having gone into government when he might have enjoyed a comfortable private life of "the pleasures he cared for, seeing his friends, playing his game of cards, his golf, and living in a sphere of activity which suited him and in which he belonged, instead of the struggles, problems, and difficulties of the world into which he came largely by chance."

With Harding's death began a slow unfolding of events that would forever tarnish his short presidency and imperil the reputation and career of the man Harding had chosen to be his assistant secretary of the navy.

On January 17, 1924, Ted received a long-distance telephone call from his brother Archie in New York City. "Of course, I may be wrong," Archie said, "but I'm afraid there's been dirty work at the crossroads on this oil business. I don't want to talk on the phone. When are you coming to New York?"

Ted said he was scheduled to speak there that evening. The story that Archie related to him after the speech had been imparted to Archie by Harry Sinclair's confidential secretary. G. D. Wahlberg had told him that at the time of the signing of the Teapot Dome lease, Sinclair had sent Secretary of the Interior Fall a check for $68,000. Wahlberg knew this to be true, he said, because Wahlberg had seen the check.

The question now was whether Archie should volunteer this information to the Senate subcommittee investigating the naval reserve oil leases.

Eleanor recalled, "It was a terrible position for Archie, and a difficult decision to make. He was only thirty years old, disabled in the war, with his way to make in the world and a wife and children dependent on him. He well knew that if he came forward with this testimony he would not only lose his job [with the Sinclair Oil Company] but would lay himself open to criticism for having betrayed his employer."

The brothers decided to seek advice from Nick Longworth and two friends who were in the Senate, Frank Brandegree of Connecticut and William E. Borah of Idaho. During a Sunday meeting at Ted's home, all agreed that Archie must tell what he knew. When it is a question of harm to the United States, the three counseled the worrying Archie, all other loyalties must be secondary. Furthermore, if Archie did not come forward with the information, his own character and honesty might be impugned. Ted phoned Senator Walsh that afternoon and arranged for Archie to appear before the committee the next morning.

Because Archie's testimony was what is known in legal terms as "hearsay" that would certainly be denied by Sinclair and Secretary Fall, Ted proposed that an attempt be made by Archie to persuade Wahlberg to come to Washington on Monday to appear at the hearing. The question was where to locate Wahlberg. Archie knew that he lived on Riverside Drive in New York, but a telephone information operator reported that Wahlberg's number was unlisted.

Feeling frustrated and anxious on a Sunday night when there appeared to be no way of contacting the man who could verify Archie's story, Ted slouched in his chair with a glum look on his face, then suddenly bolted up and exclaimed, "Of course! The Bureau of Investigation!" With a broad grin as he reached for the telephone he muttered, "God bless Father."

Sixteen years earlier, President Theodore Roosevelt had found himself dissatisfied with the inability of the federal government to carry out investigations of possibly corrupt officials, nefarious activities by trusts that flouted the Sherman Antitrust Act, thievery of public lands, and a general attitude by powerful individuals that "the public be damned." To fully address the problem TR used his executive powers to direct Attorney General Charles J. Bonaparte to create a group of detectives within the Department of Justice to be called the "Bureau of Investigation." Bonaparte had done so on July 16, 1908.

On January 18, 1924, the forerunner of the Federal Bureau of Investigation was run by a friend of Ted's. He was a tough private detective who had founded his own private investigating agency. Ted phoned William J. Burns at his home and explained the Wahlberg problem. Burns promised that his agents would find him in less than two hours.

At eleven o'clock Wahlberg phoned the Roosevelt house in Washington. Archie told him what had transpired and that Wahlberg's testimony was needed the next day. Wahlberg balked, tearfully telling Archie that he could not put himself and his family's welfare in jeopardy. Ted took the phone from Archie and bluntly told Wahlberg that if he did not testify voluntarily, the Senate would compel him to do so. He declared, "It's your plain duty as an American citizen to come forward of your own volition. How will you ever be able to look your children in the face if you don't?"

Still a reluctant witness and looking agitated and frightened, Wahlberg arrived in the capital on Monday. Archie testified to the story Wahlberg had told him about the check Sinclair had given to Secretary Fall. Senator Walsh called Wahlberg to testify.

Ted's wife observed the witness intently. More than thirty years later the scene remained vivid as she described it in her autobiography:

He was pale and his hands were shaking. Directly opposite across the table sat [one of Sinclair's lawyers, smoking a cigar], who never moved his cold blue eyes from Wahlberg's face. Senator Walsh asked if Wahlberg had knowledge of the check sent by Sinclair to secretary Fall. Wahlberg turned red, then gray. [The Sinclair lawyer] shifted his cigar to the corner of his mouth. There was a moment of breathless excitement in the room.

In a voice scarcely above a whisper Wahlberg answered, "No, Senator. Mr. Roosevelt is mistaken. I never mentioned a check for sixty-eight thousand dollars. What I said was that Mr. Sinclair had sent Secretary Fall a present of six or eight cows and bulls."

The crowd in the room gasped, then chuckled, then roared with laughter.

Over the din Wahlberg continued, "You see how the misunderstanding arose? You see how much 'sixty eight thous' sounds like 'six or eight cows'?"

One newspaper headlined the ludicrous explanation: "The Euphonies of the Oil Case."

Wahlberg subsequently amended his story. The $68,000 check was not for Fall, but had gone to the manager of Fall's ranch, Rancocas Stables. It was payment for his services as trainer of Sinclair's thoroughbred horse Zev and others, plus the trainer's share of their winnings.

What followed this fiasco was in Eleanor's view a "real witches' Sabbath" in the form of widening and deepening investigations of Harding administration corruption that has gone into history books under the collective name "the Teapot Dome Scandal." Ted found himself attacked for having been a director of the Sinclair Oil Company and having asked Harry Sinclair to hire Archie. South Carolina congressman William F. Stevenson demanded that Ted resign because as assistant secretary of the navy he'd once held shares in Sinclair Oil. The charge was refuted by Nick Longworth with Eleanor's sale receipts, dated before the granting of the leases.

When Ted heard what Stevenson said, he told Eleanor he was going to "beat up that rat." Eleanor replied, "He's a little elderly man who wears glasses."

Ted asked, "Are you sure of that?"

"Positive."

"Oh, *damn*. Then I suppose I can't do it."

Instead, Ted sat down with a pencil and on the back of a large brown envelope wrote out a statement for the press explaining why he'd asked for a job for Archie and circumstances of the stocks ownership and Eleanor's sale of them at a loss. He ended the statement with:

> Every crook should be punished regardless of politics or position. Equally crooked, however, with those who take bribes is he who, cloaking himself in Congressional immunity, willfully misrepresents facts in an endeavor to injure an innocent man. Regardless of politics, such a man should be held to strict account, and such a man is Congressman Stevenson of South Carolina. I call on all Americans, Democrat or Republican, who stand for honor, fair play, and Americanism to make it their business to drive from public life slanderers of this type.

After Senator C. C. Dill of Washington called for Ted's resignation from the Department of the Navy, and introduced a resolution to demand it, the *Spokane Review* wrote, "Someone should rise up and pickle Dill." The resolution was overwhelmingly rejected.

That summer the report of Senator Walsh's investigating committee exonerated Ted in the matter of the oil leases. This was followed immediately by speculation among Republicans and in the press that Ted would probably leave the navy post to follow in his father's footsteps by getting elected governor of New York. After that, perhaps, he might wish to become the first son of a president to be elected president since John Quincy Adams.

16

Ted's first step toward achieving his goal of the New York governorship was becoming a delegate to the 1924 Republican State Convention in Rochester. To do this he had to win the party's primary election in Nassau County. Because he'd been born and raised in the county and Sagamore Hill was listed on the voter rolls as his official state residence, this was not a problem. Winning the gubernatorial nomination was quite another matter. He went to the convention expecting that the gubernatorial nomination was likely to go to the acknowledged front-runner, Edward "Eddie" Machold. Ted's close friend, Senator James W. Wadsworth, had told Ted that Eddie would get the nod because he'd done "some splendid work for the party for years and all the boys love him." But if Machold should somehow falter, Ted's wartime comrade "Wild Bill" Donovan speculated, Ted would be "a cinch" to get the nomination.

To Ted's astonishment, Wild Bill's surmise suddenly turned into prescience. Machold lost to Ted on the first ballot. In the meantime, the Democrats had renominated their governor.

But the prize Alfred E. Smith had hoped to win in 1924 was his party's nomination for president of the United States. His name had been offered for consideration at the Democratic convention by a courageous Franklin D. Roosevelt. Four years earlier he had been stricken with polio and written off as an active politician. Instead, he stood at the podium to nominate Smith as the only man who could beat the Republicans' "Silent Cal" Coolidge.

The Democrats, however, chose a Wall Street lawyer, John W. Davis of West Virginia, who had been Woodrow Wilson's solicitor general.

The general feeling in the political world was that Smith had been denied the nomination because he was a Roman Catholic. But his religion was not an impediment in the state of New York. The majority of Empire State voters had shown repeatedly that they loved the little man with the big nose who had fought in Albany on behalf of "the little people," spoke to them with a pugnacious New York attitude in an unashamedly Lower East Side accent, sported a derby hat, and puffed away on stogies.

Alice Roosevelt Longworth telegraphed her brother about his opponent: THEY HAVE CERTAINLY HANDED YOU A FIGHT. Ted immediately sent President Calvin Coolidge his resignation as assistant secretary of the navy and launched his campaign with a schedule of speeches that Eleanor described as one that "no previous candidate for governor had ever attempted." He was expected to make more than ten speeches a day. He found himself delivering even more.

Running against Al Smith meant that Ted was aligned against his cousin Franklin. But because of Franklin's continuing struggle to cope with polio, Ted also had to contend with the campaigning efforts by another cousin. Franklin's wife Eleanor took to the hustings, traveling the state in a specially built truck with a giant teapot on top that spouted steam. Lest anyone miss the point, it was labeled TEAPOT DOME.

Alice Longworth told reporters, "It was a pretty base thing for her to do."

The other Eleanor Roosevelt on the campaign trail was content to support her candidate in the race by traveling with him, but leaving the speaking to him. She found a rapport with the reporters, all of whom promised her that Ted would win. Since the start of the tour she had worn the same hat, a black velvet beret. Examining it one day, she decided it had been rained upon so much and looked so "tired" that it should be replaced. When she told the newsmen that she was going to buy a new one, they pleaded with her not to. One warned, "It might change your luck."

At one large open-air meeting on Long Island Eleanor noticed leaflets being distributed to the crowd by members of the Ku Klux Klan. The new but powerful political force had arisen across the country and was carried along on a tide of racial, ethnic, and religious prejudice that had evidenced itself in lynchings of blacks, discrimination against Jews and Catholics in hiring and housing, segregation of the races in schools and public places, and even in the U.S. Naval Academy's yearbook.

A vestige of the years following the Civil War, the Ku Klux Klan had been organized by terrified whites in the old Confederacy out of fear of freed slaves. In the northern states whites were alarmed by an influx into their cities of blacks escaping prejudice against them in the South. Although a latter-day organization calling itself the KKK had been revived in Georgia during the Great War by William Joseph Simmons, it had found few adherents. But in 1920 Americans had flocked to see an epic motion picture made by D.W. Griffith, titled *The Birth of a Nation*. The film was inspired by a novel, *The Klansman*, in which the Ku Klux Klan of the Reconstruction period had been depicted as heroic men. Clad in white robes and white hoods, they rode in the name of Jesus Christ with the cross as their emblem to save whites from the dreaded black man. By 1924 the Klan's membership totaled nearly four and a half million men in the South, Midwest, California, and even in New York City.

The objective of the "Order of Knights of the Invisible Empire," as stated in its constitution, was "to unite white male persons, native-born Gentile citizens of the United States of America, who owe no allegiance to any foreign government, nation, institution, sect, ruler, person, or people; whose morals are good, whose reputations and vocations exemplary." The Klan also sought "to cultivate and promote patriotism toward our Civil Government; to practice an honorable Klanishness toward each other; to exemplify a practical benevolence; to shield the sanctity of the home and the chastity of womanhood; to maintain forever white supremacy, to reach and faithfully inculcate a high spiritual philosophy through an exalted ritualism, and by a practical devotion to conserve, protect, and maintain the distinctive institutions, rights and privileges, principles, traditions, and ideals of pure Americanism."

In the United States in the 1920s, wrote Frederick Lewis Allen in his popular history of that decade, *Only Yesterday*, "the time was ripe for the Klan." Here was a way for a man who felt threatened by blacks, Jews, Catholics, and "foreigners" to defend himself and the country against things and ideas that were "un-American."

Appalled that the Klan was supporting Ted's candidacy with leaflets at his rally, Eleanor showed one to Ted. He departed from his usual stump speech to reject the Klan's backing. "At this time intolerance in many forms is stirring in this country," he said. "The word *Americanism* is soiled when used by a group furthering intolerance. Such a group is the Ku Klux Klan."

His rejection of the Klan's racism was underscored on October 28 (TR's birthday) in a speech at Harlem's Mother Zion Church for Negroes.

The next day he made ten speeches in Brooklyn. On the thirtieth he addressed large rallies in Westchester County. On the thirty-first he was on Staten Island, then at the Cooper Union, and ten other rallies in Manhattan. November 1 had him in Queens and on the radio from Republican headquarters in Manhattan. He rounded out the campaign with eleven speeches on November 3 and made his last address to the audience at the rodeo at Madison Square Garden.

Back at Sagamore Hill on the fourth, he waited for the returns with Eleanor, the children, and a few close friends. The final tally showed him carrying all but six of the state's counties. But five of them were those that comprised Al Smith's home turf of heavily Democratic New York City. Smith won by 108,589 votes. (He garnered 1,627,111. Ted got 1,518,522.)

Beaten, out of a job, with small prospect for pursuing a political career because he was too independent to suit the taste of the GOP's leadership, and with no desire to resume a business career, Ted went on a postelection, two-week vacation with Eleanor in Louisiana as guests of Governor John Parker. Returning to Sagamore Hill, he announced his intention of doing what TR had done after he'd lost in his bid to be elected mayor of New York in 1886, and after he'd left the presidency in 1909.

He decided to try some exploring and hunting.

And who better to take along than TR's hardy, enthusiastic, and capable companion on the African and Brazilian expeditions?

Although Ted had done "a certain amount of roughing it" and hunting, he admitted that "compared to Kermit I am a beginner."

As to where the expedition would take them, Ted found his inspiration in a verse from Rudyard Kipling's "The Feet of the Young Men":

Do you know the world's white rooftree—do you know that windy
   rift
Where the baffling mountain eddies chop and change?
Do you know the long day's patience, belly-down on frozen drift,
While the head of heads is feeding out of range?
It is there that I am going, where the boulders and snow lie,
With a trusty, nimble tracker that I know.
I have sworn an oath, to keep it, on the Horns of Ovis Poli,
For the Red Gods call me out, and I must go.

The "*Ovis poli*," Ted explained to Eleanor, was a rare mountain sheep with enormous horns. Conceded by sportsmen the world over to be one of the finest of all game trophies, it was the "father and mother" of all the wild sheep, Ted went on. "He represents the elder branch of the family of which the American bighorn look, in comparison, a small animal. He lives beyond the barren, treeless Pamirs in Turkestan. The species had been discovered by Marco Polo, hence the name *Ovis poli*—Polo's sheep."

And so the big house of Sagamore Hill was again alive with excited talk of the romance of the wilderness, the hunt, rare specimens, campfires, meals of game, rifles, tents, packs, and pioneer spirit. Maps of Himalayan Asia produced and laid out on the floor of the gun room had exotic and thrilling names that became destinations, goals, challenges: mountain passes called Zoji, Khardong, Saser, and Muzart; names next to dots on paper: Gund, Khargil, Choong Loong, Murgu, Akh Tam, Chungtai, Tango Tash, Misgar, Gurez, Bandipur, and Srinagar.

On this trek Ted and Kermit could expect to strike all climates, from the bitter weather of snow-swept mountains to the blazing heat of sand-drifted deserts and jungle-covered rivers. The country was exceedingly interesting from a scientific standpoint, Ted explained to Eleanor and their wide-eyed children, because no comprehensive American expedition had ever covered it, and there were to all intents and purposes no collections of the region's wildlife in museums.

Because the brothers were in no position to finance the adventure themselves, they sought and obtained backing from James Simpson of Chicago's Field Museum of Natural History. Weeks of preparation followed. Permits were needed from the governments of Britain, China, and the Soviet Union. Masses of equipment had to be assembled. In addition to the clothing to be worn during their treks in the wild, they needed proper attire for meetings with local officials in the far country. They chose dinner jackets and collapsible opera hats.

Enlisted in the expedition for their expertise were noted naturalist George Cherrie and C. Suydam Cutting, a friend of Ted and Kermit who shared their zest for adventure. They would go first to England to pick up passports at the Soviet embassy, then to Paris for more supplies, on to Marseilles by rail, and aboard a Peninsular & Oriental steamer to Bombay.

The date set for departure was May 1925.

17

When Kermit went to Africa with his father in 1909, TR had taken along an assortment of leather-bound books that he called "the pigskin library." For the "Simpson-Roosevelts" expedition Ted packed clothbound editions of the Bible; Shakespeare; *Pilgrim's Progress;* Plutarch's *Lives; The Cloister and the Hearth;* works of TR's favorite poet, Edwin Arlington Robinson; Molière's comedies; and the bard and balladeer of the Far East, Kipling.

The Roosevelt brothers landed at Bombay on May 11, 1925. Three days later they were in Rawalpindi to pick up motorcars to take them to Srinagar, a city whose canals had given it the misleading title "Venice of the East." Kermit knew "a little Hindustan," but his communication with the locals was assisted by a Captain Pim, whom Kermit had known in Mesopotamia during the war. With the Englishman's assistance they made plans to march to Leh and then over the Karakoram Pass, across the plains of Turkestan, to the Tian Shan Mountains. On the way, they hoped, they could begin the scientific work of collecting specimens of the ibex, wapiti, and Siberian roe deer.

At Leh they would exchange travel by motor vehicle for sixty ponies. While waiting at Baltal for favorable conditions to cross the Zoji Pass they were, in Ted's words, "serenaded with avalanches." The slides started with a booming roar that Ted found "reminiscent of a battery of heavies [cannons] on the French front, then, if the avalanche were in sight, you would see great masses of snow hurtling down the precipices. After a short intermission another salvo of sound and more plunging snow. Two or three such outbursts would occur in diminishing violence, and then all would be quiet."

On Saturday, June 6, the four-man party divided. Cherrie and Cutting took the larger part of their caravan of guides and laden ponies on an easier route through the Khardong Pass. Ted and Kermit took a more difficult terrain. When they reached the top at 17,800 feet, it was the highest altitude they'd ever attained. They felt no mountain sickness in the thin air, but as they descended they developed severe headaches. "When we camped at night at Khardong at a height of only 13,500 feet," Ted recalled in a book he and Kermit wrote about the expedition, "we felt we were in the Low Countries."

Reunited with Cherrie and Cutting at a small village named Taghar, they moved onward to Panamik and were delighted to discover the town had a mud bathhouse. It provided the first hot water they'd had in four weeks. Washed and rested, Ted and Kermit went hunting for the bur-rhel, a member of the sheep family and a little larger than a donkey. Its colors were fawn and white, ideal camouflage in the rocky terrain. They saw quite a number of the nimble animals, but the sheep were agile targets for men with heavy guns who'd climbed from 15,000 to 17,000 feet, where, Ted noted, "there is only a hatful of air to go around, and each breath is a gasp."

Only when darkness was falling were they able to get off shots in the direction of a herd of burrhel. Their bullets killed two. But as they skinned them the next day, they found that the animals were changing from winter to summer coats. The hair came out in handfuls, making the pelts unusable as museum specimens. This realization forced a change in plans concerning their quest for the *Ovis poli*. Were they to find the elusive creature when it was shedding old hair for new, their skins would also be useless. Ted and Kermit agreed that they would seek the poli toward the end of their expedition, in late autumn or early winter.

With their plan amended, they headed for the second of the great passes on their itinerary, the Karamoram, rising over 19,000 feet, nearly half again as high as Colorado's Pikes Peak. "What might be an easy climb at 10,000 feet," Ted wrote, "at 17,000 sets the heart beating like a trip-hammer and the lungs gasping for air. At night it is very difficult to sleep. You wake every few minutes, struggling for breath, and feel as if you had been long underwater."

He found mute witness to the severity of the upward journey in the bones of pack animals that had fallen from steep paths. In some spots they were piled eight feet high. After a hard day's march over glacial streams half covered with ice, and through impeding snowdrifts, on May 17 Ted and the others made a bivouac at the head of the Sasser glacier.

"We pitched no tents that night, but rolled up in our sleeping bags, " he recorded. "The ponies and yaks were kept close together, each beside his load. A few small dung-fires glowed, over which the men cooked their tea. There was little sleep for any of us, as the altitude prevented it. Through the night the men talked and moved around."

At first light (4:30) they began the trek across the glacier. Three hours later they were off the ice and onto "a reasonably good trail into the valley." The day's only casualty was a pony that died from lack of air. As the tail of their caravan left the ice pack, a bitter wind came up. The glacier was quickly engulfed in a miniature blizzard.

By the time they reached a village at the mouth of Karakoram Pass, six more pack ponies had died and others were noticeably weakening. To ease their burdens some of the riding animals were turned into pack-bearers. The men who had each had a horse of their own, including Ted and Kermit, now shared one. As they made their way along the approach to the Karakoram, they again found the trails littered with skeletons of dead pack animals. On the last steep ascent to the crest of the pass another pony was lost when it fell off the trail. In midafternoon the caravan reached the top and started down a long, gradual slope to the north, leaving "the King of the Passes" behind them. Ahead stretched the Tibetan antelope range. The morning after entering it they saw a herd of seven grazing on their left. As they "fled like shadows across the path of the caravan," Ted shot a buck and doe. Kermit killed a buck. "This gave us not only our group for the museum," Ted noted, "but fresh meat."

It was now June 23. The next objective was the fourth of the five great passes shown on sketchy maps of the mostly unexplored region. Large sections of the maps were blank. Names that indicated places where caravans might stop turned out to be nothing but fire-blackened rocks at places, Ted noted, "where no one has ever lived or will." For nearly two weeks they had been traveling through a stretch of wilderness and mighty mountain fastnesses that were "no-man's-land" in every sense of the term.

When they camped at Ali-Nazar Khurgan on June 30 the town consisted of one family of two men and two women, dressed in "a rather grimy pink" and wearing huge headdresses like the busbies of grenadiers. Their houses were caves hollowed out of the dried earth of a hillside. Ted noted with interest that the man who seemed to be chief of the family had a large collection of trophy animal heads, including poli horns. He learned they'd been brought from the family's previous home in the Tagdum Bash Pamirs, a very long distance away.

Ahead lay the last of the passes, the Sanju. Lower than the others, it had two trails. One was known to be dangerous because of a glacier. The other was invariably closed in the summer months. When it was found to be open, the native bearers declared that the expedition must be under some special providence because they had not known the trail to be open so early in more than fifteen years. Following a path that at times sloped forty-five degrees, the caravan got to the top with no loss of animals. Ted wrote of standing at the summit of the Sanju. "There was a gorgeous view. The mountains on either side were mist cloaked, and their outlines blurred and softened. Below, zigzagging upward, was the train of more than a hundred animals, and voices of the drivers, as they shouted, came faintly to us on the gusty wind."

On the twenty-five-day climb over the Himalayas the expedition had lost thirteen animals, but no men and no vital piece of baggage. Hardly anyone had believed it possible for Ted, Kermit, and their companions to make the journey so early in the season. Certainly, no one had ever known white men to do it. Had Ted and Kermit been delayed one day in crossing the Sanju, neither would they have succeeded. Hours after they'd passed through, snow closed it.

"We had crossed 'the everlasting hills,'" Ted wrote of this first phase of the odyssey, "and we were on our way down to the plains of Turkestan."

18

For the first and second sons of Theodore Roosevelt who at Sagamore Hill had thrilled to the fireworks that always marked the anniversary of American independence, July Fourth of 1925 would be remembered as "the day of many fords." Cold, deep, dangerous, rocky, and rapid, there were sixteen of them to negotiate in getting across the Sanju River. That evening, in honor of the most auspicious date in American history, Ted noted, the expedition's cook, Jemal Shah, "called forth his undoubted culinary talents and we feasted and celebrated in orthodox fashion [Ted did not explain further], calling to mind those boyhood Fourths when armed with a plentiful supply of firecrackers we would slip out in the dark hours to disturb the sleep of long-suffering neighbors."

Had Ted and Kermit a firecracker or skyrocket to ignite to light up the valley of the Sanju River, no one but they, their men, and animals would have noticed. Over the next three days they covered more than eighty miles of barren landscape, which was broken here and there by an oasis. When they encountered natives, the locals welcomed them with apricots, curds, and unleavened bread. When the "honored guests" moved on they were escorted a mile or so by notables of the oasis. None of their hosts proved more hospitable and memorable to Ted and Kermit than the *amban* of Karghalik. Word that they were coming had preceded them, but they had not been expected so soon. Their appearance on July 18 coincided with visits to the *amban* by a group of officials called Begs. The surprised but amiable *amban* was short, squat, and cheerful, but in no way a linguist. "He did not speak even Turki," Ted recorded of their meeting, "so all sentiments had to be transmitted through Hindustance, then into Turki and Chinese. Doubtless their outlines became somewhat hazy in the process. We had hoped to avoid stopping over a day, but this proved to be impossible, for the Amban had set his heart upon giving us a *tamasha*—an entertainment." Ted's account continued:

> In preparation for this affair, we wended down to the rushing yellow river that ran near the garden in which we were camped. A large and intent audience of both sexes watched us bathe. Three of us in our modesty kept on our clothes—they badly needed a wash—but one paid no more attention to the audience than if it had not existed, and has probably joined the galaxy of country deities. Thoroughly washed, we proceeded to dig out tuxedo coats and opera hats, much to the delight of our men.
>
> The Amban arrived early to call for us. We were not ready, so he, his two sons, and entire retinue joined our own men in watching us dress. They were all greatly impressed—so much so that next morning the Amban sent his tailor armed with bundles of black-and-white striped silk. He squatted under a tree nearby busily copying the tuxedoes. The collapsible opera hats were, alas, quite beyond emulation.

The *amban*'s dinner was made even more successful when Ted and Kermit provided an assortment of bottles from a small supply of brandy and liqueurs they'd brought for just such an occasion. They mixed up palatable cocktails with fruit juice, brandy, and sloe gin.

The host provided two bottles of his own. On the labels were pictures of pretty Chinese women. One was "Girl Brand Orange Champagne." The other, "Girl Brand Rose Champagne."

"It was not easy to describe the taste," Ted wrote.

It was nothing like the champagne he and Kermit had been served at the White House or in the restaurants of New York and the bistros of Paris. But in July, in the lands north of the Himalayas, nothing they found was like anything at home.

On the third of August the expedition traversed Muzart Pass. To Ted it represented "the last barrier to the promised hunting grounds." Nine days later they reached Chin Ballak in the heart of the Tian Shan Mountains. "There are many ibex in the Tian Shan," Ted wrote, "but anyone who believes that a good head is therefore easy to get makes a very real mistake. It is one thing to see them through the field glasses, and another to get them and bring them back in triumph to camp. Stalking the big ibex is hard and tricky work."

As the Roosevelt brothers made their way through the Himalayas and into vast unknown territories that lay beyond them, in search of the *Ovis poli,* periodic reports of their adventures made fascinating reading in newspapers for countless Americans who admired their courage and spirit of adventure. That a pair of young men of privilege of the 1920s whose father had been president of the United States would go halfway around the world to shoot wildlife, and then be lauded for their deeds, would seem to some Americans at the beginning of the twenty-first century to be an enterprise to be condemned. But Ted and Kermit had not gone to Central Asia for the purpose of slaughtering the animals of the region, just as TR had not ventured on a safari to West Africa to enjoy killing lions and elephants. In both instances the expeditions served natural science and fostered general knowledge of the geography, people, and fauna of previously obscure parts of the world.

"Though hunting in itself is great sport, without the scientific aspect as well it loses much of its charm," Ted wrote in the introduction to the book he and Kermit wrote about their journey, *East of the Sun and West of the Moon,* published in 1926. "Our thoughts turned to central Asia. This had always been the Mecca of our desires."

It was the land about which they'd read as boys, envisioning at their father's urging the Mongol tribes who'd swept out of the region like flame over Asia and half of Europe. Through it had run the great caravan routes carrying treasures of the East to grace the parlors of the West. To get there the sons of Theodore Roosevelt would have to traverse the exotic land of the Kipling stories and poems they'd had read to them, then read again themselves, and that they would read to their own children.

And there was Marco Polo himself, writing of the land he'd seen north of the Himalayas, "There are great numbers of wild beasts, among others wild sheep of great size, whose horns are a good six palms in length." Doubters had classed such animals with the unicorn and phoenix, as wholly mythological. But six hundred years after Marco Polo an English army officer, Lt. John Wood, shot a sheep in that country that proved Marco Milione had told the truth. Even later the emir of Afghanistan gave a visiting English nobleman a head with horns measuring seventy-five inches.

The season and mountain-sheep biology had forced Ted to postpone seeking *Ovis poli* until the Himalayan autumn. After a summer in the Tian Shan, the time came to seek it. In mid-September the hunters left the mountains by again passing through the Muzart Pass. On October 6 they were at a tiny settlement named Bulun in typical Pamir country of sandy valleys dotted with tufts of dried grass, and snow-covered hills and mountains. There were many tracks across the snow left by wolves, marmots, some kind of small mountain cat, and even a mouse. When Ted and Kermit caused five large hares to speed off, the brothers remembered a southern custom which held that a running rabbit meant luck, but only if you took off your hat. They removed their caps in the hope that their luck would take the form of the *Ovis poli*. A few minutes later, as they were plodding along, one of their men jumped off his yak and pointed excitedly to a slope some six hundred yards away.

Running along the hillside were two small poli rams with horns about twenty inches long. They were the first *Ovis poli* Ted and Kermit had seen in the flesh. Too young to be shot, they cantered up the slope and disappeared over the crest. Ted thought they were "very handsome with their gray backs and white chests and legs."

Presently, they spotted six females with four young. Because Ted and Kermit were looking for males, they left them undisturbed. As darkness fell, they returned to camp encouraged by the poli they had seen. There had been enough females to make them feel reasonably certain that mature males were nearby.

The next day they encountered more of the sheep, but they were too far away. Ted used field glasses and a telescope to observe the males stepping delicately among the rocks, nibbling grass, and halting now and then to glance around and sniff the wind. Occasionally, one would clamber on a rock and stand sentinel-like, his head thrown back until the massive spiral horns seemed to rest on his shoulders. Ted thought they looked like the very spirit of the mountains. There were eight males. He estimated the horns of six of them to be about forty-five inches in length. Those of the others appeared to be more than fifty inches. Ted and Kermit agreed that if they tried to shoot at them, they would have been as likely to hit the moon as the poli.

They would try tomorrow. When it dawned, the whole country was blanketed with snow. The sky was steely gray and threatening more. They trudged to the place where they'd seen the poli and found them at the end of a valley. They were moving slowly up a steep slope.

Ted and Kermit lay still, barely breathing as they watched the eight poli breast the crest and stand for a magnificent moment outlined against the sky. They disappeared one by one on the far side of the hill. As soon as they were out of sight, Ted and Kermit rose to follow them. They pushed through waist-deep snowdrifts, then climbed up slippery snow-covered shale slopes so steep that Ted wondered how the snow could stick. Snatching for handholds and gasping for air they climbed to 17,000 feet and despaired of finding their agile quarry. But as they were about to give up, Kermit spotted them on the opposite side of the valley, about a mile away. The sun was out, warming the fresh snow and creating a heavy, hanging mist. Carefully advancing to a little ravine flanked by a steep ridge from which he felt he could get off a good shot, Ted was sweating heavily despite a bitter wind that cut through his soaked clothing.

Peering into the valley, Ted saw a snowstorm sweeping upward. Realizing with dismay that it would be upon them in minutes, he decided it was "now or never." Both he and Kermit got off one shot. As the startled rams bolted away, the brothers thought their shots had hit. Then they saw that the scrambling poli were headed in their direction. Ted pulled off his gloves to get a better grip on his rifle. His hands were so cold he couldn't feel the trigger. Suddenly one poli came into his view from behind a huge buttress of rock. Others followed in single file, the big rams in the lead. They were about 250 yards away, going at a plunging canter through the snowdrifts, heads held high, the great spiral horns flared out magnificently.

In his book Ted described what happened next:

We began firing at once at the two leaders. First one and then the other staggered and lost his place in line. Though hit hard, they pulled themselves together, joined the herd, and all but disappeared over a nearby ridge. Clutching our rifles, we stumbled after them. When we reached the trail we found bloodstains. We put every ounce of strength we had into the chase, for these were the trophies we had traveled 12,000 miles to get. The going was very bad. Every few steps we floundered in armpit-deep snow. It was the tied-foot race of nightmare. Try as we would, we could not make time. Suddenly the wind rose, snow began to drift down, and the trail was blotted out in the swirling white of the storm. We could do no more and had to give up to make for camp.

Working their way down to the valley, they found their yaks so frosted with snow that they looked like animated birthday cakes. Two native hunters had seen the rams cross the ridge and told Ted and Kermit they were confident that the poli were mortally wounded. They felt sure they would be found the next day, provided the storm did not obliterate their trails.

Ted feared that during the night the dead animals would be found by wolves that would destroy the skins. For the sportsman the horns were the trophy, but for the *Ovis poli* to be put on display in a museum the whole skin was needed.

"It was growing late," Ted wrote of his anxious trek back to camp. "The snow drifted in stinging particles against our faces. It was a moment when we fully appreciated the beards we had grown. Though far from ornamental they were great protection. When we got to our tent they were stiff and heavy with ice and snow. After as hot a supper as we could get, we rolled up in our bedding. Storm or shine, we made up our minds to be off early next morning to the point where we had last seen our poli."

The day broke gray but snowless. Stars still glittered over the white mountains. When the sun broke through, its slanting rays gave the snow a coppery glow. Fragments of the trail led up and over a crest. Following it with great difficulty, Ted and Kermit found no trace of their quarry and were about to give up. But one of the native hunters asked for field glasses and volunteered to go ahead a way to study ravines and cleft hillsides for tracks of wolves that might have trailed the wounded sheep. He returned presently to report success. He had spotted seven wolves near the head of a small ravine and knew at once that at least one of the poli would be there. He found two. They were the pair Ted and Kermit had shot. They had lain down together after crossing the ridge and had died during the night.

The brothers were thrilled. The poli they'd seen and shot had good heads with horns that Ted had estimated at fifty inches. When measured in the camp, those of one were fifty-one and a half inches. The second's were forty-nine and a half.

Unfortunately, the wolves had gotten to the animals and ruined the skins.

This disappointment was assuaged elsewhere a few days later when they came upon a large herd of females with four rams nearby. Adults, they were strolling leisurely along a slope toward a ravine. After tracking them, and fearing for a time that they had lost them, the hunters came upon the herd. As the animals began to run away, Kermit opened fire and dropped one. A second later, Ted hit another. It rolled down the steep slope like a giant rabbit.

Although the horns of Kermit's poli were a disappointing forty inches in length, and Ted's even shorter, they were adult poli with large heads and perfect skins.

Ted wrote, "We had our sportsman's trophies, the two big heads. We had our poli for the museum. The essential part of our work with the poli was done. We stood around the small fire in our camp, the melting ice and snow dripping from our beards and clothes." Their total tally during their seven-month expedition would include eight *Ovis poli* and more than seventy other large animals of twenty different species, and nearly two thousand specimens of birds, small mammals, and reptiles.

In that time they had not been in touch with the wives and families they'd left behind. "We could not have been farther away or more cut off from communication than we had been," Ted wrote. Once he'd tried using a Chinese telegraph line, sending a message to a friend in Peking and asking him to relay it to New York. He learned later that the message got only as far as Peking, and that had taken eighteen days.

Before leaving New York in May, Ted and Kermit had promised Eleanor and Belle that if they were to come to India and be at Srinagar on November 9, their husbands would have ended their excursion beyond the Himalayas and would be there to meet them.

Still in their hunting togs and with beards intact, they kept their word.

An amazed Eleanor noted that she and Belle had traveled halfway around the world and had arrived at the appointed place on the same day as their husbands.

The excited, sketchy report Ted gave Eleanor reminded her of a line from Kipling:

But it was all pure delight—the wandering road, dipping and sweeping about the growing spurs; the flush of the morning laid against the distant snows.

19

The Roosevelts spent a month in Kashmir. Their headquarters was three houseboats tied together in the Jhelum River. Hunting stags in a private game preserve was by permission of the maharajah of Kashmir. At the end of this respite Kermit and Belle moved on to Delhi, while Ted and Eleanor set their sights on Peshawar. Gateway to the fabled Khyber Pass and one of the most fabled towns of the Indian Northwest Frontier, Peshawar had even been cited in Arthur Conan Doyle's adventures of Sherlock Holmes as the place to which Dr. John H. Watson was sent for treatment of a wound he'd suffered in the Battle of Maiwand in the Second Afghan War. The pass linking India to Afghanistan and the West had known the tread of the marching feet of the armies of Alexander the Great, Genghis Khan, Tamerlane, Babar, and Queen Victoria. After a few days of investigating the pass; touring the ancient city's huge Balahisar Fort; marveling at the imposing Mhabat Khan Mosque; and exploring the bazaars and the Street of the Storytellers, they made a long train journey to join Kermit and Belle in Delhi.

They arrived at six in the morning and found that their hotel room had a bath with a big porcelain tub. Ted hadn't seen such an amenity in months, and Eleanor was so pleased that she didn't mind the two-foot-long lizards that darted about the wall. They later moved into a bungalow offered by Chief Forest Officer Sir Henry Farrington. Overseer of the Allapilli Forest, he allowed them to collect a representation of Indian fauna for the Field Museum, including a tiger. But none of the animals cooperated by putting in an appearance.

Hoping for better luck, they left India for Nepal. The remote country was normally off limits to western tourists, but the maharajah granted the sons of America's venerated president Theodore Roosevelt an exemption. As members of a large hunting party that killed eight tigers, Ted and Kermit each managed to add one to their inventory of exhibits for the museum.

They were at last on their way home. The James Simpson–Roosevelts–Field Museum Expedition to Central Asia had been, they believed, a smashing success.

Eleanor would write of their return to New York, "When we reached home there was excitement and much publicity about the expedition, with stories on the front pages of the *New York Times, Herald Tribune,* and other newspapers as well as in the Sunday rotogravure sections. A Chicago paper carried a picture of Ted and his biggest *Ovis poli.*"

Ted was so unrecognizable in his bushy beard as he posed next to the animal and three of the party's professional hunters that the editor wrote a caption for the picture that read, "The *Ovis poli* with four natives."

Even America's beloved humorist Will Rogers took note of Ted's prize. He asked the readers of his popular newspaper column, "You don't know what an *Ovis poli* is? It's a political sheep. You hunt it between elections."

Observers of the American political landscape and its fauna in the spring of 1926 had no problem grasping Rogers's point. Speculation that the leader of the Central Asia expedition was in the running again for governor began even before Ted set foot on his native soil. Invitations to him to address civic, veterans, and patriotic groups flooded in. One came from the Reserve Officers Association asking Ted to speak at luncheon a on April 7, 1926, on the topic of the nation's military preparedness. The Churchwomen's League of Patriotic Service sought his views of "citizens' training camps" of the kind at which Ted and his brothers had prepared to go to war in 1917. The Bureau of Advertising of the American Newspaper Publishers Association had no topic in mind for Ted's address on April 23. He used the opportunity to both assail the Volstead Act (which implemented Prohibition) and criticize the courts for "coddling criminals" by not enforcing the letter of the law.

In this Ted emulated his father's attitude during TR's years as police commissioner. TR thought a law banning sale of alcoholic drinks on Sunday encouraged police graft, but he said, "The law is the law and it shall be enforced," and enforce it he did.

Asked by reporters on May 17, 1926, if he were a candidate for governor, Ted answered that he was not. The only activity in which he was involved, he said, was fulfilling a contract he and Kermit had with Charles Scribner's Sons for a book about their Himalayan expedition.

To be closer to Kermit while working on the book, he set up an office in the Manhattan home of Eleanor's mother. Assisting him by taking dictation and typing was his former secretary in the Navy Department, Margaret Hensey. She found that the brothers' work on the book often was sidetracked by talk of organizing another adventure in unexplored wilds, perhaps the part of Asia to the northwest of French Indochina where the Himalayas gradually descended to tropical plains. They could push in by the Bhamo-Talifu trail from Burma to Yunnan.

If luck proved to be with them they might find one of the most mysterious animals in the world—the giant panda. Almost nothing was known about it. Its existence had been reported in 1868 by the French missionary-scientist Père David. Noted British traveler Brig. Gen. George Pereira, the first Englishman to go from Peking to Lhasa, had hunted the panda for three months in the early 1920s with no success. A few skins of animals said to be giant pandas had been trapped by natives, but no specimens had been collected scientifically. The "giant pandas" in some museums might be another variety of bear or even raccoon.

Keeping their idea of going after the giant panda to themselves, Ted and Kermit worked on *East of the Sun and West of the Moon* while quietly accumulating data about the region where the panda was believed to roam. While Kermit was engaged in book-writing and planning, he also pursued his shipping business. Ted concentrated on the book, kept speaking engagements, continued to deny he harbored political aspirations, and went to Oyster Bay for family weekends.

In a book that Ted would publish in 1929, titled *All in the Family,* he gave his readers a glimpse of life at Sagamore Hill and a portrait of himself as family man. He attempted this even though, as he wrote on page four of the book, "It is very difficult to get a picture of the family from literature [because the homes] pictured are usually either too good or too bad, too rich or too poor. It is not the writer who is to blame for this, but the reader, for the reader does not wish a story dealing with the humdrum of every day."

Writing that a family without children is "as unthinkable as a drum major without a band," he offered readers a family of Roosevelts living at Oyster Bay during the previous forty years:

Naturally Father and Mother play an important part. Then come my brothers and sisters, Kermit, Archie, Quentin, Alice, and Ethel. Later all our wives and children appear on the scene. We certainly never lacked in numbers. Today there are over twenty.

Our family is certainly no different in any material way from thousands and thousands of others from Walla Walla to New York. We have the requisite number of children of both sexes. What is more, the stories and incidents, the proverbs and allusions in use, have been handed down from the generations before us, who were probably not greatly different from us.

How many readers of *All in the Family* believed that their families and their lives were no different from those of the Roosevelts of Oyster Bay, the Groton School, Harvard, the New York governor's mansion in Albany, the White House, and romantic adventures in the wildernesses of Africa, Brazil, and Rudyard Kipling's "world's white rooftree"? Probably none. But without question, many thousands enjoyed a vicarious kinship with them. They'd gleefully made Theodore Roosevelt into "Teddy." They'd fallen in love with Alice and chuckled at all of her iconoclastic ways and tart tongue. They'd prayed that ten-year-old Ted would recover from his pneumonia. They had adored Archie and his White House–gang antics. They had grieved for Quentin and wept over his father and mother's broken hearts. And for nearly a year, while Kermit and Ted poked around in places most people had never heard of, they had crossed their fingers, hoped, and prayed that they would come back to their wives and kids in one piece.

In the book about his family Ted wrote, "One of the greatest institutions of the civilized world is the family dining table." The words appear on page twenty-one. Their inspiration was found on page three in a quotation from Kipling's *The Jungle Book:*

For the strength of the pack is in the wolf,
And the strength of the wolf is in the pack.

Seated at his father's table while growing up, and as a burgeoning young man, Ted had been at first a listener, then a participant, in conversations that ranged as far as the mind of the man at the head of the table cared to go. As a father himself, Ted tried to emulate TR in raising Grace, Teddy, Cornelius, and Quentin. This included welcoming their views. "If table talk is handled properly it has endless possibilities," he wrote. "If the parents will make the effort, there is any amount of opportunity to interest the child in subjects of every kind."

Throughout 1926 and into 1927 the children of Ted and Eleanor Roosevelt began hearing their father talk about going on another expedition, this one in the hope of finding an animal that seemed to them a lot more interesting than a shaggy-haired sheep with a big head and enormous set of horns. This time the talk was about looking for a bear of some sort, and bears were always much more interesting than a big sheep.

The children learned that no white man had been able to shoot a giant panda. No one could declare with certainty where they could be found. Some naturalists held that the animal did not exist. But, Ted reminded the children, the same had been said about the *Ovis poli*. If the giant panda existed, it would be found only in the area that he pointed out on a sketchy map of East Asia. Why there and no place else? By finding the giant panda and observing its habitat, he might be able to answer that question.

Fascinated by the distribution of wildlife, Ted touched on the subject in the June 1927 issue of *Field and Stream* magazine. The article dealt with game he'd observed in New Zealand on his way home from India. Of factors affecting where animals thrived, some were reasonably plain. Food was the most obvious. "There are many times, however," he continued, "when there seems to be no explanation why certain animals do not spread their range. No one has ever given me what seemed a satisfactory reason for the distribution of the Himalayan ibex. It is found in many different mountain ranges, while in country that is not only contiguous but practically identical in every way it does not exist. The range of the *Ovis poli* is confined to the Pamirs, a tableland in Central Asia, though it is hard to see why it does not spread east and west where conditions seem much the same."

Determined to find the giant panda in its unique habitat, Ted and Kermit turned again for financing for the expedition to the Field Museum. At a dinner meeting to discuss the venture the president of the museum, Stanley Field, introduced them to William V. Kelly, president of the Miehle Press and Manufacturing Company. By the time brandy was poured and cigars lighted the deal was done, and the sojourn had been named the William V. Kelly–Roosevelts Expedition to Eastern Asia for the Field Museum.

It would have two divisions. Ted and Kermit would specialize in large animals, including the search for the giant panda. A young scientist from the Harvard Museum, Harold J. Coolidge Jr., would lead a team to collect birds, small mammals, and reptiles in unexplored regions of northwestern Indochina. The date for their departure was set for the autumn of 1928.

It had to be after the presidential election, Ted insisted, because he had commitments. He had promised the Speaker's Bureau of the Republican National Committee to hit the hustings to help elect the GOP slate of Herbert Hoover and Charles Curtis. But of just as much interest to Ted as keeping Republicans in the White House was the man whom the Democrats had chosen as their presidential standard bearer.

20

Democrats in 1928 gave their presidential nomination to the man the party had shunned four years earlier. At the party's convention in Houston, as in 1924, Franklin Delano Roosevelt spoke on behalf of the nomination of Al Smith. He cited the governor of New York as "a leader who grasps and understands not only the large affairs of business and government, but in an equal degree the aspirations of the individual, the farmer, the wage earner."

"The Happy Warrior," declared Roosevelt, was a man who had not just the will to win. "Victory," he said, "is his habit."

A year before Smith was nominated, everyone who followed politics had assumed that whoever won the Democratic nomination in 1928 would face President Calvin Coolidge and go down to defeat. But in August 1927 while vacationing in the Black Hills of the Dakotas he had handed a group of reporters a statement: "I do not choose to run for President in 1928."

The terseness of the declaration by the man known as "Silent Cal" reminded Coolidge's former assistant secretary of the navy of a delightful story that Ted hadn't been able to confirm.

A woman seated next to Coolidge at a White House dinner had turned to Coolidge and said, "I have a bet with a friend that I can get you to say more than two words."

He replied, "You lose."

Suddenly, with ten unexpected words, Coolidge had closed the door to what Ted believed would be easy reelection based on a four-year record of unparalleled prosperity. The Coolidge administration had weathered the revelations of corruption in the Harding years, practiced fiscal prudence in managing the government, and substantially reduced the national debt. Coolidge's expressions of optimism about the economic state of the union had contributed to a booming stock market and a general feeling of national well-being.

Ted assumed that the immediate front-runner for the GOP nomination was Coolidge's capable secretary of commerce. Born in West Branch, Iowa, in 1874, Herbert Clark Hoover was the son of a blacksmith. He'd earned a degree in engineering at Stanford University, managed gold-mining operations in Australia and China, and headed his own engineering firms, which had supervised projects in several countries. But it was his chairmanship of a commission for relief in Belgium after the Great War, and his term as head of the United States Food Administration, that had thrust his name into headlines. His renown as a great humanitarian was reinforced by his work as secretary of commerce to improve child health and eliminate child labor.

Although a "Stop Hoover" campaign was promptly organized by old-guard members of the GOP, he arrived for the nominating convention in Kansas City with more than 400 of the 1,084 votes needed to win. When the first ballot was completed, he had 827. His message to the American voter was that America was nearer to the final triumph over poverty than ever before in the history of any land. "We have not yet reached that goal," he said, "but, given a chance to go forward with the policies of the last eight years [of Republican administrations], we shall with the help of God be in sight of the day when poverty will be banished from the nation."

On the issue of repeal of Prohibition he pronounced "the great experiment" of a drink-free America "noble in motive and far-reaching in purpose."

His Democrat opponent strenuously disagreed. But prosperity proved more potent as an issue than quaffing beer and booze without threat of arrest. The Roman Catholic Smith lost to the Quaker Hoover in the popular vote by more than six million. But as the ballots were tallied on election night for president, Ted was just as interested, and perhaps more so, in the outcome of the New York gubernatorial race. For the second time in history there was a Roosevelt on the ballot for governor. In the hope of keeping the Albany Executive Chamber in party hands the Democrats had turned to TR's admiring cousin Franklin.

The choice, anointed by Al Smith, of "a cripple" had shocked many in the party, but Smith had blunted the issue by declaring in his Lower

East Side grumble, "A governor does not have to be an acrobat. We don't elect him for his ability to do a double backflip or handspring."

As Ted followed state returns on election night it appeared that Franklin had gone down in the Hoover landslide. But the picture brightened for Franklin the next morning. When all the votes were counted, he'd won by 25, 564 votes out of 4.25 million. In the house on Sagamore Hill, planning an expedition to search for the giant panda of Asia, Ted noted that cousin Franklin had taken another step forward in TR's footprints. Now that Franklin had been elected governor of New York in the year of a GOP landslide, he had to be regarded as the de facto leader of the Democratic Party. As such he would have to be counted a serious contender for the presidential nomination in four years.

Might the American people decide in 1932, after twelve years of Republican faces in the White House, that the time was ripe for a change in the form of a Democrat named Roosevelt?

And what of the political future of the Republican Roosevelt?

The author of a recent book about Al Smith and a clever writer for the popular magazines *New Yorker, Harper's, American Mercury, World Work,* and *The Outlook* offered his analysis of Ted's political fortunes. In an essay called "Chore Boy of the G.O.P.," published in his 1928 book *Big Frogs,* Henry F. Pringle wrote, "A theory is frequently advanced that the political future of Theodore Roosevelt, 'the young Colonel,' as Al Smith rather nastily refers to him, lies entirely in the past. It is said that the 'fighting son of a fighting sire,' to quote a phrase evolved by campaign press agents, has fought his last battle. He has proved, the wise ones say, a washout, a dud, a flop. It no longer profits him to cry 'Bully! Delighted!' or to wave his battered hat like a Rough Rider charging San Juan Hill. The people have learned that the king is dead and that there is no king."

Ten years ago, "while the youthful Teddy" was fighting in France, Pringle continued, the leaders of the Republican Party dreamed dreams and saw visions. "Crystal gazing, the G.O.P. bosses saw vistas of young T.R. returning from the war, T.R. bowing to demands that he enter public life, T.R. in the State Assembly at Albany, as Assistant Secretary of the Navy, as Governor of New York, as Vice-President of the United States, as President! It was to be an almost line-for-line repetition of his father's career. For a time the program was smoothly followed."

But "the man of destiny" who was "still the fighting son of a fighting sire" had lost to Al Smith in 1924 and "was forced to leave on an expedition to hunt the *Ovis poli*, the Ibex, the Goitered Gazelle, and the Asiatic Wapiti in the Himalayas."

Conceding that "the young Colonel's prolonged banishment to private life is the result of a peculiar situation in his party and is not due to any widespread belief that he had been found wanting," Pringle continued with an accurate portrait of the firstborn son of an American icon:

> It is superfluous to point out that a young man starting life as the eldest son of Theodore Roosevelt, particularly when his name as the same, was certain to face untold difficulties. The younger Theodore knew this; at least in his earlier years. There is more than a touch of pathos in a remark he made in 1910:
>
> "I will always be known as the son of Theodore Roosevelt," he said, "and never as a person who means only himself."
>
> A timid youth would have lived wretchedly as the son of Roosevelt. But though he was less than brawny, physical fear never took hold of Theodore, Jr.
>
> The most casual analysis of the record of Theodore Roosevelt reveals that he was rushed along too swiftly. He should have remained in Albany for several additional years and there learned the A.B.C.'s of the political game. He was far from mature, politically, when he went to Washington and was additionally handicapped, all the while, by comparisons to his father. Roosevelt is still immature. Just turned forty, he still has little conception of what it is all about.

At one point in the 1924 campaign Al Smith cracked, "If bunk was electricity, the young Colonel would be a powerhouse."

Since being defeated in 1924, Pringle opined, Ted had been waiting for something to happen. But any theory that Ted was politically dead, Pringle warned, was based on a fallacy. He remained "an asset to his party."

Less than a week after Herbert Hoover won the presidency and Franklin D. Roosevelt the New York governorship, Ted and Kermit boarded the liner *Homeric* bound for Europe on the first leg of the voyage to Indochina. They were accompanied by Harold Coolidge and the trusty companion from the *Ovis poli* odyssey, Suydam Cutting. Unfortunately, at the end of the first stage of the expedition, Kermit was compelled by business conditions to return to America and Cutting fell ill, leaving Ted and Coolidge to carry out its second stage, collecting the region's wild oxen. Despite these complications, the expedition was an unqualified success. It resulted in the collection of more than forty big mammals, including the giant panda.

Ted and Kermit had found its tracks in a light fall of snow. When they came upon the panda, it had just awakened. They each fired one shot. The giant panda was not a species of bear, but a member of the raccoon family. Confirmation of its existence caused a sensation in the zoological world and among naturalists who had not believed it existed. To assure that the rare animal would not be hunted into extinction the Chinese government eventually imposed restrictions on killing them, and placed limitations on the numbers that could be trapped and removed to zoos.

In addition to the panda and other large mammals the expedition collected more than five thousand birds and reptiles and two thousand small mammals. Nineteen of these were unknown species or subspecies. A previously unknown muntjak deer was named by the Field Museum after the brothers who discovered it: *Muntiacus rooseveltorum.*

According to Ted's plan, Eleanor was to meet him in Saigon at the end of his expedition in the summer of 1929. The children would be left in the care of their grandmothers. Grace was now seventeen, Teddy fourteen, Cornelius thirteen and Quentin nine. She reached the capital of French Indochina on schedule to learn that Ted would be delayed in arriving.

That night Eleanor had just sat down for dinner at the American Consulate with the U.S. consul, Henry S. Waterman, and his wife when she heard a strange sound of howling outside. From where she sat she could see the figure of a man at the front door, shaking its ornamental ironwork with both hands. Waterman feared it was "some sort of crazy native." Eleanor recognized Ted, but barely. He was dirty and his body was wasted from fever. He was delirious. Not since Ted had been gassed in France had Eleanor seen him look so sick. A doctor examined him and diagnosed malaria and dysentery.

Plans for a visit to Peking were canceled, although Ted's condition improved enough to permit a tour of Angkor. From Saigon they sailed on a small Norwegian freighter, the *Prosper,* to Hong Kong. From there they went to Shanghai to board the U.S. steamer *President Grant* for Tokyo. From Japan they sailed for home and toward a new job for Ted.

In May 1929, while Ted was looking for giant pandas in China's bamboo jungles, President Hoover had appointed him governor of Puerto Rico in the expectation that Ted would assume the post as soon as possible after his return.

He did so on Monday, October 7, 1929.

The Roosevelt children. Ted is seated on floor. Left to right: Ethel, Alice, Quentin, Kermit, and Archie. (Author's collection)

TR during a visit to the civilian training camp at Plattsburg, New York, where Ted was preparing to become an army reserve officer prior to World War I. The officer is TR's old friend Gen. Leonard Wood, with whom TR had organized the "Rough Riders" cavalry in the Spanish-American War. (Author's collection)

"The lion and his pride." TR with (left to right) Ted, Archie, Quentin, and Kermit, taken when TR was president. (Author's collection)

In the tradition of the Victorian Era of young boys being dressed like girls, two-year-old Ted posed with "Father" in 1889. (Theodore Roosevelt Collection, Harvard College Library)

Twelve-year-old Ted at Albany
Academy in 1900, while TR
was governor of New York.
(Author's Collection)

Ted with his mother, Edith
Carow Roosevelt, after a
morning's ride. (Author's
collection)

Snap-shot taken at Harvard 2nd Exeter game last Saturday. Exeter won easily 11 – 0

"Teddy" Roosevelt Jr

Snapshot of Ted taken at Harvard-Exeter game. Harvard lost 11 to 0. (Theodore Roosevelt Collection, Harvard College Library)

Ted in 1910 with his fiancée, Eleanor Alexander. (Author's collection)

The three Theodores: Ted, his son (called Teddy) and proud grandfather, the former president of the United States. (Theodore Roosevelt Collection, Harvard College Library)

Mrs. Theodore Roosevelt Jr. (the former Eleanor Alexander) in her YMCA uniform during World War I. (Theodore Roosevelt Collection, Harvard College Library)

Ted instructs army recruits in bayonet practice at Plattsburg in 1917. (Author's collection)

Sketch of Maj. Ted Roosevelt made in Paris in 1918. (Theodore Roosevelt Collection, Harvard College Library)

Ted (Lieutenant Colonel) with Eleanor and the commander of the 1st Division, Brig. Gen. Frank Parker, at Romagne, France, 1918.(Theodore Roosevelt Collection, Harvard College Library)

Ted and his family. Left to right: Cornelius, Mrs. Roosevelt, Grace, and Teddy, with Quentin II on the ground. The dog next to him was named "Donald." The small one held by Grace was "Binkie." (Author's collection)

Ted as Republican candidate for governor of New York in 1924. He ran against Democrat Alfred E. (Al) Smith and lost. Because Ted's distant cousin Franklin D. Roosevelt backed Smith, the campaign marked the start of a feud between the Roosevelts of Oyster Bay and the Roosevelts of Hyde Park. (Theodore Roosevelt Collection, Harvard College Library)

Caricature of Ted in 1928.

Ted (on the right) with his *Ovis poli* and native guides. (From *East of the Sun and West of the Moon*.)

The *Ovis poli*. This one's horns measured fifty-three inches. (From *East of the Sun and West of the Moon*)

Ted (left), his friend Suydam Cutting (center), and Ted's brother Kermit at the end of their trek in the Himalayan Mountains for Chicago's Field Museum in search of the elusive mountain sheep *Ovis poli.* (From Ted and Kermit's book, *East of the Sun And West of the Moon,* 1926)

Colonel Theodore Roosevelt Jr., commander of the 26th Infantry, with son Quentin II, also a member of the 1st Division, June 1941. Quentin was named after Ted's brother, who, as an army aviator in World War I, was killed when his plane was shot down over German territory in France. (U.S. Army photo)

Brigadier General Theodore (Ted) Roosevelt, 1941. (Theodore Roosevelt Collection, Harvard College Library)

Ted as a brand-new brigadier general with Quentin in front of Ted's tent during 1st Division maneuvers in 1941. (Theodore Roosevelt Collection, Harvard College Library)

North Africa, 1943. Brigadier General Roosevelt with Maj. Gen. Terry Allen, commander of the 1st Division, and their new boss, Lt. Gen. George S. Patton. (U.S. Army photo)

Ted receiving a decoration from the French for his services as liaison officer in North Africa in early 1944. He was soon transferred to England to become second in command of the U.S. 4th Division on D day. (Theodore Roosevelt Collection, Harvard College Library)

The U.S. high command of the D-day invasion of Normandy: Left to right, Dwight D. Eisenhower, supreme commander; Lt. Gen. Omar N. Bradley, commander, First Army; and Maj. Gen. J. Lawton Collins, commander, VII Corps. (U.S. Army photo, *Utah Beach to Cherbourg*)

Commander of the 4th Division, Maj. Gen. Raymond O. "Tubby" Barton. Ted told Eleanor that Barton was "a very fine character of a real American type." When Barton let Ted lead the troops ashore on Utah Beach, he "never expected to see him alive again." (U.S. Army photo, *Utah Beach to Cherbourg*)

Troops of the 4th Division at the Utah Beach seawall on D day. For leading them ashore and directing their actions on the beach, Ted was recommended for the Congressional Medal of Honor. It was presented posthumously to his wife, Eleanor, by President Franklin D. Roosevelt. (U.S. Army photo, *Utah Beach to Cherbourg*)

In the film *The Longest Day*, Ted was portrayed by Henry Fonda. This scene from the movie captured Ted's spirit and heroic actions that day, including Ted's use of a cane. Ted went ashore with a knit cap on his head because he hated wearing a helmet. (Author's collection; 20th Century-Fox)

Part 4: Governing

My brother knows it is not easy to be a chief.

—*Rudyard Kipling*

21

Hailed by jingoes as a prize of "the splendid little war" with Spain in 1898, the island of "Porto Rico" (hereafter Puerto Rico; the spelling of name would be officially changed in 1932) had proved to be a headache for United States presidents since the first day the Stars and Stripes flew over its picturesque capital of San Juan. Instead of gaining possession of a paradise and a location for harboring advance elements of the Atlantic Fleet that the jingoes had wanted, the former Spanish colony presented its American governors with seemingly intractable problems of poverty, unemployment, malnutrition, and disease. To make matters worse, the year before Ted's ship sailed into San Juan harbor and glided past its old overlooking fort, El Morro, the island had been ravaged by an exceptionally destructive hurricane. Villages that had been wrecked were still in ruins. Factories and schools had been hard hit. The fruit, coffee, and sugar crops had been decimated. But on the day the guns of El Morro boomed a salute to the new governor, a holiday was in effect. The waterfront was crowded with welcomers. They happily thronged the car that took Ted and Eleanor to the capitol, where a platform with a roof of palm leaves had been set up for Governor Roosevelt's inaugural address.

He was the first of the island's American governors to begin a speech with *"Señores y Señoras."* (His limited Spanish had been learned in a crash course during the voyage home from Asia.) Halfway through the speech a torrential rain began, immediately drenching the audience and pouring through the palm roof to soak everyone on the platform.

Most of the people stayed as Ted soldiered on to the end of his only slightly abridged remarks. Just as he finished the sun came out.

Of the first speech by the new man in San Juan the *New York Times* correspondent, Harwood Hull, reported:

The Governor's speech was largely a discussion of the island's economic needs. It was a message to the people. By no means did he ignore the politicians, but he talked to their constituents. Immediately the people knew the new Governor had much basic information regarding them and their island. He spoke openly of handicaps and hardships which for years have been officially ignored, if not officially denied. He acknowledged and praised the many fine qualities of his island fellow citizens, and set them and himself new tasks which they know will require every ounce of energy and all the faith, optimism, and courage which collectively may be summoned if they are to be performed.

The Roosevelts would reside in the half-palace, half-castle Government House known as La Fortaleza. Built a hundred feet above the water in 1529, it had two round towers with circular staircases, and its eight-foot-thick walls held several secret passages. Its most magnificent room had been designed in regal style for the Spanish governors. When Eleanor found that its glories had been painted over in American navy battleship-gray, she set herself the task of restoring it to its historical grandeur.

Ted's goal was to limit the time spent in La Fortaleza and to go out into the countryside to meet as many Puerto Ricans as possible. Nights before these ventures were spent learning more of their language. He made mistakes, the worst of which was his introduction of the head of the U.S. War Department's Bureau of Insular Affairs. He meant to say in Spanish that Brig. Gen. Francis Parker was a bachelor. The word he used meant "tapeworm."

With the intention of alerting the American people to the plight of the Puerto Ricans, he wrote about his experiences in exploring the island and its problems in an article for the *New York Herald Tribune Sunday Magazine:*

I have stopped at farm after farm where lean, underfed women and sickly men repeated again and again the same story—too little food and no opportunity to get more. Sixty percent of the children are undernourished. Many are slowly starving. On the roads time and again I have seen little groups carrying tiny, homemade coffins. One public school in San Juan, the capital city, has an enrollment of 710 boys and girls. Of these 223 come to school without break-

fast. Two hundred seventy-eight have no lunch. We are able to provide in the school lunchroom food for just fifty-four. The rest go
hungry.

He continued, using the personal possessive:

Our island will turn the corner in the near future. We look forward
to greater prosperity for our people. But that is in the future, not
the present. It will come too late to save the lives of many of our
children, too late to prevent disease from permanently damaging
those who will live.

The result of the article was shock and anger. An embarrassed Bureau
of Insular Affairs cabled him to stop all further public discussion of the
conditions he had found during his six-week inspection of the island's
conditions. Ted cabled back that he would continue to speak out until
something was done by Washington to deal with the situation. The occupant of the White House who had supervised American relief efforts
in Belgium after the Great War asked that a commission of the American Child Health Association go to Puerto Rico to study the problems.
President Hoover also asked Congress for two million dollars in loans to
farmers and a million for road repairs and new construction.

The report of the Child Health Association substantiated Ted's sum-
mary of conditions and called for assistance from several philanthropic
organizations. They responded with formation of the Porto Rico Child
Health Committee, which announced its intention to raise more then
seven million dollars to finance a five-year program dealing with health,
feeding, and the related problems that Ted had delineated. Another
group, the Golden Rule Foundation, launched a campaign to raise
$50,000 for immediate use in school lunchrooms and for establishing
milk stations for babies.

All these good intentions were to be impeded by the effects of a day
in October 1929 that became known on Wall Street as "Black Tuesday."

The crash of the stock market would eventually cause a banking crisis in Puerto Rico in 1931 that confronted Ted with his greatest challenge
as the island's governor.

In the meantime he sought to tackle the underlying cause of all of
Puerto Rico's ills, the crushing poverty that smothered the hopes of the

people for better lives. A promising source of income for them, he believed, was in having small plots of ground on which to grow food not only for themselves, but for sale. In studying the island's economic structure he found that the main industry was agriculture for export—sugar, coffee, and citrus fruit—but the main diet of the people was rice, beans, codfish, and salt, most of which was imported. He learned that the value of fresh vegetables imported by the United States amounted to $12 million. Yet in 1928 and 1929 the island had shipped only 388,163 pounds of produce to the mainland. Why should a large part of U.S. imports not come from Puerto Rico? He reasoned that if people who labored for the big sugar, coffee, and fruit plantations were given parcels of land for truck farming, they could feed themselves and their families and market the excess. After persuading the employers to participate in the experiment, he discovered to his dismay that some of the people who were given land preferred to grow sugar cane, rather than vegetables.

He wrote in frustration to his mother on December 10, "Last week I went out visiting little farms. It was very interesting, but only increased my grasp of the difficulties of our problem. It consists in not simply changing the condition of the people, but in addition changing their attitude of mind in such fashion that they may take advantages of the new opportunities. Indeed, it is the old story—we have to protect the poor not only from the oppression of the rich, but also from the equally disastrous foolishness they are guilty of themselves."

The truck-farming idea slowly made inroads, so that the year after its inception Puerto Rico tripled its exports of vegetables. The program was ultimately developed further by a new Bureau of Commerce and Industry.

In examining the structure of Puerto Rico's educational system Ted found that its main purpose was educating children to take white-collar jobs, of which there were very few. What was needed, he proposed, was vocational schools that would teach the three R's and provide the children practical grounding in skills that would enable students to graduate into paying jobs. Accordingly, the national curriculum in schools was revised to provide boys with training in trades. Girls learned the skills of home economics. Clothes making, embroidery, and other crafts were taught that could be profitable in another aspect of the Roosevelt program for economic development—tourism.

Although twenty-first-century Puerto Rico and other Caribbean islands thrive on tourism, it was not always so. In 1929 Ted found that in the previous year Puerto Rico had been visited by only thirteen cruise ships. Envisioning the island's potential as a haven for winter-weary Americans, he directed his aide, Maj. Cary I. Crockett, to look into encouraging cruise lines to push Puerto Rico as a vacation paradise that Americans could enjoy and still be on United States soil. As a result of Crockett's efforts thirty cruise ships would visit the island in 1930. When they put into the harbor at San Juan the startled but delighted disembarking passengers were often greeted on the dock by the governor of Puerto Rico himself, or invited to meet him and his wife at La Fortaleza that evening.

Just how financially strapped the government of Puerto Rico was at the start of 1930 was driven home to Ted when an official of the treasury informed him the coffers were empty. They would remain depleted until taxes came in later in the month. This meant there were no funds to pay government employees. Ted also learned that without wages, fathers employed by the government probably would not be able to buy Three Kings Day gifts for their children. Ted knew that in Spanish tradition January 6 was the present-giving day celebrating the arrival of the three wise men who had followed a star to a stable in Bethlehem to see the newborn King of the Jews. Determined that Puerto Rican children should not be denied their happy day because the government was broke, the man who as a boy had enjoyed Christmases in the comfort of the big house on Sagamore Hill endorsed a note for two hundred thousand dollars to cover the payroll.

But this was not Ted's only gesture in respect of the holiday. In an article published in the *Baltimore Sun* in January 1930 a future governor of what would then be the Commonwealth of Puerto Rico wrote that when Ted heard that efforts were being made to officially displace Three Kings Day as the date for marking the birth of Jesus, and require recognition of December 25 as the proper date, Ted promptly declared January 6 a public holiday. When he heard of an order from the superintendent of schools that money was to be spent on small American flags for children to wave when "the American governor" passed by, Ted directed the schools to spend the money on breakfasts for the kids.

Funds provided to pay the governor of Puerto Rico's salary amounted to ten thousand dollars a year. He was allowed another ten thousand for running and maintaining La Fortaleza. When he and Eleanor arrived in October 1929, three-fourths of the fund for the residence had already been spent in the first three months of the fiscal year. This meant that the expenses for the nine remaining months had to come from Ted's pocket. Eleanor noted in her book that La Fortaleza needed painting. "Considerable entertaining had to be done" because "the Puerto Ricans "loved a good party." Ice cost $115 a month. Two limousines were immediately disposed of, replaced with the Roosevelts' own Model-A Ford driven by a policeman. The limousine chauffeurs were reassigned to guard duty.

Housekeeping at La Fortaleza was handled by a staff consisting of a maid, two cooks, two laundresses, and four houseboys. They were augmented by eighteen convicts. Marched to the residence each morning from a prison, they did the heavy work of scrubbing floors and tending to the expansive grounds. Eleanor thought they looked like "such nice men." When she asked the attorney general what crimes they'd committed, he replied, "Mostly voluntary homicide."

She asked what that meant.

The attorney general smiled slyly. "Oh, they say their hands slipped."

Use of criminals to do work around La Fortaleza did not bother Eleanor until she found out that ten-year-old Quentin had made friends with some of the men. "As this was not precisely the circle we would have chosen for him," she wrote, "at first we thought of putting him in an American day school in San Juan but realized he would be with American boys and would not have the best opportunity to learn Spanish."

Quentin was sent to the San Augustine Military School at Río Piedras. It had American teachers and Puerto Rican students. He stayed there during the week and spent Saturdays and Sundays at La Fortaleza when the prisoners were back in their cells. After a few months at the school he was speaking Spanish "exactly like a Puerto Rican, with characteristic gestures."

Grace was in New York with Eleanor's mother, taking a business course and preparing for her debut. Teddy and Cornelius were students at Groton. All made brief visits to San Juan in the summer. On an outing by Cornelius and Teddy in pursuit of butterflies for their collections on the island of Caja de Muertos off the south coast, they found a new subspecies of lizard and named it for their mother, *Ameiva wetmorei eleanore*. An usual fly that was captured was named for Ted, the boys explained, because it was "a good fly, it did not harm citrus fruit, and it has beautiful eyes."

None of the children were in residence at La Fortaleza in March 1931 when President Hoover made history by being the only sitting president to visit Puerto Rico (TR had been there but as an ex-president). The three-day visit began with the arrival of the USS *Arizona* to the booming tribute of El Morro's cannons. Accompanying Hoover were Secretary of War Patrick J. Hurley, Interior Secretary Ray Leyman Wilbur, military and naval aides, White House physician Joel T. Boone (a navy captain and later vice-admiral), the president's secretary (Lawrence Richey), a group of "kodak creatures" and their newsreel cousins, and a pair of newspapermen who had managed to become friends of the Roosevelts during Ted's gubernatorial campaign, Mark Sullivan and Richard V. Oulahan, both of the *New York Times*. Mrs. Hoover had chosen to remain in Washington.

Dinner for twenty-four at La Fortaleza that evening was stag, except for Eleanor. She had engaged a small orchestra to play *"música brava"* during the meal. A reception for officials of Puerto Rico was at nine, followed by a public reception. In order to avoid overcrowding and traffic jams, Eleanor arranged for everyone at the receptions to go through the palace and out on the seawall, where they found refreshments. They were "discouraged" from going back inside. Keenly aware that some Puerto Ricans resented their island's having gotten its freedom from the Spanish, only to be taken over by Americans, and remembering what had happened to President McKinley in a reception line in Buffalo in 1901, she had "many policemen on duty." They were so "tactful," she observed, "that people did not realize they were being managed."

After shaking hands without stopping until eleven o'clock, the president went up to bed. Half an hour later, guests were persuaded to go by the orchestra's playing "Home, Sweet Home."

The next day Ted spoke in Spanish to introduce Hoover to an immense crowd at the capitol. Hoover spoke briefly, translated by Carlos Chardon, chancellor of the university. In a report for the *Times* Richard Oulahan noted, "The crowd became very enthusiastic when it heard the Spanish version of the President's complimentary references to Gov. Roosevelt. So prolonged was this demonstration that the governor, sitting by Mrs. Roosevelt, was obliged to rise and bow his acknowledgments."

Eleanor thought that was "just as it should have been."

Hoover was then taken on a tour of El Morro and other San Juan sites. After lunch at La Fortaleza he left aboard the *Arizona* for Ponce and a continuation of his visit. Upon its conclusion another journalistic veteran of Ted's 1924 campaign, Mark Ethridge, a Democrat, wrote in the *Macon (Georgia) Telegraph,* "President's visit to Porto Rico has served, in addition to its other purposes, to do justice to an American citizen who has been the victim, in other days, of none too friendly criticism and much too low an estimate. That American is Theodore Roosevelt, governor of Porto Rico."

But attacks on Ted were by no means a thing of the past. In October 1931, after Ted had been governing Puerto Rico for two years, a former mayor of San Juan whom Ted had helped to oust from office because of incompetence, thereby placing San Juan under a commission form of rule, accused Ted of using government money for his family expenses. The accusation was rightly dismissed immediately by the Puerto Rican people as a baseless charge by "a disgruntled former mayor."

The outrageous slur on Ted's character was further undermined the following month. Ted and Eleanor were on an official trip to Washington at the request of President Hoover when Ted got a cable from San Juan informing him that a financial panic was sweeping the island. He returned to San Juan by plane to learn that the principal local banks had closed and another was in such bad shape that without additional funds it would be forced to close the next day. People all over Puerto Rico had taken their money from the banks and put them in strongboxes and in some instances had buried it.

Ted summoned the insular treasurer and handed him a personal note for $100,000, to be used to secure that amount in government paper which would be deposited immediately in the threatened bank. The hundred thousand was about a quarter of Ted's fortune. He then went on the radio to tell the panicky population what he'd done and urge them to have confidence. The panic ended.

The solid fiscal foundation of the island's government was later evidenced when Ted was able to announce that for the first time in seventeen years Puerto Rico's budget was balanced.

In January 1932 the reason for Ted's November trip to Washington became known when President Hoover announced that he was sending Ted to an even more troublesome prize from the Spanish-American War. He would be governor general of the Philippines.

22

Seven months after TR's charge up the San Juan Heights and Spain's loss of her major colonies, in the Philippines a shot was fired by a Filipino at a U.S. soldier in what would be a three-year war fought guerrilla style in the jungles and swamps of the maze of islands that formed the new American colony. TR's literary friend Rudyard Kipling sneeringly called the United States government's efforts to squelch the rebels "setting bulldogs to catch rabbits." He mocked the American imperialists as racists:

Take up the White Man's burden—
Send forth the best ye breed—
Go, bind your sons to exile
To serve your captives' need:
To wait, in heavy harness,
On fluttered folk and wild—
Your new-caught sullen peoples,
Half devil and half child.

For the jingoes the annexation of the Philippines meant expanding the U.S. sphere of influence across the Pacific. The new possession would open the door to China and immense economic opportunities for American manufacturers. The Stars and Stripes over the capital of Manila would also be a warning signal against adventuring in the region by Germany. The flag was also a caution to the Japanese against attempting to extend their "Empire of the Rising Sun" south and east.

Should either Germany or Japan choose to dominate the Pacific, they would first have to deal with the United States Pacific Fleet. Despite the naval disarmament agreement forged at the Washington Conference while Ted was assistant secretary of the navy, the navy remained a formidable force capable of waging a two-ocean war.

To suppress the Philippine uprising in the aftermath of the Spanish-American War the United States Army deployed 70,000 men against an almost equal number of rebels, but by the end of 1899 the contest was being fought mostly man against man in jungle skirmishes that went on for three more years. When hostilities ceased, a report of the "Philippine Commission" set up to find a way out of the morass recommended ultimate independence for the islands, but not until the Filipino people were deemed "ready for self-government."

Of the men who had been appointed governor general since the islands were annexed, Theodore Roosevelt (Ted by now had dropped the "Jr.") was the youngest (age forty-five). Facing a month-long crossing of the Pacific on the USS *President Taft,* he again used some of the time to try to learn the dominant native language of the people he was expected to govern (Tagalog). When the United States took over the islands in 1898, English was decreed the language of the government and commerce. It was also taught as the national language in schools. Because Ted had scored a hit with his limited Spanish in Cuba, he hoped that being able to say something in Tagalog would prove equally helpful in winning the support of Filipinos.

The trip from Seattle included ports of call in Yokohama, Japan; Shanghai, China; and the British colony of Hong Kong. Each stop provided Ted an education in the geopolitics of the Far Pacific, along with glimpses of the military and naval situation. He learned his first lesson from the passenger manifest of the *President Taft.* Besides the Roosevelts (Ted, Eleanor, and Grace), the ship had only eight first-class travelers. The reason for this was Japan's invasion of China's Manchukuo province and fighting between the Chinese army in and around Shanghai. This dangerous situation, Eleanor noted with delicious understatement, "was quite enough to stop tourist travel."

In Japan the Roosevelts were granted a rare audience with the emperor and empress, but Ted could not fail to notice a pervasive martial atmosphere in the seat of Japan's empire, or that the backbone of the empire was its modern fleet of warships. When the *Taft*—despite the fierce fighting that had been raging on the banks of the Whangpoo River—was permitted by the Chinese to go to Shanghai, Ted observed, as the ship entered the mouth of the Yangtse to proceed to the Whangpoo, that several Japanese destroyers were lying at anchor. Warships of other nationalities were also there, American, British, French, and Portugese—but only on the Japanese ships, he noted, were the crews exercising or drilling. At Shanghai he found little river traffic and none of the thousands of sampans he remembered from his visit to the city en route home from Indochina. A few distant rifle shots, he assumed, came from snipers.

After a call at Hong Kong, the *President Taft* reached Manila on February 29, 1932. To the large crowd that greeted him on the pier—said to be the world's longest—he shouted, *"Mahbuhay,"* the Tagalog word of greeting. Noting this later, a Manila newspaper said, "The cheer that answered him eclipsed all others and continued until the roar of artillery sounded in the seventeen-gun salute."

Drawn up in front of the Malacanan Palace, the governor's residence, for Ted to review was an honor guard of Philippine constabulary. That night there was an inaugural ball at the Manila Hotel. The next day at a press conference Ted declared that he intended to follow his Puerto Rican policy of familiarizing himself with the islands by visiting them. Until he did that, he would say nothing about specific problems. One of the reporters was less interested in what he said than in the appearance of the new governor:

> His smile is the most attractive feature about him. The lines about his keen steel-blue eyes deepen, and those framing the corners of his mouth widen. Not only the eyes and lips but the whole expression breaks into an infectious smile that is irresistible. But there is something in those steel-blue eyes and the set of the jaw which says that the former can bore through one, and that the latter can set like a steel trap when occasion demands it.

In a story written fifty-seven years earlier by a reporter who covered the New York City Police Department, the father of the new governor general of the Philippines had been similarly described. When TR seized the reins at the NYPD's Mulberry Street headquarters, purchasers of the *New York World* had read, "His teeth are big and white, his eyes are small and piercing; his voice is rasping. It is an exasperating voice. It is a voice that comes from the tips of the teeth and seems to say [to policeman TR had caught misbehaving or not doing their duty], 'What do you amount to, anyway?'"

During Ted's gubernatorial campaign he had been criticized for "deliberately" copying TR's bold and distinctive mannerisms. Making the point in "Chore Boy of the G.O.P.," Henry Pringle noted that when Ted spoke he used his hat in the same way as TR. He wrote, "He wore out a hat in five days by snatching it from his head, crushing it in iron grip, waving it, whacking it against his hand for emphasis."

Although Pringle's assessment of Ted had been scornful, it contained truths about the burdens that went with being born the son of the most colorful and exciting public figure of the day. "Historians may one day assail the greatness of Theodore Roosevelt, the first, as President of the United States. But none, it is likely, will question his greatness as a father. The elder Roosevelt was a hero to his children."

Thirteen years, one month, and twenty-three years after TR died, his son spoke to a crowd assembled in the Luneta, Manila's largest public square. He told them while his father had been governor of New York he had written to his friend Henry Cabot Lodge that he did not want to be vice president of the United States because his ambition was to be governor general of the Philippines. Now that the post was his, Ted said, his purpose was to contribute to the eventual independence of the Philippines by following a policy of governance that would promote justice, health, education, business progress, and development of Philippine culture.

Unlike the situation Ted had found in Puerto Rico, conditions in the Philippines in 1932 were good. During thirty years of U.S. rule the standard of living in the islands had become the envy of other Asian countries. Eleanor noted as she traveled with Ted that every sizable town had its hospital, dispensary, and high school. There were playgrounds, movie theaters, radios, and lots of automobiles. Most of the resentment that had erupted in rebellion at the turning of the century was gone. But not all of it. Factions of public opinion and some political figures were impatient with the promise of independence and demanded a definite date.

Late in March Ted began inspection trips to the provinces that spread out over forty-nine islands. He began on the biggest, Luzon. Because a Manila newspaper was serializing one of his books on hunting, he was invited to test his marksmanship against the wild carabao. He knew that the variety wandering in the jungle was not really "game." It was a domesticated animal that had simply strayed into the forests. In the scientific sense there was no such species as a "wild" carabao. Although he believed he would look foolish "hunting" one, he found he had no choice but to do so. His hosts had arranged an elaborate event with so many people, including reporters, that Ted told Eleanor, "This is going to be too conspicuous. I'd hate to shoot and miss. It would be really disastrous if I hit a carabao and then found it had a brand on it."

As the hunt plunged into the wild, with Ted slipping and sliding and occasionally falling in thick mud, one of the animals "bounded like a porpoise" through bushes and the tall grass a hundred and fifty yards away. Ted felled the fleeting animal with one bullet.

Noting that Ted was promptly nicknamed "One-shot Teddy," the newspaper *Philippines Herald* observed, "A governor general who does not mind being bitten by jungle mosquitoes, who can fall into wild carabao wallows and like it, who can drink Igorot wine and lick his chops, who can be really human without losing his grin—he is some governor general."

In the summer eighteen-year-old Teddy and Cornelius, going on seventeen, arrived on vacation from school. At noon on their first day in Manila their father was meeting the press. When he saw the boys, so tall that they towered over their mother, he beckoned them into the office to meet the reporters. "And you, too, Eleanor," he called. When she shook her head and attempted to walk away, Teddy and Cornelius lifted her by her elbows and carried her in. She recalled in her memoirs, "The reporters were delighted but tactful enough not to mention such unseemly frivolity."

A traveler to Manila who called at the Malacanan Palace that summer as he paused on a round-the-world cruise was George Bernard Shaw. He and his wife, Charlotte, were met at the dock by Ted's military aide and technical adviser, Maj. Matthew Ridgway. At various ports on the way to the Philippines the irascible Irish playwright had let loose with a string of blasts at the British Empire in particular, and colonial powers in general. As a result, the U.S. governor general of the Philippines braced himself for a Shavian broadside at American occupation of the islands. Instead, Shaw announced that he had witnessed "the most extraordinary of all things, independence pending for a people that don't want it."

For a memento of the visit the relieved governor general gave Shaw a signed copy of *East of the Sun and West of the Moon* with little expectation that the sophisticated author would actually read about the travails of a pair of brothers on the hunt for the *Ovis poli*. The book was given because Mrs. Shaw had requested it.

Another caller who presented no cause for alarm was the composer Rudolf Friml. He was a guest in Manila of the head of the Philippine phone company, Joseph Stevenot. When Stevenot was asked to bring Friml to the Malacanan, he doubted that Friml, "a shy figure who dislikes meeting people," would come. Friml also hated dressing up in a dinner jacket and being expected to arrive on time.

Eleanor and Ted asked Stevenot to tell Friml that, should he come, dress would be informal and he could arrive at whatever time he wished. Dinner would wait.

The famed maestro appeared at a reasonable hour, casually attired.

Ted handed him a cocktail and began talking about the heroes of Friml's native Bohemia. From Ted's mouth flowed a litany of names: Ottokar, "the great King Charles," and Jan Hus. As they went in for dinner they were discussing "the victorious march of the Bohemian Hussars through Germany to the Baltic in the fifteenth century." Over soup the topic was the Czechs in Russia and Serbia in the Great War, "fighting Bolsheviks and Hungarian ex-prisoners every step of the way."

At one point Friml called across the table to Stevenot, "Joe! Why did you not tell me it would be like this? He knows all our history. What a man!"

Fresher history was on Ted's mind in talks with Major Ridgway.

In violation of the Washington disarmament treaties, flaunting the Kellogg-Briand Pact and the Covenant of the League of Nations, the Japanese, on September 18, 1931, had sent their army flooding into Manchuria. On January 4, 1932, they had completed military control of South Manchuria and renamed the region Manchukuo.

The reaction in the United States had been a statement by Secretary of State Henry L. Stimson. Immediately characterized in the press as the Stimson Doctrine, it pledged that the United States would not recognize any treaty or agreement that might impair the "sovereignty, the independence, or the territorial and administrative integrity of the Republic of China" and the "Open Door" policy.

Four weeks after this warning the Japanese attacked Shanghai and expelled the Chinese army. On February 23 Stimson sent a letter to Ted's friend, Senator Borah, chairman of the Senate Foreign Relations Committee, declaring that the United States would stand by its treaty rights in the Far East.

Less than a month later, the League of Nations adopted a resolution that embraced the Stimson Doctrine. The Japanese responded by pulling out of Shanghai.

The bluster from Stimson notwithstanding, the secretary of state told the U.S. ambassador in London on November 19, 1932, "We do not intend to get into war with Japan."

On March 27, 1933, Japan served notice to an increasingly anxious world that it was no longer a member of the League of Nations.

During this worrying scenario, the United States was engaged in its quadrennial exercise of electing a president. The Republicans proposed that the incumbent deserved to be reelected. The Democrats had chosen as their standard bearer the man who had run for vice president in 1920 on a ticket headed by James M. Cox. Now governor of New York, Franklin D. Roosevelt cast aside the custom that the presidential choice not appear at the convention to accept the nomination. He told ecstatic delegates in Chicago, "I have started out on the tasks that lie ahead by breaking the absurd traditions that the candidate should remain in professed ignorance of what has happened for weeks until he is formally notified of that event many weeks later. You have nominated me and I know it, and I am here to thank you for the honor."

Proudly calling himself the "bearer of liberalism and progress," he claimed leadership of the country's "uninterrupted march along the path of real promise, of real justice, of real equality for all our citizens." He closed the address with "I pledge you, I pledge myself, to a new deal for the American people."

In Manila as Ted read the text of his distant cousin's speech he noted with a smile that Franklin was still emulating his political ideal. TR had promised a "square deal."

23

During Ted's years at Groton and Harvard he had considered the members of the press meddlesome stalkers. His attitude changed when he entered politics. Just as TR had despised and denounced reporters for intruding on his private life, then embraced them as "Teddy" the office seeker, governor, and president, Ted Roosevelt grasped the importance of having the press on his side. As in Washington, D.C., reporters had organized socially in the form of the Gridiron Club. Its president was Carlos Romulo, a young man whom the world would come to know as a brigadier general and comrade of Gen. Douglas MacArthur, and afterward Philippine ambassador to the United States following independence. Because Ted could not take a large group of reporters to accompany him on his tours of the islands, he asked Romulo to choose one to go along and to share his observations with the others. The main question on the minds of the Manila press corps in the summer of 1932 was whether Ted would take off his governor general's hat and put on his political one by going home to help his party.

After Russell Owen was picked by Romulo to cover one of Ted's inspection tours, the correspondent of the North American Newspaper Alliance wrote, "Campaigning is hard work, but if Colonel Theodore Roosevelt, governor general of the Philippines, goes home in September to stump for President Hoover, he probably will look upon it almost as a vacation. For no campaigning trip could hold a candle to the recent inspection tour Colonel Roosevelt made through the Philippines during hot weather. If he was tired he did not show it. Later it was learned that he is never tired. He weighs 145 pounds, all muscle. He is lean and hard. He waved his hat and the crowd cheered and waved. The governor general appealed for co-operation and told of the necessity for economy, and was answered with the cheers of the people to whom his vigorous personality apparently makes a tremendous appeal."

During one of these ventures Ted was informed that the island of Jolo had been hit by a freak hurricane. The island was the headquarters of the Moros. While the vast majority of the people of the Philippines were Christians and, as George Bernard Shaw had observed, content to be living under United States rule, the Moros were Muslims who wanted to be independent of everyone. Despite warnings of personal peril if he went to Jolo, Ted rushed to survey the storm's toll in lives, injuries, and property damage. He found that two hundred people had been killed and destruction was extensive. A few weeks later he was back in Jolo. A twelve-member police patrol had been ambushed and killed by Moros. This attack had been followed by a punitive police raid on the Moro headquarters. In the company of Major Ridgway, Ted interviewed witnesses to the slaughter of the police patrol and then went on foot to the scene of the massacre.

"The fact that the governor general had come himself without delay, disregarding the danger," Eleanor noted, "was said to have deeply impressed the outlaws and convinced them that he would really get them if they caused more trouble."

Civil unrest was also a problem in central Luzon. Disorder had broken out in several places because rice farmers objected to being taxed. The anger was largely fueled by communist outsiders. To explain why taxation was needed and how the money was being used, Ted chose to have the kind of town meetings he'd observed when he was a student in New England. He arranged for "assemblies" at which he appeared, along with experts on agriculture, domestic animals, poultry, fishing, sanitation, land laws, and the acquiring of homesteads.

The *Philippines Herald* said of one of these local conclaves: "The big way Governor Roosevelt put over the first community assembly in Malabon yesterday proved the great possibility of such public meetings in the government's effort to solve the people's needs, and in checking the nefarious signs of paid [communist] agitators in this country."

The assemblies were not restricted to discussions of problems. One held on June 6, 1932, Ted reported in a letter to his mother, was more like a party. "In addition to the lectures," he said, "we had local music. It is customary here in the small barrios that are too poor for bands for some of the people to get together and form what they call 'banda de boca' (mouth band). This has no instruments and renders all the tunes vocally, various individuals taking the part of various instruments. There was also a splendid bamboo band of thirty pieces in which the instruments were made of bamboo or gourds."

Commenting on the governmental program outlined in Ted's first message to the Philippine legislature, given on July 16, 1932, the *New York Herald Tribune* editorialized, "No single item on his reform agenda is conditional upon independence, autonomy, or the persistence of present relations with the United States. Since the Filipinos have developed no partisan feeling on any question that is not linked up in some way with the independence issue, Mr. Roosevelt has afforded no party leader an excuse for opposing him on any familiar political score. Having completely disarmed all possible criticism by making himself the champion of the small farmers, who constitute an overwhelming majority of the electorate, Governor Roosevelt puts the professional politicians in such position that the only competition among them must now be for the distinction of giving his plans the heartiest approval."

In the *Manila Tribune* Carlos Romulo declared, "Governor General Theodore Roosevelt has established the first 'Era of Good Feeling' our government has ever known."

But as these verbal bouquets were being tossed Ted's way, he found himself caught in a political windstorm blowing from the United States.

In the thirty-year history of American governors of the Philippines, none had been asked to interrupt his duties in Manila to go home to take part in a presidential campaign. But almost as soon as the Republican convention concluded with its endorsement of Herbert Hoover for reelection, Ted received telegrams from party leaders telling him it was "imperative" that he come home to go on a national speaking tour on behalf of the president. Ted responded that if he took off for three months and were not in Manila to lobby for his Reorganization Bill, it would fail in the legislature. He sent letters to his old friends Patrick Hurley, the Secretary of War; Lawrence Richey, the president's personal secretary; and GOP national chairman Everett Sanders.

Further pleas came from Hurley and Sanders. Instead of their cables being couched in coded language, they were transmitted "in the clear." They informed Ted he would have no choice but to return to campaign for Hoover. The contents of the messages immediately found their way into the hands of reporters both in Washington and Manila.

The political press rubbed collective hands and licked collective lips in hungry anticipation of a delicious battle like the one in 1924 between a Roosevelt from Oyster Bay and a Hyde Park Roosevelt. Then it was Franklin's wife as his surrogate, puttering around New York state in a car with a rooftop teapot. In 1932 it would be man to man, or in the language of Puerto Rico that Theodore had recently mastered, *mano a mano.* The only scenario better than Ted on the hustings and blasting his cousin Franklin on behalf of Hoover in the fevered imaginations of the press would be a race for the White House in which the Republicans' candidate was also a Roosevelt. Of course, should Franklin Roosevelt win—or lose, for that matter—they had 1936 to look forward to.

In Manila, faced with what appeared to be an edict sanctioned by the president himself, Ted gave out a statement to the members of the Gridiron Club that he would accede to the order from Washington. This provoked such criticism in both countries that President Hoover's men declared that Governor General Roosevelt had not been ordered home. They said he was coming on his own volition. No one believed it.

A few days later, an embarrassed Hurley cabled:

AFTER FULL CONSIDERATION OF THE SITUATION AS PRESENTED BY YOU, THE PRESIDENT HAS REACHED THE CONCLUSION THAT YOU SHOULD NOT LEAVE YOUR DUTIES AS GOVERNOR GENERAL FOR THE PURPOSE OF PARTICIPATING IN THE CAMPAIGN IN THE UNITED STATES. HE HAS THEREFORE ASKED ME TO ADVISE YOU THAT UNDER ALL THE CIRCUMSTANCES HE BELIEVES IT TO BE YOUR DUTY TO REMAIN AT YOUR POST.

At this point the wisdom that had guided Ted in resisting leaving Manila seems to have failed him. A few days before the presidential election he went on the radio from Manila in a broadcast to the United States on behalf of Hoover's reelection. The speech made history as the first radio broadcast across the Pacific. But it infuriated the Democrats. And it made the Hurley cable with its high-minded placing of duty over party, and the president on whose behalf it was sent, an even bigger target of ridicule.

The question whether barnstorming the nation for Hoover by Theodore Roosevelt would have made a difference in the outcome of the election was both moot and doubtful. The Hyde Park Roosevelt with the nose glasses and toothy grin who had followed Teddy Roosevelt's foot-steps to Harvard, into the office of assistant secretary of the navy, on a run for vice president, and to the chair in the New York governor's cham-ber, beat Herbert Hoover in a landslide of equal proportions to the one in which Hoover had buried the presidential aspirations of Franklin D. Roosevelt's beloved "Happy Warrior" in 1928, Al Smith.

The last vote had barely been tallied when political circles buzzed with speculation as to the fate of the Roosevelt occupying Malacanan Palace. Belief that "FDR," as the president-elect was now identified in the short-hand of newspaper headlines, might keep Ted Roosevelt in the Philip-pines was fueled by a report that Ted's brother Kermit had gone on a cruise with FDR on Vincent Astor's yacht, the *Nourmahal*. Kermit's pur-pose in going sailing with FDR, it was said, was to persuade him to reap-point Ted.

On FDR's inauguration day, March 4, 1933, the *New York World Tele-gram* columnist William P. Smith quoted Philippine public opinion on the question of Ted's staying. "Retention of Colonel Roosevelt is all the more important right now," he said, "because the relationship between the islands and the United States is about to undergo a radical change. He or his successor seems likely to be the last American governor the is-lands will have. The American Congress has voted the independence of the Philippines, and within the next two or three years the Filipino peo-ple are scheduled to accept or reject the independence measure, and second to frame and ratify a constitution of their own. It would seem a most inopportune time, therefore, to send out a new governor general."

As was the custom for presidential appointees on a change of ad-ministrations, Ted sent in his resignation. FDR accepted it immediately.

When a reporter asked him exactly what relation he was to FDR, Ted replied, "Fifth cousin about to be removed."

Twelve days after FDR was sworn in as the thirty-second president, Ted and Eleanor boarded the steamer *Arayat*. It sailed past the peninsula fortress called Corregidor, bound for Macassar. It was the first destina-tion on their return-home voyage that would take them constantly west-ward through storied but familiar places of the Far Western Pacific, South and Central Asia, again to Peshawar on India's Northwest Frontier, through the Khyber Pass into Afghanistan, Persia and an audience with the shah, Damascus, the Antioch of St. Paul of the New Testament, Is-tanbul, Venice, Florence, Rome, Paris, and finally to London, where they were entertained by Mr. and Mrs. Rudyard Kipling.

The author whose stories TR had read to Ted as a boy and whose poems Ted could recite perfectly asked Ted what he planned to do next.

Ted spoke of an expedition to unexplored territory in Tibet.

Kipling asked, "Aren't you getting a little too old? I think you should leave that sort of thing to younger men."

24

Forty-five years old, fit in body, mind, and with adventuresome spirit, Theodore Roosevelt returned to New York in the fall of 1932 in need of a job. Finding one that would take advantage of his knowledge of world affairs, proven administrative talents, and his record in both high finance and banking proved easy. He was barely unpacked when Winthrop W. Aldrich, chairman of the Chase National Bank and married to Eleanor's cousin Harriet, put him on the board of directors. This would lead to chairmanship of the American Express Company.

Civic and patriotic organizations also sought him out. Having served on the National Council of Boy Scouts since 1919, he accepted its vice presidency and seats on nine committees.

When Irving Berlin turned over the past, present, and future earnings of "God Bless America" to the Boy Scouts and Girl Scouts, he insisted that the funds be administered by a committee of three—a Catholic, a Jew, and a Protestant. Those chosen were Ted, Gene Tunney, and Herbert Bayard Swope. The National Health Council made Ted its leader and coordinator of links to seventeen national health groups. He became a member of the National Citizens' Committee of Mobilization for Human Needs, national chairman of the Citizenship Educational Service, and member of the national Civil Service Reform League. This was meaningful to Ted because TR's entire political career had been devoted to civil service reform. He was named a director on the board of the National Association for the Advancement of Colored People (NAACP), as well as honorary president of the National Health Circle for Colored People and a trustee of Bethune-Bookman College. At the request of Newton B. Baker, who had been Wilson's secretary of war, Ted went on the board of the National Conference of Christians and Jews.

Shortly after his return from the Philippines, he was elected president of the National Republican Club. He found that half its members had drifted away and the club's budget was in deficit by three thousand dollars a month.

None of these activities kept him from taking the summer of 1935 to again follow in his father's footsteps with an expedition to Brazil. The difference was that Ted did not go for the purpose of exploration. He went as a hunter to get a good jaguar specimen for the American Museum of Natural History. The quest was frustrating. After six weeks of fruitless hunting in the jungles of the Matto Grasso, he was resigned to going home without his quarry. But three days before he was to leave he found and collected an excellent specimen weighing three hundred and forty pounds. Not yet fifty years old, he did not think of the adventure as being his last chance to be a boy again, but he did return from the arduous experience feeling more sympathetic to the view of Kipling that such undertakings were more suitable for younger men.

Another manifestation of the continuing powerful influence of TR on his namesake was Ted's lifelong passion for reading. To an interviewer who asked how he found the time, he answered, "I read in bed. I read in my bath. I read in the train. I read in the subway. I would feel as desolate without a book in my pocket as I would if I had lost my trousers."

Like TR, he was also a prolific writer. He turned out many magazine articles, best-selling books about his explorations, a popular volume about life as a Roosevelt (*All in the Family*), and a compendium of poems. Compiled in collaboration with sportswriter and World War veteran Grantland Rice and published in 1932, *Taps* contained works by Rice, Rupert Brooke, Kipling, Alan Seeger, Herbert Asquith, Robert Frost, C. Fox Smith, Edith Wharton, and the Roosevelts' favorite poet, Edward Arlington Robinson. An anonymous work proved especially meaningful to Ted because it seemed to have been written for his brother:

TO AN AVIATOR KILLED IN ACTION
I like to think that as you winged your way
Up through the dusk of that deep darkening day
That God leaned down and took you by the hand
And led your soul into that other land.
Because He saw, engraved across the sky,
The paths you made where others dared not fly;

And saw you dim the distance of the west
A little nearer than the rest.
And when, above some flaming battle's wake,
My soul shall stand nor know which path to take,
I like to think I'll find, above the fray,
That God has taken you to show the way;
That, standing head erect, with wings outspread,
Between earth and sky, you watch the dead;
And when their souls, confused, bewildered, rise
They find you there to point them to the skies.

The book was published by Doubleday, Doran and Company. Its president was Nelson Doubleday. A friend of Ted, he was impressed by both his love of books and experience in world affairs. Because the reading public was demonstrating an increasing interest in public affairs and international issues, he invited Ted to join the publishing firm to help develop books on those topics. An announcement that Ted was joining the company was made in the fall of 1935. When a reporter asked Ted if he could be satisfied seated at a desk in the firm's Garden City offices, he replied, "It's time I settled down. I like to work with the public, and the publishing business is, after all, a way to reach the public."

Ted also noted that he was now a grandfather.

In March 1934 Grace had married William McMillan, a young Baltimore architect whom Ted and Eleanor had met on their way home from the Philippines. McMillan and a friend had been tiger and elephant hunting in Indochina. A few weeks after the Roosevelts returned, Ted complained that he no longer saw his friend McMillan because William was so busy courting Grace. The wedding was held at Christ Church in Oyster Bay. Teddy and Cornelius were ushers. Quentin was too young, but was given a pair of gold cuff links like those worn by his brothers. The newlyweds settled in Baltimore. Their daughter Eleanor was born there in December 1937.

Because Ted's publishing job took him to England from time to time, he was able to renew friendships he'd made during the war, and to forge new ones with the prominent figures of the British government at a time when they and the other leaders of the allies in the world war were anxious about alarming events in Germany. On a visit in March 1936 at a dinner given by Lord and Lady Astor at their house in St. James's Square, the table talk was the threat posed by the Nazis and the dictator

Adolf Hitler's brazen retaking of the Rhineland in violation of the agreements that had concluded the war. As Ted took in the scene, in which the table glittered with gold plate and the Astors' servants and footmen wore knee breeches, white silk stockings, and powdered wigs, his mind filled with dark memories of France in 1918 and worries that someday England and France might again have to turn to the United States to save them from a Germany on the march. If so, his sons would be of the age to be called to fight. It was a possibility that left him feeling depressed . . . and determined to do all he could, if that time should come, to keep the United States out of it.

Having plunged into the world of publishing, Ted found himself drawn into the company of authors who had emerged on the American literary stage after the war. One of the brightest of these new literary lights, F. Scott Fitzgerald, had called them and everyone who had been in the war "the lost generation." He'd dazzled readers in 1920 with *This Side of Paradise,* followed in 1922 by *The Beautiful and the Damned* and *The Great Gatsby* in 1925, but his novel *Tender Is the Night* in 1934 had gotten a lackluster reception. Faring much better was Ernest Hemingway. His tragic novel *A Farewell to Arms* was the story of two lovers in the war. Most recently, Ted had enjoyed his tale of big game hunting, *The Green Hills of Africa.*

Among the recent best-selling nonfiction works were *The Epic of America,* prompted by the Wall Street crash of 1929 and the ensuing economic depression that had propelled FDR into the White House; *Wake Up and Live,* a plea to Americans to cheer up; *Life Begins at Forty,* an indirect answer to Kipling, who questioned Ted's desire to explore Tibet at age forty-five; and *While Rome Burns,* a wit-filled collection of anecdotes and whimsies by Alexander Woollcott.

The founder of the famous (some said infamous) literary lunches at the Algonquin Hotel known as "the Round Table," Woollcott had been the *New York Times* drama critic. Declared physically disqualified to serve in uniform during the war, he went over as a medical volunteer. He'd served at Base Hospital 8 and done so well that he'd been made a sergeant. In 1918 he was transferred to the AEF's weekly newspaper, the *Stars and Stripes,* and became its star reporter at the front. With the war over, he returned to the *Times* and published his first book, titled *The Command Is Forward,* a collection of his wartime stories. Since then he had become one of the most famous literary names in America and a radio celebrity through a weekly program on CBS. *The Town Crier* consisted of Woollcott's opinions on whatever subjects struck his fancy.

Residing in a house on Fifty-third Street overlooking the East River that he called "Wit's End," he was fat with a small mustache and wire-rimmed glasses that made him resemble an owl. Among a strangely assorted confluence of people invited to his "salons" and dinners were Round Table literary-world compatriots Dorothy Parker, Robert Benchley, George S. Kauffman, Charles MacArthur and his actress-wife Helen Hayes, Mark Connolly, Franklin P. Adams (a veteran of the *Stars and Stripes* and later editor of *The New Yorker*), "Wild Bill" Donovan, Alice Roosevelt Longworth, and the fascinating vice president of Doubleday, Doran, Ted Roosevelt, and his charming, sophisticated, and lively wife Eleanor.

Convinced that Americans liked poetry, Aleck, as his circle called him (some said Smart Aleck), suggested that Ted and Alice compile an anthology of verses people had clipped from magazines and newspapers and put away in a desk, or carried in their wallets. He would help in the gathering of the material by telling his vast radio audience to send their favorite verses and poems to Ted's office. The next mail delivery brought thirty thousand. The resulting book was titled *The Desk Drawer Anthology*.

Woollcott's successes had enabled him to buy an island in Vermont. Used as a summer retreat, it was called "Bomoseen" and became an extension of Wit's End. Among the friends who spent long periods there was Harpo Marx. Whenever he was visiting, Woollcott saw that there was a harp available. Recalling a visit to the island when Harpo was present, Eleanor wrote, "I asked nothing better than to sit doing embroidery and listening to him play the most beautiful improvisations while everyone else was busy with croquet or badminton."

In the late summer and fall of 1936 Ted was again asked by the Speakers' Bureau of the Republican National Committee to take to the political hustings, this time to campaign for the GOP presidential candidate, Governor Alfred (Alf) M. Landon of Kansas. FDR, in accepting the Democratic renomination in Philadelphia, had railed against "economic royalists" who complained that the intent of FDR's "New Deal" program was the overthrow of the institutions of America. "What they really complain of," said FDR, "is that we seek to take away their power."

Some political commentators recalled that TR had coined a phrase for such people: "the malefactors of great wealth."

TR's son believed in the aim of the New Deal to provide a more abundant life for all, but he feared that some government assistance programs discouraged industry, thrift, and initiative. He felt as had another Democrat president, Grover Cleveland, that the government's purpose was not to support the people, but vice versa. His criticism of his distant cousin's program was that New Deal policies would saddle succeeding generations with a huge, permanent debt and burden the people with federal regulations affecting every aspect of their lives.

Describing the bitterest presidential election since the 1896 contest between McKinley and Democratic candidate William Jennings Bryan, the 1930s historian Frederick Lewis Allen wrote in *Since Yesterday,* "To hear angry Republicans and angry Democrats talking, one would have supposed the contest was between a tyrant determined to destroy private property, ambition, the Constitution, democracy, and civilization itself, and a dupe of Wall Street who would introduce a fascist dictatorship."

With the political jousting centered on domestic issues, little attention was paid to world affairs. Millions of unemployed Americans had no interest in what the Nazis and fascists were doing in Europe, nor in Japanese aggression in China and whether Japan might have designs on other territories in the Pacific. They were even less concerned about the Soviet Union, which FDR had formally recognized in November 1933. On the questions of a possible European war and the ambitions of Japan, the president promised to "isolate" America. In a speech at Chautauqua, New York, he said, "I have seen war on land and sea. I have seen blood running from the wounded. I have seen men coughing out their gassed lungs. I have seen the dead in the mud. I have seen cities destroyed—I have seen two hundred limping, exhausted men come out of the line— the survivors of a regiment that went forward forty-eight hours before."

It was a speech that Ted could have delivered. He'd received numerous invitations to join organizations and committees formed by liberals to protest Nazism and fascism and had turned them down because he felt they were problems for Europeans to solve, and secondly, because the groups were silent on the evils of communism and the ideology's chief exponent, the Soviet Union and its brutal dictator, Josef Stalin.

During three weeks of barnstorming the country on behalf of Landon, Ted knew that he was engaged in a doomed cause. Few people in the country believed the Republicans had even a slim chance. When the votes were in, Landon carried two states, Maine and Vermont.

In 1938 Ted and Eleanor agreed to stop living in apartments or renting houses and build their own near the home TR had built at Sagamore Hill. Although Sagamore Hill was Ted's inheritance, it remained Edith's home. It had been built at a time when hiring and paying for domestic help was not a problem. It was also much too large for their needs. Choosing Bill McMillan to be their architect, they decided to build a house nearby on land of an old apple orchard. The site gave the house its name, "Old Orchard."

As work began on it, Eleanor was advised by her doctor that she was "badly run down" and in need of a complete rest somewhere away from the activities that were the cause of her condition. Ted said, "Why don't you go to China? A month at sea going out, a month there, and another coming back would do you a lot of good. Take Quentin. It would be a splendid trip for him before he goes to college in the fall."

While she was there, he continued, she could do him a business favor. He was editor of a book by the wife of Chiang Kai-shek, the "generalissimo" who was the country's ruler. For special editions of the book he needed Madame Chiang Kai-shek to autograph two hundred and fifty blank pages that would then be bound into the volumes.

"I don't want to trust them to the mails," he told Eleanor. "Don't return without them."

Her plan to go to Peking was vetoed by the U.S. ambassador in Tokyo, Joseph Grew. He reported that fighting between China and Japan had broken out near Tientsin. If she went to Peking, he warned, it might be impossible to get her out. She and Quentin went to Shanghai and then on to Nanking to meet Madame Chiang Kai-shek. With the pages signed, they returned to Shanghai. From a window of the Cathay Hotel overlooking the Woonsung River, Eleanor and Quentin observed four warships—two British, one French, and the Japanese flagship *Idzumo*.

As they peered at the ship, Eleanor recalled, its antiaircraft guns "broke loose in a deafening racket." To get a better view of what was happening, she and Quentin left the hotel to go to their car and drive to the Canton Road apartment of a friend, Dr. William Gardiner. When they got there, a flight of six Chinese bombers flew by, dropping bombs in the river. Their target was the *Idzumo*. They missed, but some of their bombs fell among terrified refugees around the spot where Eleanor's car had been parked. Had she and Quentin been in it a few minutes earlier they would probably have been killed. At dinner that evening Dr. Gardiner asked Eleanor her religious denomination. She answered, "Presbyterian." Gardiner chuckled and said, "I don't think that any woman would have stood there and watched the bombs fall unless she had been born and raised a Presbyterian."

Not until many hours later was she able to send this cable to Ted:

ALL SAFE. LORD LOVE A DUCK.

She told Quentin, "Goodness only knows how mad he is at us now."

In her book she wrote of nearly being killed in China. "In spite of everything, from a purely personal point of view our journey had achieved its purpose and more. We had come back alive. We had Madame Chiang Kai-shek's two hundred and fifty autographs in both Chinese and English. We had collected some good possessions. What was more, as a rest cure for me the trip had been an outstanding success."

Another result of the trip was to draw the attention of Americans who read about her harrowing escape in newspaper accounts, and an upsurge in sympathy for China. A few months later Ted became head of the American Bureau for Medical Aid to China and national president of the United Council for Civilian Relief in China. To raise money he started "Bowl of Rice" parties to raise money for China relief.

In April 1938 they moved into their new house. It was built in Ted's favorite Georgian style, with high ceilings and a wide hall that ran front to back. Constructed of old brick, it was to have been painted white, but they liked the color and painted only the shutters white. The front door was eighteenth century, found in the backyard of a parish priest in Dublin who'd rescued it from an old house that was being demolished.

"Ted loved the house so much," Eleanor wrote, "that he could hardly bear to leave it to go to work while we were getting settled. Every afternoon, unable to wait until he got home, he would telephone me to ask what progress I had made since morning in arranging furniture. He spent every evening for a week putting books on the shelves in the library."

After an inspection Aleck Woollcott wrote to Eleanor of "that lovely house of yours":

My thoughts have revisited it so often that I think of many of its rooms as rooms I already know. To be any good a house must be self-sprung as a bear. Yours was indisputably yours as your toothbrush.

But that really doesn't tell the story. It is so clearly a part of this house's quality and secret that all the family had hands in making it. For instance, so much of its color and character derives from what Ted had done and is.

Between portraits of four generations on the walls stood flags of the governor general of the Philippines, the governor of Puerto Rico, assistant secretary of the navy, and the colors of Ted's command in the war, the 26th Infantry.

Ted and Eleanor had waited twenty-eight years to realize their dream house.

They would live in it together for only three years.

Part 5: Our Cause

It was like the magnificent climax of a great play.

—*Quentin Roosevelt II, July 14, 1944*

25

In a letter written in 1940 as armies were again arrayed, guns were booming in Europe, and voices across America called for the United States to once more save civilization by taking up arms, the eldest son of the Theodore Roosevelt to whom war had been the glorious test of manhood wrote to a friend, "More than twenty years ago, with some two million other young Americans, I went to Europe to fight a war to end wars. At that time I thought I was fighting to make the world safe for democracy. Theoretically we won the war. One glance at the world today is sufficient commentary on the value of our victory. The sober truth is that no one wins a war. The victor loses as well as the vanquished."

By remaining neutral, he argued, the United States "can best serve not only ourselves but the other people in the world as well." The primary mission of Americans, he said, was to preserve "our representative self-government." It had been badly shaken in the last war and might not survive another one. "If we preserve it, it will be a beacon towards which other nations can struggle from the mires of dictatorship. If it perishes the light will have gone out of the world."

Despite his great sympathy and liking for England, he told his brother Kermit as Kermit prepared to volunteer to go to England and again enlist in the British Army, his first duty was to the United States and her citizens. He feared that should the country get into the war, irrevocable damage to the nation and its institutions would result. By being "a strong neutral" the United States would be of "inestimable help at the peace table."

In 1940, after Alice Roosevelt Longworth helped to found a neutrality group called the America First Committee, the organization's membership rolls quickly grew to eight hundred thousand across the nation.

Its chief spokesman was the famed aviator Charles A. Lindbergh. In 1927 "Lucky Lindy" had taken off from Roosevelt Field in a tiny silver airplane, *Spirit of Saint Louis*, on an historic solo flight across the Atlantic to Paris. Second in demand as a speaker only to Lindy at America First rallies, Ted supported the aims of Alice's committee by touring the country to advocate neutrality so that the United States would be in a position to broker peace. But as he talked with America First leaders and rank and file, he found that three fourths of them advocated refusing to enlist or fight if the country were drawn into a war. Appalled by this attitude, he severed his relationship with America First, saying, "I have fought and will fight our entrance, but if and when we are committed, then I feel that every last one of us have got to do all we can to bring the war to a successful conclusion."

Since the end of the Great War he had retained his army reserve commission by going to yearly summer training camps. Although he had been known by many titles since 1919 he preferred, like TR after the presidency, being addressed as "Colonel." He had also worked to maintain friendly relations with men he'd known during the war, in connection with the American Legion, in his government posts, and in contacts with men who had remained in military service. Among these was the captain who had been amused and touched by Eleanor's appeal on Ted's behalf to be shipped to France as soon as possible in 1917, and who, as a major, had saved Ted from feeling the brunt of Black Jack Pershing's displeasure with a training exercise in 1918. George Marshall was now a general and chief of staff of the army. Watching events unfold in Europe and the Pacific in 1940, and believing the United States dare not repeat the mistake of unpreparedness that left the country scrambling to mobilize in 1917, the fifty-four-year-old ex-commander of the 26th Infantry, 1st Division, petitioned Marshall to return him to active duty with his old outfit.

Eleanor looked back on the years 1939 and 1940 when Ted advocated neutrality and was a speaker on behalf of America First and remembered him being "roundly attacked" as a Nazi sympathizer, "white-livered coward, and traitor." She found it "indeed ironic to see how many people who had abused him and were younger than he had no idea of volunteering for military service to uphold the cause they had championed so frantically. Or how many of them, when they or their sons were drafted, used influence to escape the inconvenience of combat or even of overseas service." Yet her husband, still feeling effects of wounds of the last war, a father and grandfather, well into middle age, and who could have petitioned for a civilian post in the War Department, had appealed to once again command troops in battle.

As Ted waited anxiously to learn whether General Marshall would grant his petition, his wife and children prayed that he would. They felt that Ted believed that in rallying to this new cause by taking up arms for his country, he would be the legitimate heir to his father's spiritual estate. Being in uniform again, and possibly having to "pay with his body for his heart's desire" by going into the line of fire, would be an emotional homecoming.

The answer from Marshall in April 1941 granted Ted's request by ordering him to join the 1st Division, in training at Fort Devens, Massachusetts.

Two months later, twenty-year-old Quentin was commissioned second lieutenant in the regular army and was assigned to the 33d Field Artillery, 1st Division, also at Fort Devens.

The fact that a father and his son, the direct lineage of Theodore Roosevelt, were in the same division was so irresistible a news story that *Life* magazine sent a writer and a "kodak creature" to capture the phenomenon for its readers. When the team arrived, they also found a story in Eleanor. To be near husband and son she had settled nearby at the Groton Inn.

In October the 1st Division was ordered to North Carolina for maneuvers. Following them in her car, Eleanor stayed in the town of Pinehurst. Each morning she drove to the scene of the day's maneuvers with a box of raisin cookies, a bottle of Coca-Cola, and an apple for her lunch in the hope of finding Ted or catching a glimpse of Quentin. Sometimes on the way back to town she picked up soldiers hitchhiking toward the town's general store. Without saying who she was she maneuvered their conversation to comments on their commander. One of the men related in awe that Colonel Roosevelt had "the legs shot out from under him three times in the last war." Another said he'd heard that one of Roosevelt's lungs had been totally destroyed by mustard gas, yet he was still able to keep up with everyone on maneuvers. The "Old Man," another said, was the first CO he'd seen who believed in good food for the men.

"When I left them," Eleanor wrote, "I would tell them I was the colonel's wife and watch their grins as they waved me out of sight."

Back in Fort Devens, Ted was promoted to brigadier general and made deputy commander of the division. This entitled him to an orderly, driver, and a small bungalow on post. It had a few pieces of well-worn furniture, an electric stove, and a refrigerator. Eleanor bought kitchen utensils and tableware at a five-and-dime store in Lowell. Days after they moved in, the Japanese attacked Pearl Harbor.

Brigadier General Theodore Roosevelt's cousin Franklin was now commander-in-chief of an army at war. Acutely conscious that they had been engaged in political combat since the 1920s, and that the nation's press had taken great delight in characterizing relations between the "Roozavelts" of Oyster Bay and the "Rose-a-velts" of Hyde Park as a family feud, Ted asked to meet FDR for the purpose of "burying the hatchet" and ending press talk of the feud continuing between a president and a general with the same family name. The president extended Ted an invitation to the White House. When Ted emerged to be thronged by reporters in a scene that was reminiscent of those of his Groton and Harvard days, he publicly ended the feud.

"This is our country," he declared, "our cause and our president."

By then Ted's first son and TR's first grandson, Teddy, was in the navy and undergoing training for a commission at the naval base at Jacksonville, Florida. Grace's husband, Bill, was also in the navy. Cornelius would soon join them as a naval officer.

With her husband and three sons in uniform, Grace married, and with the 1st Division on maneuvers at Hershey, Pennsylvania, while awaiting orders to head to England, Eleanor closed most of Old Orchard and moved into a maid's quarters "for the duration." As she did so, she felt that a chapter in her life with Ted had ended.

With fifteen hundred men as advance guard of the 1st Division, Ted sailed to England in June 1942. The remainder of the men, some sixteen thousand, were scheduled to follow aboard the refitted liner *Queen Mary*. One of those on the ship, which was so crowded the men had to sleep in three shifts, was second lieutenant of artillery Quentin Roosevelt. But he and his father were not the first Roosevelts to go to England's aid.

Kermit had gone there in 1940. With assistance of his friend, Prime Minister Winston Churchill, who appreciated Kermit's valor under the Union Jack in fighting on the Near East front in the last war, Kermit was commissioned in the British Army. Churchill helped even though Kermit was a shadow of the dashing hero who had captured Turks by waving an officer's baton at them. Churchill recognized that Kermit's condition was the result of the toll alcohol had taken on him physically and spiritually. The prime minister also recognized that Kermit's volunteering was an expression of a no-longer-young man's desire to restore the heroic character he'd shown in his wartime experiences, as the youth who had dared the wilds of Africa and Brazil with his father, and as the young man who had conquered the Himalaya Mountains with his older brother.

In addition to these admirable achievements Kermit Roosevelt had built and run a great steamship company. Always in love with literature and the great poets, he'd written books and poems that garnered praise from critics and good sales. But somewhere, somehow, everything had gone wrong. He'd sought escape from his troubles in a liquor bottle and in the arms of a mistress. Hit hard by the effects of the Great Depression and unable to write because of drinking, he had periodically left Belle for a woman named Carla Peters.

In this Kermit proved to be more like his uncle than his father. TR's brother Elliott had been an alcoholic, had taken a mistress, and in an attack of delirium tremens had tried to kill himself by jumping out a window. When he died in convulsions, TR remembered Elliott's "old sweetness" and with a broken heart said to their sister, "I suppose he has been doomed from the beginning."

Whether Winston Churchill saw Kermit as a man on the brink of doom is not known. If Churchill's intention in aiding Kermit to obtain an army commission reflected a belief that he could be saved, he soon had reason to believe that his faith would be justified. The veteran of mountain climbs with Ted in search of the *Ovis poli* proved he still possessed the quality of valor by taking part in Churchill's plan to thwart an invasion of Norway by the Soviet Union. But before the mission could be mounted, the Norwegians surrendered to Germany. A second British attempt to get a hold in Norway, in which Kermit took part, failed. But in the evacuation of British commandoes Kermit helped extricate men and equipment. He even carried some of the wounded on his back. He'd done all this while staying sober.

Sent on a mission to North Africa in 1940, Kermit found German patrols, but none of the exciting action he desired. Bored, he resumed drinking and became ill. He was ordered back to England, where he was diagnosed with a flare-up of malaria he'd contracted while on the Brazil expedition with TR. He was also found to have an enlarged liver. Because of these illnesses he was discharged from the British Army in early 1941.

Back in New York in June and reunited with Belle, he vanished almost immediately. An appeal by Belle to FDR put the FBI on his trail. He was found in July, beaten up after a fight with a taxi driver. After two commitments to a sanitarium, he went to California with Carla Peters in early 1942. When the FBI traced him again, agents reported finding him "stumbling drunk" and reciting the Edwin Arlington Robinson poem "Richard Cory," about a young man who seemed to have everything but went home one night and put a bullet through his head.

Appeals by Belle and brother Archie to FDR and General Marshall resulted in Kermit's being sent to an army air corps base at Fort Richardson, Alaska. He had no specific duty, but he persuaded pilots to take him along on bombing missions against Japanese forces on small islands in the Aleutians. He also helped organize Eskimos and Aleuts into a militia, in case the Japanese attempted to overrun the islands. Sober and feeling good about himself, he wrote to Ted that the war was his "fountain of youth."

The third son of Theodore Roosevelt to seek the assistance of Franklin D. Roosevelt in getting into the war was Archie. At the age of forty-eight he'd been deemed unsuitable for army service because of his wounds in what was now being called the First World War. Desperate to join the fight, he wrote to the president that there might be places and times in the war where FDR would like to have the son of TR "and someone with your name to share the dangers of soldiers or sailors or marines in some tough spot." Of course, one son of Theodore Roosevelt (his namesake) and three of TR's grandsons were already serving. But this fact and Archie's disabilities did not keep FDR from granting Archie's appeal. He was commissioned lieutenant colonel and given command of the 162d Infantry, 41st Division.

As if these requests by the Roosevelts of Oyster Bay were not enough family problems for the Hyde Park Roosevelts in the White House, FDR learned in August 1942 from the adjutant general, Col. Thomas Jefferson Davis, at the U.S. General Staff Headquarters in Grosvenor Square, London, that Ted's fifty-three-year old wife had flown over by Pan American Clipper as a volunteer with the Red Cross. Told that Ted's division was based at Tidworth on Salisbury Plain, she rushed to see him. She found the area a lonely and desolate region even in summer. Ted informed her there were no recreation facilities for the men and instructed her to "start something." He put her in touch with Maj. Gen. Richard H. Dewing, senior British representative on General Eisenhower's staff. The ultimate result was a servicemen's club called Tidbury House. Eleanor ran it for ten months. Her work ended when the 1st Division packed and moved out to a destination known only to Eisenhower, his highest-rank-ing officers, Prime Minister Churchill and his senior advisors in the War Office, their American counterparts on the staff of Gen. George C. Mar-shall, and the president of the United States. The code name assigned to the plan that commenced on November 8, 1942, was Torch.

26

As American troops flooded into England throughout 1942, the first question everyone asked was: "When will they fight?" The second: "Where?"

With the Red Army engaged in a life-and-death struggle with the Germans on Russian soil, Josef Stalin demanded that a second front be opened in the West by an immediate Anglo-American attack across the English Channel. To this Churchill replied, "Why stick your head in the alligator's mouth [in France] when you can go to the Mediterranean and rip his soft underbelly?" The way to get at that more vulnerable region was from North Africa. Unfortunately, British forces in the region's vast stretches of deserts and mountains that were engaged with Germany's Afrika Korps, and with troops of Germany's ally, Italy, had suffered a humiliating defeat at Tobruk in Libya. In pursuit of his "soft underbelly" strategy, and to redeem Britain's honor, the prime minister campaigned for an American invasion of North Africa.

Eisenhower told General Marshall and the president this would require complete reversal of thinking and drastic revision in planning and preparation aimed at a cross-Channel invasion of France in the region of Normandy sometime in 1943. "Instead of a massed attack across narrow waters," he wrote after the war, "the proposed expedition would require movement across open ocean areas where enemy submarines would constitute a real menace." The target would not be a restricted front where they knew the enemy terrain, facilities, and people as they affected the military operations, "but the rim of a continent where no major military campaign had been conducted for centuries." FDR sided with Churchill.

The last German bullet aimed at an American had been fired on November 11, 1918, in France. Now troops fresh from the United States who had heard the sounds of guns only on their firing ranges and during training exercises were being ordered into combat against the battle-seasoned Afrika Korps. The best trained of the "green" invaders were Ted's 1st Infantry.

The landings were to be made in Algeria near the city of Oran, site of the Tafaraoui and La Siena Airfields. Taking them would provide facilities for bringing in supplies and equipment and additional troops and bases for Allied air cover. The first unit ashore was a British infantry brigade. It landed near Algiers and met no resistance from forces of Germany's French allies. Nor was there serious opposition when Ted's 1st Infantry moved ashore. The greatest danger was that troops overloaded with equipment might drown as they stepped from boats into deep water.

Their commander was Maj. Gen. Terry de la Mesa Allen. Although he had attended West Point, he'd dropped out in his last year and completed his education at Catholic University in 1912. As a student at the army's Command General School at Fort Leavenworth, Kansas, he finished 221st out of 241. At the top of the class had been Dwight D. Eisenhower. As a leader of troops Allen was liked by enlisted men because he did not demand strict adherence to the army manual for maintaining discipline and order. Among some officers his reputation was that of a "slapdash and reckless" soldier concerning his own skin, but a commander who was too solicitous of the safety of those under him. Famed war correspondent Ernie Pyle, the self-styled champion of the "dogface GI," would write of the commander of the 1st, "Major General Terry Allen was one of my favorite people. Partly because he didn't give a damn for hell or high water; partly because he was the only general outside the Air Forces I could call by his first name. If there was one thing in the world Allen lived and breathed for, it was to fight. He had been shot up in the last war and he seemed not the least averse to getting shot up again."

Allen was in these respects very much like his second in command. But Ted Roosevelt and Terry Allen differed in other aspects of character. Allen was a hard drinker and an easy man with profanities. Of this "picturesque" language Pyle noted, "No writer can fully capture him on paper, because his talk was so wonderfully profane it couldn't be put down in black and white."

Examples of Allen's vivid language and his solicitude for his men presented themselves two days after the landing. At Saint-Cloud on November 9 French artillery pounded the 18th Regimental Combat Team.
When its commander, Col. Frank Grier, ordered three battalions pulled
back to regroup while U.S. artillery prepared to shell the town, Allen
rushed to the area. With spicy language he called off the bombardment.
Rather than kill four thousand civilians, and who could say how many
Americans, in an attack, he decided to bypass the town. This decision,
his first of the war, would be seen by other commanders as "pampering"
his men.

Another instance involving a decision to shell or not shell a town was
related by Eleanor in her book. She recounted the arrival at the American hospital at Salisbury, England, of a group of wounded men from
the 1st Division. They told her that after the heights above Oran had
been captured, the city still held out. The question for Ted was whether
to bombard it into submission. He ordered nothing be done for the moment and drove into town to give it a chance to surrender. His jeep flew
a flag of truce in the form of a white undershirt. "If I'm not back in two
hours," he told artillery officers, "give it all you've got."

The holdouts gave up and Ted returned unscathed.

Eleanor was "inclined to think that this story was merely one of the
legends growing up around Ted." After the war she asked Ted's aide, Bill
Gordon, about the tale. "They got only one detail wrong," he said. "It
wasn't a jeep, it was a half-track. I know, because I drove it."

During the first months of fighting in Tunisia the character of the 1st
Division changed as men were killed or wounded and replacements arrived. Eisenhower also delegated the British general Kenneth Anderson
to organize an offensive against Tunisia by combining British troops with
the 1st Division. This reshaping put Ted in command of three battalions
of the 26th Infantry; a company of American light tanks; U.S., British,
and French artillery batteries; and six thousand Arab irregulars with
French officers. Ted's chief of staff was French. The mongrel outfit was
named Groupement Roosevelt.

In New York City on January 14, 1943, Alexander Woollcott sent Ted
a chatty letter. In a postscript he noted an interesting bit of history about
the place where Ted's troops had landed in North Africa:

In May of 1919 at least one transport started back to Brooklyn from
Marseilles. Aboard it were sundry very recent civilians, including

ex-Private Harold W. Ross [he returned to start *The New Yorker*] and Sergeant Alexander Woollcott (Ret.). En route, where it stopped for coal, it was delayed for five days by a longshoreman's strike. This port was Oran. Did you know that part of the last AEF strayed as far as Oran? Curious one-piece bathing suits in wide alternate stripes of shell-pink and baby-blue were available at five francs each. Clad in these, both Ross and I aroused unfavorable comment as we sported in the waves of the gulf of Mers el Kebir.

The day before Woollcott wrote to Ted, he'd written to Ted's son Quentin. Beginning with the salutation "Son of Heaven," Woollcott said that if Quentin had not heard from him earlier, it was "not because some letter from me went to the bottom of the sea." He had failed to write for various reasons, "chief among them my sense of that unbridgeable gulf between soldiers and civilians."

This inhibition, he continued, had been partly the result of a recent letter from Thornton Wilder. Serving as a captain in air force intelligence, the three-time winner of the Pulitzer Prize (*The Bridge of San Luis Rey*, 1927; the plays *Our Town*, 1938, and *The Skin of Our Teeth*, 1941) had written to Woollcott, "Nothing so lifts a soldier's morale as getting a letter from home, and nothing so depresses him as reading it."

In a letter "made up largely of oddments," Woollcott told Quentin that he had recently "tottered to Washington on sundry pieces of mischief, and was kindly lodged by such of your relatives as now live in the White House." (FDR was so fond of Woollcott and his radio shows that he was a frequent overnight visitor, and sometimes remained longer.) "My host and hostess were hardly on the train to Hyde Park when I invited an out-of-season Roosevelt [Quentin's brother Cornelius] over for breakfast [in the White House]. I found the ensign in tip-top shape. I had always known that he was the sport of the family, no Roosevelt at all really. Cornelius is so like your mother in every mannerism and gesture and look that I would have thought she was sitting there telling me where I got off."

The letter ended, "Of course you are always in my thoughts, and so's your old man."

Woollcott's letters would be greatly delayed in reaching the Roosevelts. That month the Germans counterattacked in a thrust into the Ouseltia Valley and with a two-pronged assault on Americans around Kasserine. Orders from Allied headquarters to the 1st Division were to keep Rommel and his Afrika Korps from breaking out and driving the American forces back into the Mediterranean Sea.

The German advance was covered from the air by Messerschmitt fighters. Swooping low, they strafed troops as they scattered for cover. One of the scrambling figures who was hit was Lt. Quentin Roosevelt II. A piece of shell struck him in the chest, pierced a lung, and lodged in his liver. He was evacuated and examined in the only field hospital that had not been ordered to pull back. A surgical team tried to remove the fragment, but decided to leave it for surgeons at a hospital in the rear. It would be at least several days before he could be evacuated.

On the third day after Quentin was wounded, the news reached Ted that his son's temperature had reached one hundred and four degrees and that he was in danger of dying. The fighting had subsided, permitting Ted to drive sixty miles to the hospital. Fearing the worst, he found Quentin asleep on a cot in a tent with a dirt floor. Doctors reported that his fever had eased and he was doing better, permitting transfer to a hospital in Oran. Because an infection developed in his lung, he stayed four months before going home. He arrived at Sagamore Hill in June 1943.

To help his grandmother Edith nurse him back to health, Eleanor resigned her Red Cross position in England and went home. She found Quentin vowing to get back into the war. He did so eight weeks later, in command of his battery in the 33d Field Artillery in Sicily.

In February 1943 a momentarily homesick Ted wrote to Eleanor:

When I'm riding in my jeep or rolled up in my blankets I plan what we'll do after the war. Here's my plan, God willing.

The arrival in the morning. Then, a very good barber for a short haircut, a manicure, a shampoo, and so forth. Squash-racquets at the River Club for a big sweat and rub-down. Then upstairs to your room in the Club where we doze and read, the children popping in and out. Meanwhile, my uniform has been cleaned and pressed, my shoes polished until they're brown mirrors, and clean—spotlessly clean—linen is laid out. Then we get dressed, you and I. Here comes a hitch.

I can't decide what you ought to wear, your Red Cross uniform or your best clothes.

The children have been all doing the same and we meet in the bar, ostensible purpose to have a cocktail, real purpose to have friends admire us—three Navy blue or white uniforms, two army.

Next dinner. Here again I'm not sure. The dinner must be good, but obviously there must be people to look at us, and some will get up to greet us. We'll be very nice to them! After dinner—Madison

Square Garden or a play. Probably a play, though Madison Square Garden would provide more people to look! Then 21 or the Stork Club. More people of a different kind would be the reason for the Stork Club (I've been there only once).

Finally, all into cars and out to Oyster Bay, where next day we'll all revert to type.

The timetable laid out by Eisenhower for quickly capturing North Africa and taking the island of Sicily as a stepping-stone toward landing in Europe by way of Italy had been thrown off by the battle at the Kasserine Pass. Three thousand GIs had been killed or wounded, 3,700 men captured, and 200 tanks destroyed. This first real measure of the fighting ability of the American troops had been seen as a disastrous and embarrassing fiasco.

Blaming the field commander, Gen. Lloyd Fredendall, a shaken Eisenhower turned to an old friend to replace him. To restore American prestige and give GIs back their self-respect as a fighting force, he chose a cocky, spit-and-polish general, George S. Patton. He had been based at Casablanca and charged with planning the invasion of Sicily.

Patton's priority was to galvanize the troops who would carry it out by improving their discipline, dress, and the condition of their weaponry. To achieve this he visited every battalion in four divisions to make it clear that winning battles depended on every soldier being obedient. This meant following all regulations, from wearing leggings and helmets to adhering to military etiquette by saluting. In all of these matters he found no outfit more lax than the 1st Division.

During an inspection of Allen's headquarters he noticed slit tenches and foxholes. He asked Allen what they were for. Allen replied that they were for use during air raids.

Patton asked, "Which one is yours?"

Allen showed him. Patton urinated in it.

Zipping up his fly, he said contemptuously, "Now try to use it."

According to Patton biographer Carlo D'Este in *Patton: A Genius for War,* sentries who observed this took it as an insult to Allen and to General Roosevelt. They released the safeties of their machine guns and were ready to open fire on Patton on a word from either Allen or Ted. Patton quickly departed.

The flamboyant two-star general with specially tailored uniforms and a brace of pistols with ivory grips was not alone in finding fault with the 1st Division's military image. An aide to Eisenhower, Maj. Gen. John

Lucas, noted in his diary, "The division has been babied too much. They have been told so often that they are the best in the world, [but] as far as real discipline is concerned they have become one of the poorest. They look dirty and they never salute an officer if they can help it." Ike blamed Allen for this and told Patton to order Allen to shape up his men.

If Sicily were to be taken, the Afrika Korps had to be beaten first. Patton explained how to achieve this at a supper for division generals and commanders of artillery and armored units. The Allen-Roosevelt 1st Infantry would join the 1st Armored Division to attack Gafsa and Meknassy.

During the night of March 16, Ted's troops marched for forty-five minutes in pouring rain, drove out the Germans, and secured Gafsa in the morning. They then marched ten miles and took the town of El Guettar and found themselves facing two divisions of panzer tanks. When the fighting ended, the enemy was in retreat and thirty tanks were in flames. The victory erased the idea that Americans could not fight.

So pleased was Patton with Terry Allen and Ted Roosevelt's squared-up division that in the plan for invading Sicily, code-named Husky, the 1st was given a crucial assignment. More than seven Allied divisions were to land along one hundred miles of coast. At the center, where the greatest German resistance was anticipated, the 1st would have as its objective the town of Gela. Patton's message to the troops stressed the pride they deserved for having been selected to share the privilege of attacking and destroying the enemy. They had in their hands "the glory of American arms, the honor of the U.S. Army, and the future of the world." He concluded, "See that you are worthy of this great trust."

As Patton was exhorting the troops, Brigadier General Roosevelt was getting around with the help of a cane. Before returning to active duty in 1941 he had complained to Eleanor of pain in his hip. Doctors studied X-rays and found marked traces of arthritis around an old football injury that had been aggravated by his playing squash for years on hard courts. They had advised him to stop all strenuous physical exercise. But when another doctor told him that wild horses with similar arthritic problems were known to go through their life-span without being crippled, Ted continued his regimen of daily strenuous exercising. The result was increasingly nagging pain that he did not report to army doctors. The need for the cane was explained away as "a temporary thing because of a minor sprain."

D day for the invasion of Sicily was July 10, 1943. Right on schedule the 1st Division went in. But this was not Oran. The resistance was fierce from German and Italian divisions. They were driven back only by heavy naval fire, but were expected to attack again the next morning. Knowing that holding Gela depended on the 1st Division, Patton came ashore at 9:30 A.M. and drove to the town for a conference with his two generals, Allen and Roosevelt. After their men met and repelled the expected attack, Patton said that only the "battle-experienced division could have withstood and turned it back."

Eleanor learned a few details of the action in a letter from Ted's aide, Lt. Marcus O. Stevenson, known to everyone as Stevie:

> For the second time the General hit a beach at H-Hour [the first was at Oran] and established the advanced Division Command Post. The operation went well until afternoon when the Germans attempted to split our land forces with a tank attack before our anti-tank equipment had been put ashore. The General saw it coming, huge clouds of dust from oncoming tanks. He rushed in his jeep on a parallel road back to the C.P. and gave the alarm. On his way back he met the 18th Infantry cannon company, put them into position, and personally directed our counterattack. This saved the landing from being pushed back into the sea.

At some point in the twenty-three days of hard fighting in Sicily Ted was hit by a spent fragment of a mortar shell and had two teeth broken.

In late July the 1st Division assaulted the town of Troina. The troops did so with all the pride and self-confidence for which the division had become famous, or, in the view of some observers, notorious. Among those who believed the Allen-Roosevelt outfit had become too big for its britches was the supreme commander of the Sicilian campaign, Gen. Omar Bradley. A classmate of Eisenhower at West Point, he had taken command of the II Corps from Patton in North Africa. He'd proven his mettle on May 7 at Bizerte when troops under his command took 40,000 prisoners. He had none of Patton's swagger and little patience for such showboating. He had even less tolerance of recklessness in his generals. In reviewing the performance of the 1st Division in Sicily he came to the conclusion that under General Allen it "had become increasingly temperamental, disdainful of both regulations and senior commands, [and] thought itself exempted from the need for discipline by virtue of its months in the line."

As for Allen, he had become too much of an individualist to submerge himself without friction in the group undertakings of war. The

1st Division under Allen's command had become "too full of self-pity and pride."

To "save Allen both from himself and from his brilliant record and to save the division from the heady effects of too much success," Bradley decided to "separate them."

A persuasive case can be argued that Bradley was angry and perhaps jealous. Anger came from the fact that Allen had never been part of the inner circle of the West Point graduates who turned out to be generals in the greatest war in history. Nor did Allen's personal demeanor of carousing with his staff in off-duty hours sit well with Bradley. The jealousy stemmed from the successes of the 1st Division and the popularity of Allen and his aide, Ted Roosevelt, with their troops and war correspondents whose accounts of the 1st Division's actions contributed to the division's image as "the best and the fightin'est in the army."

In deciding to relieve Allen of command Bradley cited the Allied assault on Tunisia in May 1943 in which Allen "foolishly ordered his division into a completely unauthorized attack and was thrown back with heavy losses." Allen then "ran amok along the entire coast of North Africa from Bizerte to Oran." But the final straw was the assault on Troina in Sicily when Allen "miscalculated the enemy's strength and verve and was thrown back with heavy losses." In the seven days of heavy fighting that ensued "he attempted to operate much as he had in the past, as an undisciplined, independent army, unresponsive to my wishes—or in some cases, orders."

None of these sins in Bradley's eyes tainted Allen's second in command, but military form dictated that when the top man was fired, the deputy went with him. Allen was sent back to the States and a training command. On December 18, 1943, Ted was appointed Eisenhower's chief liaison officer between the U.S. Fifth Army under Gen. Mark Clark and the French Expeditionary Corps under Gen. Alphonse Juin.

While the French were still in Africa preparing for the planned invasion of Italy, Ted was detached on a mission to Sardinia to deal with an Italian parachute division that was holding out on the island and refusing to surrender. Unarmed, he visited them and found the soldiers to be "good, plug-ugly roughnecks," not unlike the cowboys of TR's Rough Riders. He went from unit to unit to talk to them in personal terms, asking where and how they had got their medals, inquiring about families, and telling them that he knew them to be good fighters and that they could be put to good use in driving the Germans out of their beloved Italy.

Observing this was Lt. Col. Serge Obolensky of the OSS (Office of Strategic Services, the U.S. wartime spy agency headed by Ted's friend Wild Bill Donovan). Obolensky would write of Ted's performance that day, "By the sheer force and charm of his personality and an exhibition of the coolest gallantry he won the wavering troops to a wild personal ovation."

Ten years later in a conversation with one of the Italians, Obolensky wrote in his book of memoirs, *One Man in His Time,* he learned that six of the paratroopers had been designated to kill Ted and Obolensky, but the Italians had been "so impressed by his manner and the fact that we were alone and unarmed that they were delighted to become our allies."

Shortly before Christmas, Ted accompanied the French Expeditionary Corps into the line in Italy near Cassino. He wrote to Eleanor of his admiration for the troops and their commander, Alphonse Juin, whom he called "a front-fighting general." Of the action he wrote, "It has been bitter, with every foot of ground paid for in blood. Attack and counter attack have succeeded one another in unending sequence. Day has merged into night and night into day until time seemed to have no periods. I've been at the front every day, usually with Juin. My memory of this part of Italy will always be a series of rugged hills, the valleys between filled with smoke and echoing with the rumble of artillery and the rattle of small-arms."

Getting around this rugged terrain was by way of a jeep pulling a half-ton trailer, which served as his home. With him were Stevie and a driver, Kurt Show, who'd found a bucket of white paint and adorned the front of the jeep with the words *Rough Rider.* Although Ted was afraid this would be interpreted by war correspondents and photographers as a brazen attempt to remind the world that Ted was TR's son, out of respect and fondness for Kurt Show he left the name on the jeep. Its windshield soon had a German or Italian bullet hole in it.

When Ted received orders from Eisenhower's headquarters to leave Italy for England at the end of February 1944, General Juin wrote to him, "There is no one in the Corps from the lowliest private to the most be-starred general who does not know and love you. At our most exposed places, such as the front line of battle, you appeared every day at one point or another with your great calm, your wide smile, and your good words, to see that all was going well and to attend to necessary liaison. It is with profound distress that I see you go."

He left the campaigns in North Africa, Sicily, and Italy entitled to wear on his uniform the Bronze Star with Oak Leaf Cluster and his second French Croix de Guerre.

On the sixth of January 1944, the twenty-fifth anniversary of TR's death, while Brig. Gen. Ted Roosevelt was at the front in Italy in his jeep "Rough Rider," Lt. Col. Archibald Roosevelt, commanding a battalion of the 162d Infantry, 41st Division, was half the world away. Deep in an uncharted jungle on the island of New Guinea, together with units of the Australian 3d Division, Archie's men had driven the Japanese from Salamauna. At the end of the battle he asked his comrades to pause for a few moments of remembrance for his father. The Australians decided that the best way to pay tribute to Theodore Roosevelt would be to name the ground on which they stood "Roosevelt Ridge."

His Aussie comrades admitted that when it came to guts, they had never seen the likes of Archie. He acted as if he were an immortal, impervious to the perils of combat. To locate Japanese gun placements he'd gone out in the open in a boat with binoculars, a pencil, and a map to mark the spots from which they fired at him. When an accompanying soldier flattened himself on the bottom of the boat, Archie told him, "Don't worry. You're safe with me, kid. I was wounded three times in the last war, and that's a lucky charm."

A few days later, shrapnel from a Japanese grenade slammed into the knee that had been shattered in World War I. The wound resulted in the third son of TR being declared one hundred percent disabled for the second time, making Archie the only man in the long saga of Americans at war to have earned that distinction.

While Archie slogged through Pacific jungles and Ted fought across the wastelands of North Africa and the lush landscapes of Sicily and Italy, their beloved brother Kermit had been drinking from his metaphorical "fountain of youth" and imbibing wine in saloons in Alaska. But early in 1943 he had suffered internal bleeding as a result of his diseased liver. Returned to the States by the army for treatment, he drifted back into heavy drinking. At the request of his wife, Belle, who hoped being on duty again would help him stop, the War Department ordered him back to Fort Richardson. On the night of June 3, 1943, he went to his room, put an Army Colt .45 automatic pistol under his chin, and fired.

In keeping with TR's belief that "where a tree falls, there let it lay," he was buried at Fort Richardson in Grave 72, Plot A, with an army-issue white headstone.

One year and three days later, Kermit's brother Ted and Ted's son would gain a place in American military annals by being the only father and son to be in the first wave of troops going in on the beaches of Normandy.

27

Throughout Ted's tour of duty as U.S. liaison officer to French forces in Italy, Eleanor recalled in her autobiography, he wrote to Gen. Omar Bradley and Ike's chief aide, Gen. Walter Bedell Smith, pleading for a return to action. Feeling certain that the long-delayed cross-Channel invasion of France was imminent, he dreaded that he might be left out, as his father had feared missing the invasion of Cuba in 1898. He asked Eleanor to go to Washington to carry his request to General Marshall. When she questioned the propriety of "pulling strings," he assured her it was all right to ask a favor in order to get him a more dangerous job.

When he received orders late in February 1944 to report to London for reassignment, he told Eleanor he was "overjoyed." But on his way to England the bright anticipation of getting a new combat command dimmed. Soon after boarding the plane for the first leg of the four-day journey, he felt ill and started running a fever. During a layover, an army doctor found his temperature well over 103 degrees. He diagnosed pneumonia and recommended hospitalization. Ted pulled rank and refused. When he arrived in London, he again balked at going to a hospital. He demanded transportation to Eisenhower's Grosvenor Square headquarters to see General Smith. Assured that he would be placed with troops as soon as he was well, and that he would not find himself left behind on D day, he checked into a hospital.

Although he had what his doctors called the worst type of pneumococcus and would be in the hospital at least three weeks, he was glad to rest in a clean, warm place where the food was hot and plenty of books were available to keep him occupied. His only complaint was with the nurses. In a letter to Eleanor he griped, "They are kittenish and arch, and always say brightly, 'Well, how are we today?' One has patted me three times on the head. I suppose it's what elderly generals like, but it shrivels me up inside. If she does it again I'm going to pat her hard, not on the head."

At the end of the predicted three weeks in the hospital he was pronounced ready to be discharged and to accept his new post. His orders were to report to Maj. Gen. Raymond O. Barton, commander, 4th Infantry Division. A regular army outfit, it had arrived in strength in England in January and was based at Crompton. It came with an illustrious record.

Formed in December 1917 under the command of Maj. Gen. George H. Cameron, it went into action in the Aisne-Marne campaign, which began on July 18, 1918. In the next four months, both on the line and in reserve, it was the only U.S. division to serve in both French and British sectors of the Western Front. By Armistice Day it suffered 14,500 killed and wounded.

Reactivated on June 1, 1940, at Fort Benning, Georgia, the 4th found itself sharing training areas with the newly organized 2d Armored Division, commanded by George S. Patton. But the 4th was a very different outfit from that which had fought in France. The table of organization had been changed to reflect the army's new doctrine of moving quickly and being more responsive to combat conditions. This meant paring division strength to 15,000. Gone was the old brigade structure. There were now three infantry regiments, each with about three thousand men, divided into three battalions. This "triangular" structure allowed commanders much more flexibility and could be customized for particular missions. The three regiments were the 8th, 12th, and 22d Infantry.

Artillery battalions were the 20th, 29th, 42d, and 44th. In addition there were the 704th Ordnance Company, 4th Quartermaster Company, 4th Signal Company, 4th Medical Battalion, 4th Engineer Battalion, 4th Counterintelligence Corps Detachment, a military police platoon, and the 4th Reconnaissance Troops (Mechanized).

From June 1, 1940, to late 1943 the division had served as an experimental division to implement theories developed in the 1930s concerning combining and restructuring units. These ideas and others were tested during maneuvers at Fort Benning and in war games, which involved 400,000 troops in Louisiana in August 1941.

Its uniform arm patch was a triangle with four ivy leaves, giving the division the nickname "Ivy Green." Its men also called it "the Fighting Fourth."

• • •

As part of VII Corps, the role of the 4th Division in the assault on the Normandy beaches of France was to take and hold the westernmost sector, code named Utah; break out; and proceed up the Cotentin Peninsula to capture the port of Cherbourg. Landings would be preceded by intensive air and naval bombardments. This bold amphibious attack against Germany's so-called "impenetrable Atlantic Wall" was an invasion plan of a magnitude that had never been tried in the history of warfare. Dress rehearsals for the big day were to be staged at the Assault Training Center at Woolacombe, England, and at Slapton Sands. Infantry units and combat engineers ran through exercises with code names Duck, Fox, Tiger, and Fabius.

The objective of these run-throughs, wrote D-day historian Stephen E. Ambrose, "was to make the men believe that combat could not possibly be worse than what they were undergoing, so that they would look forward to their release from training and their commitment to battle."

It was after one such exercise that Ted wrote to Eleanor of spending the day shivering in soaked clothes in a small boat, and that if his health were being tested, he'd proved he was fit.

Most of the men under his command were draftees. Joseph S. Blaylock Sr., of Wiggins, Mississippi, had been called up on November 6, 1941. His expectation that he would serve one year was sunk a month and a day later, along with most of the ships of U.S. Pacific Fleet in the Japanese attack on Pearl Harbor. In late May 1944 he was with the 4th Division, 4th Motorized Division, 20th Field Artillery, B (Baker) Battery. When orders came to pull out of Compton into marshaling areas, he recalled, "the whole town turned out to say good-bye to us, because they had the feeling and we had the feeling that this was the real thing." When they reached their destination, most of their time was spent in tents. The talk among the men was "This is it," and that they'd made good preparation. "It was time for us to do the job that we were trained for."

In his contribution to the "oral history" of D day compiled at the Eisenhower Center for Leadership Studies at the University of New Orleans, Blaylock continued, "On June 3 we were called into a big tent and were given a talk by General Barton, and then some of the commanders took over and broke us into groups and told us where we were going to land. It was Utah Beach, and they also explained to us where Omaha Beach would be and where the French and English and the Canadians would be—and they told us about Normandy."

• • •

In books and stories of war when it was glorious, in Shakespeare's plays, in histories of Britain, and on maps old and new that had enthralled Ted Roosevelt as a boy at Sagamore Hill, the name Normandy had been writ large. Julius Caesar's legions had claimed it for Rome. In the third century Christianity was the conqueror. Then came the Franks, and then the Norsemen, who gave their name to the peninsula and whose chief, Rollo, was the first duke of Normandy. From there in 1066 went William, duke of Normandy, to lay claim to Britain, earn the name "Conqueror," and begin a series of struggles for its possession between the English and the French until the land was permanently ceded to France in 1450. It was in France that Shakespeare gave the English king Henry V the greatest exhortation to battle in all of literature:

We few, we happy few, we band of brothers;
For he today that sheds his blood with me
Shall be my brother; be he ne'er so vile
This day shall gentle his condition;
And gentlemen in England now abed
Shall think themselves accursed they were not here.

From geography studies Ted knew Normandy was a region of farmlands, forests, and gentle hills. Its great cities were Rouen and the ports of Le Havre and Cherbourg, the latter at the tip of the Cotentin Peninsula, which jutted north into the English Channel like a thumb. Normandy's pleasure beaches were Deauville, Granville, and Etretat. Beaches marked on the map shown to Joe Blaylock and the other soldiers who would assault them were named, right to left: Utah, Omaha, Gold, Juno, and Sword. Utah would hold the right flank, Juno and Sword the left. Omaha was in the center.

What the troops of the 4th Division did not know was that in the original grand plan there had been no Utah. When the plan was drawn in the summer of 1943, it was felt that there would not be enough resources and manpower to launch an attack on the Cotentin. But when General Eisenhower assumed supreme command in January 1944, it seemed to him and his subordinate commanders that swift capture of the peninsula and Cherbourg's port were vital to the success of the invasion.

The mission was assigned to VII Corps, commanded by Gen. J. Lawton Collins. His superior was General Bradley. As chief of the First U.S.

Army his command consisted of VII Corps on Utah and V Corps, which was to land at Omaha. On Bradley's left flank was Second British Army under Lt. Gen. Miles C. Dempsey. The two armies together formed the 21st Army Group. Its overall ground commander for the assault phase was British general Sir Bernard L. Montgomery.

Transporting the troops, providing protection from the sea, and breaching of underwater obstacles were the responsibility of U.S. Navy Task Force U, commanded by RAdm. Don P. Moon. While the troops were training and then awaiting their orders to board ships, Moon and General Collins and their staffs were finalizing details of the operation in a fenced-in Quonset-hut camp on Fore Street in the port of Plymouth. Task Force U would consist of twelve convoys totaling 825 large vessels and small craft. To reach nine loading and sortie points most of the convoys would be divided into three or four sections and sail from different ports.

The ships designated for conveying the troops landing on Utah Beach were the *Barnet, Bayfield, Dickman,* and *Empire.* The commander of the 4th Division, General Barton, would be on the *Bayfield.* Troops from it and *Barnet* would land from the west on a portion of Utah Beach designated "Uncle Red Beach." The men from the other ships would go ashore at "Tare Green" and "Victor." Between high and low watermarks the approximately three-mile-wide terrain was smooth with a shallow gradient and compact gray sand. It was backed by a four- to eight-foot-high masonry sea wall that stretched 10,000 yards. Sand was piled against it in many places, forming a ramp to the top, which held a wire fence. Gaps in this barricade provided access to roads that led to the beach, but these openings were closed with huge concrete blocks. Behind the wall were sand dunes ranging from ten to twenty feet in height. Beyond the wall low flatlands had been flooded. They were shown on planning maps as "inundated areas" and could be easily defended from their western banks and exits by relatively small enemy forces.

The blocked roads leading from the beach through these areas were called "exits" and numbered 1 to 4. The main towns beyond inundated areas were Pouppeville (1), La Houssaye, (2), Turqueville (3), and St. Martin-de-Varreville and St. Germaine-de-Varreville (4). Largest of the inland towns was Ste. Mère-Eglise. This key location was to be attacked on the night before the landings by the 101st Airborne Division with the objective of capturing it and blocking the eastern approaches to the Cotentin Peninsula. At the same time the 82d Airborne was to land west of the town of St. Sauveur-le-Vicomte to seal western approaches.

Access by sea to the beach was hindered by obstacles in the form of stakes and piles that slanted seaward. They were placed from 50 to 130 yards from the beach. Barricade-like gates made of steel angles and plates and mounted on small rollers were known as "Belgian gates." Defenses behind the seawall were pillboxes made of tank turrets mounted in concrete, firing trenches, a bigger German version of foxholes known as "Tobruk pits," and bunkers. These were laid out to provide interlocking fields of fire. Aerial reconnaissance had also revealed that new open field battery emplacements were under construction. About two miles inland were several coastal and field batteries. This zone of defense was the responsibility of the German Seventh Army, commanded by Col. Gen. Friedrich Dollmann. Intelligence estimates placed the enemy strength at two infantry divisions (the 709th and 243d.) The 709th was situated generally along the east coast. On the west was the 243d. Two other divisions, the 716th and 352d, east and south of the peninsula, were not deemed capable of affecting the landings. These forces were augmented by the 91st Division to the rear of the 709th. Its appearance had caught Allied planners by surprise and forced modifications in the deployment of VII Corps and the mission of the 82d Airborne. But the mission of VII Corps as defined in Field Order No. 1, dated May 28, 1944, remained the same: "VII Corps assaults Utah Beach on D Day at H Hour and captures Cherbourg with minimum delay."

For Brigadier General Roosevelt, planning of a far different kind had been on his mind in the months leading up to his appointment with Utah Beach. He learned in March that Quentin had become engaged to a young woman from Kansas City who was in the Red Cross. Her name was Frances Webb. Despite the certainty that Quentin would soon be taking part in the invasion and acknowledging that he might be killed, and even the likelihood of it, they planned to get married on April 12. Eleanor heard the news from Ted. "Don't worry about Quentin," he wrote. "Just feel happy about him. All is well."

That Quentin and Frances were not the first to let Eleanor know was the fault of military censorship. Both had written her letters, but they had been impounded because of the impending invasion. Eleanor informed the surprised and pleased parents of the prospective bride.

With Ted as best man, Quentin and Frances were married at the Church of St. Peter and St. Paul in Blandford, England. Ted wrote to Eleanor, "Thank God I was here at this time, but I miss you something awful. I am not used to being two mothers and two fathers all at the same time. I feel as if I should flit from place to place dressing first the bride, then the groom, then giving the bride away and acting as best man. With all the work I must do I have so little time to help them." The wedding breakfast was given by Quentin's former outfit, the 33d Field Artillery.

Ted described the scene at the unit's headquarters in a letter to Eleanor:

It was very touching, for everyone from the battalion CO to the junior cook had done their best. At home perhaps it wouldn't seem much, a shabby barracks, card tables and chairs, coarse food, bad punch, harsh coffee in thick cups, heavy cake—but no one thought this, least of all the bride and groom. To them and to all it was wonderful—a breakfast arranged with every effort possible and respect and affection.

We sang songs—we had the 26th Infantry orchestra—and Q played his accordion. We drank toasts to the bride and groom, to the two mothers, the two fathers, and the best man, and finally I proposed a toast to the absent wives. After that I kissed them both good-bye, and to the rattle of tin cans they drove away. They've gone on their honeymoon to a seaside resort for five days, and Frances has an evening dress!

And, bless their hearts, they're very happy. There are shadows when they stop to think, but Frances believes God could not be so cruel.

On D day Quentin would be in a far different environment from that which confronted his father. Omaha Beach was a heavily defended, narrow stretch covered with small, smooth rocks (shingle) backed by bluffs that provided the enemy enfilade fire that covered the entire landing area. The GI hitting the beach in the first wave at Omaha, historian Stephen E. Ambrose noted, would have to get through minefields in the Channel without his ship blowing up, then be under fire as he debarked from a Higgins landing craft, and work his way through waist-deep water strewn with obstacles and mines to cross a tidal flat that was being raked by machine-gun and cannon fire from both sides and in front. High ground commanded all approaches to the beach. Any advance by U.S. troops from the beach was limited to the narrow passages

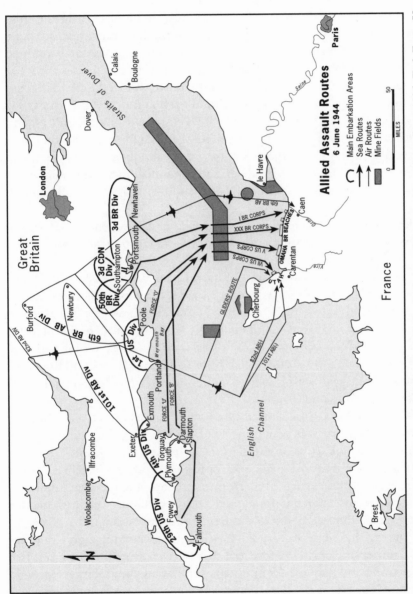

Allied Assault Routes
6 June 1944

Main Embarkation Areas
Sea Routes
Air Routes
Mine Fields

0   50
MILES

Allied assault routes across the English Channel. Ted sailed aboard the troop transport *Barnet* with Task Force U from the port of Torquay to land on Utah Beach with VII Corps.

between steep bluffs. Pillboxes were situated in the draws to crossfire east and west.

"If the GI was not killed getting off his landing craft or crossing the tidal flat," wrote Ambrose, "if by some miracle he made it to the shingle," Field Marshal Erwin Rommel, the German commander and planner of the defenses known as the Atlantic Wall "wanted him wounded before he got there. If not wounded, paralyzed by fear."

Omaha was between the Cotentin Peninsula and a flat plain in front of the vital city of Caen. Linking Utah Beach and the British and Canadian beaches (Gold, Juno, Sword), it was assigned to V Corps's 1st and 29th Divisions, supported by the 5th Ranger Battalion and 5th Engineer Special Brigade. The objective was to gain a lodgement area between Port-en-Bessin and the Vire River and then push forward to sever German communications at Caumont and capture a major railroad junction at St. Lô.

Naval historian Samuel Eliot Morison later called Omaha Beach "the best imitation of hell for an invading force" that American troops would encounter anywhere in the war.

This enormous cross-Channel enterprise had begun in early 1944 with a staff of planners known as Group Two, XI Amphibious Force, based in England, and code-named Neptune. Before Eisenhower left the Mediterranean front he'd sent members of his staff to formulate the plan for landings termed "Overlord." By February 3, 1944, Neptune had U.S. Navy bases as far west as the Welsh ports of Milford Haven and Rosneath and in the English seaside cities of Falmouth, Dartmouth, Salcombe, Appledore, Instow, and Plymouth.

On March 6, 1944, Admiral Moon and his forward echelon staff arrived in the port from which the Pilgrims had set sail in the *Mayflower.* With his headquarters on the *Bayfield,* a ship manned by the U.S. Coast Guard, Moon had overseen a pair of full-scale rehearsals of Task Force U in late April and early May. Troops and equipment embarked in the same ships and left from the same ports to which they were assigned for an invasion that seemed likely to happen in early June.

During the night of April 26–27 the ships passed through Lyme Bay with minesweepers in the fore as if they were crossing the Channel. Two destroyers and five smaller gunboats kept a watch for German torpedo boats (E-boats). As the fleet maneuvered in Lyme Bay around midnight on April 27–28, nine subs out of Cherbourg that had slipped past patrols

moved in to attack. A few minutes after two o'clock, a torpedo hit landing ship LST-507. It burst into flames, rolled over, and sank. A battle ensued in which the destroyers engaged the E-boats for about half an hour
while the troopships escaped under a cover of smoke. LST-289 took a
hit from a torpedo but managed to make port. In this brief fight that
many considered the first action of Neptune-Overlord, 197 sailors and
441 soldiers were killed.

By the middle of May the plans for the invasion were complete, but
subject to change to accord with altered or unexpected conditions, such
as bad weather. On the fifteenth a final review of the plan was held at
Montgomery's headquarters, with King George VI and Prime Minister
Churchill attending. Minutes of the meeting called the group "the
greatest assembly of military leadership the world has ever known."

Eisenhower told them, "I consider it the duty of anyone who sees a
flaw in the plan not to hesitate to say so." The meeting ended with no
changes made.

Beyond the walls of Montgomery's headquarters few men of the millions of soldiers, sailors, and airmen gathered into camps in southern
England knew when and where the plan was to be tested. But after the
meeting the circle of knowledge widened as briefings were held. The one
for Ted Roosevelt's 4th Division was conducted using a huge sponge-rub-
ber replica made to scale of the Cotentin Peninsula. Laid out in minute
detail were its coasts, hills, rivers, bridges, hedgerows, roads, communication and power lines, strategic sites, landmarks, fortifications, and
places of enemy deployments.

For a briefing by General Bradley nearly a thousand officers crowded
into a vast hanger and took seats by rank. Lowly lieutenants were in the
back, captains and majors in the center, and colonels in front rows. Generals were on the platform. "Gentlemen," began Bradley, "this is going
to be the greatest show on earth. You are honored by having ringside
seats."

A voice from behind him blurted, "Ringside, hell. We'll be in the
arena."

Every officer and gentleman in the hanger heard Ted. As they
laughed, so did the general who had so recently relieved Ted of his command.

Long before Theodore Roosevelt Jr. took his seat in that hangar he
had learned that the success of any military operation, from a handful

of infantrymen on patrol to the movements of regiments and divisions, depended on two factors: terrain and weather. The skies above the hangar as Bradley spoke were clear, the air warm, the winds mild.

The fair weather didn't last.

28

Task Force U was to load troops in five ports between Plymouth and Tor-cross. Ted was to board the APA *Barnet,* a transport designated for the 2d Battalion. Late at night in the town of Torquay, he stood beside Capt. George Mabry watching the men march down a street toward the dock. A two-man mortar team passed. One of the men was tall and burly and had the tube of the 88mm mortar on his back. His short comrade carried the heavy steel baseplate.

Observing this Abbott-and-Costello-like duo, Ted tapped his cane on the ground and said to Mabry through a grin, "Isn't that typical? The big man always gets the small load and the little man always gets the big load."

The short soldier hunched the weighty base a little higher on his shoulder, peered at the slightly built brigadier general, noted that he was no taller than himself, and replied with a big grin, "That's right, General Roosevelt, but we can take it, can't we?"

Mabry found the situation typical of the attitude of GIs who served under Ted. "General Roosevelt loved soldiers," he said, "and he was a soldier's general."

The armada was to organize for the Channel crossing into twelve convoys. Loading was scheduled for June 3. Timing depended on the phase of the moon and its effect on tides at the landing sites. Eisenhower noted in his diary, "My tentative thought is that the desirability for getting started on the next favorable tide is so great and the uncertainty of the weather is such that we could never anticipate really perfect weather coincident with proper tidal conditions, that we must go unless there is a real and very serious deterioration in the weather."

That seemed to be exactly what was happening. Beautiful conditions that had prevailed while Ted listened to General Bradley's briefing had turned ugly. Proving the truth of a warning from Ike's meteorologist, Group Captain J. M. Stagg, that "weather in this country is practically unpredictable," southeast Britain was experiencing wind-driven, relentless rain. Even the largest ships in the invasion armada arrayed in the ports bobbed upon churning water like corks. Aboard them was an armed force that Ike saw as a "mighty host," tense as "a coiled spring." It poised eagerly and anxiously for his signal to go.

Waiting with them, Ted wrote to his wife about General Barton's having given him permission to land at Utah with the first wave of troops and of his concerns for Quentin going in at H-Hour on Omaha, where "it may be worse than when I go in." As he penned the letter he was at sea with the men of the 4th Division. Their ships circled off the Isle of Wight while Task Force U listened for word from naval commander in chief Adm. Bertram Ramsey to proceed to Utah Beach. As they awaited the signal, Eisenhower weighed the problems of stormy weather and the lunar calendar. The intention had been to launch the invasion on June 4. Weather had forced a delay. At a final conference on conditions Stagg forecast a break in the storm, but a brief one. It was a window of opportunity that would rapidly close and remain shut, as it turned out, for more than a month. At that moment thousands of men were, as Ted wrote to Eleanor, "buttoned up" in ships. At his headquarters, surrounded by the high command of the Allied Expeditionary Force, Ike asked of them and himself, "How long you can hang this operation at the end of a limb?"

The generals and admirals did not reply.

At 9:45 P.M. Ike gave the answer. "Okay, let's go."

After signaling the armada, Admiral Ramsay wrote in his diary, "Thus has been made the vital & crucial decision to stage the great enterprise which [shall?], I hope, be the immediate means of bringing about the downfall of Germany's fighting power & Nazi oppression & an early cessation of hostilities."

Under no "delusions as to the risks involved in this most difficult of all operations," he saw success "in the balance" and placed his trust in "invisible assets." He wrote, "We shall require the help that God can give us & I cannot believe that this will not be forthcoming."

At 0415, June 6, 1944, the *Barnet* made way. At 1045 she slipped into place in a column of warships off Plymouth bound for France. As she plied the turbulent waters of the Channel, Brig. Gen. Theodore Roosevelt leaned on his walking stick on deck and joined the men in singing "Onward Christian Soldiers" and "The Battle Hymn of the Republic."

As *Barnet* and the other ships in the convoy proceeded eastward along the southwest coast of England, weather and seas became, in the words of Maj. Robert P. Tabb III, a leader of a beach-obstacle demolition team, "increasingly uninviting." All hands were constantly checking the tie-downs of heavy cargo. Pitching decks were wet and slick.

When Tabb slipped and fell, the result was a badly sprained ankle. He had it heavily and tightly wrapped by a combat medic (the first of many instances of aid that he would render in the coming hours).

"I was determined to get on that beach and not be left behind," Tabb recalled. "I also had heard stories about people being able to walk out sprains if they could stand the pain."

A conspicuous example of a man enduring bodily aches in the interest of getting into battle on D day could be seen in the figure of Brigadier General Roosevelt. Everyone in the 4th Division had somehow heard of his remark to General Barton that if the men saw him hobbling ashore with his cane they would find encouragement. Most knew of his gallantry in North Africa and Sicily and they assumed that his need for a stick was connected to arthritis and being wounded in France in 1918. They did not know, nor did anyone in the army, and not even Eleanor, that for a long time he had also been having chest pains. Fearing that a "heart condition" would keep him from being in uniform again, he'd taken no one into his confidence. If a young officer commented that he appeared a bit out of breath or that he looked a little tired, he dismissed the remark with the celebrated smile of two generations of Theodore Roosevelts and pointed out that he was, after all, middle aged and old enough to be the officer's father.

He was almost fifty-seven, a fact that entitled him to the distinction of being the oldest man, and the only general, to hit the beach with the first wave of troops on June 6, 1944.

With everyone else on the *Barnet* that morning he had spent a sleepless night. Those who were capable of dozing off were awakened in the early hours by the engines of landing vehicles being checked, antiaircraft guns being tested, and the drone of high-flying bombers and transport planes carrying paratroopers to be dropped into the midst of the enemy.

"Most people were seasick," noted Tabb, "so not too much stuff was given to eat."

At 4:30 elements of the 4th and 24th Cavalry landed on a small island off Utah Beach called Îles St. Marcouf. Their mission was to destroy a German observation post. They found the island mined, but without enemy soldiers.

At 5:50 ships of Task Force 125 began bombing German shore batteries. More than four thousand 250-pound bombs were to be dropped on seven targets on the beach.

When air and naval bombardment ceased at H-Hour (0630), the plan was for thirty-two swimming tanks (DDs) to go in first, carried in LCTs under the covering fire of one thousand rockets. They were to be followed by the 2d Battalion, 8th Infantry, in Higgins boats, each with a thirty-man assault team. After them in waves at precise intervals would go combat engineers and navy demolition teams, some with Sherman tanks and bulldozers.

This activity was directed by primary and secondary control vessels for each beach. They left the transport area at approximately 0455, but the secondary control vessel for Red Beach fouled her propellor on a buoy and was unable to continue. An hour later, while more than seven thousand yards from the beach and about a quarter hour late, the primary control for Red Beach was sunk, probably by a mine. Some of the landing craft that depended on them slowed. Observing this on the secondary control vessel for Green Beach, number LCC 60, Howard Vander Beek and Sims Gauthier brought it about to guide the LCTs closer to the beach. They also announced through a bullhorn that they would lead all amphibious tanks. The LCTs were to be in position at five thousand yards. Because their landings were behind the time line, they were guided to within three thousand yards. Ten LCTs on the right were to go to Tare Green Beach. Ten on the left were intended for Uncle Red, about a thousand yards south. All that was to happen thereafter was keyed to their landings, set for 0630: H-Hour.

This makeshift operation was complicated by a strong tidal current and thick clouds of smoke, dust, and sand thrown up by the naval bombardment. The result was great difficulty in identifying markers on the shore. Troops of the 2d Battalion, 8th Infantry, were expected to land on Uncle Red opposite Exit 3. The 1st Battalion's objective was opposite a strongpoint known as les Dunes-de-Varreville. Both units came in astride Exit 2, about two thousand yards south.

Not everything was going according to plan on Ted's transport. Coordinating the loading of the troops was Captain Mabry. The men had

The 4th Division D-day plan for the assault on Utah Beach at 0630, June 6, 1944. The plan went awry and the troops found themselves two thousand yards south of their objective. When Ted realized this after coming ashore, he ordered, "We'll start the war from right here."

trouble climbing down netted rope ladders in the dark to landing craft bobbing below in extremely rough and cold water. Mabry recalled for an oral history archive cited in World War II–historian Gerald Astor's *The Greatest War: Americans in Combat 1941–1945:* "On two occasions just before men were to turn loose and jump into the boat, a foot would get hung up in the rope and hang the man upside down. The boat would come up and smack the soldier on the shoulder or the head, even while those already in the boat tried to push the man up. You'd see the landing craft high up on a wave, almost halfway to the rail of the ship, and then suddenly so far down in a trough you could dimly see it."

When time came to go, Ted yelled to trusted aide Stevie, "Where's my life belt?"

"General, I don't know," Stevie replied in exasperation. "I've already given you three."

"Dammit," Ted barked, "I don't care how many you've given me, I don't have one now."

Seeing Ted with the life belt around his waist and a knit watch cap instead of a helmet as he went to the rail to go over the side, Mabry asked if he had all his armament. Ted patted the holster of his Army Colt .45 automatic and said, "I've got my pistol, one ammunition clip with six rounds in it, and my walking cane. That's all I expect to need."

The landing craft awaiting him held part of E Company, 2d Battalion, 8th Infantry. To get into it Ted would have to jump down about five feet to the deck. A hand reached up to assist. The soldier said, "Here, General, let me help you."

Ted tapped him on the arm with his cane and growled, "Get the hell out of my way. I can jump in there by myself. I can take it as well as any of you."

If any of the young men in the boat doubted it, none dared say so. With the short, sort of pug-nosed, sinewy, grinning, cane-carrying, helmetless, one-star general safely on board, the Higgins landing craft moved away from the transport and made for the beach. In the rehearsals for the landing the procedure was for their boat to trail swimming tanks ashore, but the navy coxswain running Ted's craft grew impatient with the slow-moving vehicles and steered past and ahead of them. Consequently, the men of E Company and their brigadier general found that they were headed for the distinction of being the first Allied infantry outfit in the invasion to set foot in Normandy.

Sergeant Melvin Pike was in the right rear of another boat. Hunkered down, he heard the snap of bullets over his head and the chatter of the boat's two .50-caliber machine guns. Looking for the man who was firing it, he saw no heads, only the hands steering the boat and one hand on each of the guns. "Lieutenant," he said with alarm to his platoon leader, "these guys aren't even looking where they're going or shooting."

The boat slammed into a sandbar about two hundred yards from the shore opposite Exit 2. An attempt to move closer failed against another sandbar. When the coxswain lowered the ramp at the front of the craft, it stuck. The lieutenant shouted, "Okay, let's go." He jumped over the side. Pike followed and found himself in waist-deep water about two hundred yards from the beach. Sergeant Pike recalled, "You couldn't run, you could just kind of push forward."

Major Robert Tabb's LCT touched the bottom and dropped its ramp. Tabb's swimming tank, called a weasel, quickly sank. In water up to their shoulders Tabb and his partner, Sergeant Newsom, were forced to abandon all equipment except a radio and Tabb's map case and musette bag. "We moved directly shoreward," Tabb remembered, "and never looked back. When we reached the waterline, I was somewhat surprised that the beach obstacles were light. Of course, this was because we had landed at an unlikely spot, which was not heavily prepared."

The errors made in guiding the landing craft had fortuitously put the troops on part of the target beach that was less heavily defended. Sergeant Pike attributed lack of serious opposition to the Germans' being "all shook up from the bombing and the shelling and the rockets and most of them just wanted to surrender."

Having dashed for the cover of the seawall, Capt. Howard Lees of E Company peered over it and saw terrain that was nothing like the sand-table model he'd studied. Then he saw Ted Roosevelt walking toward him. Pistol in one hand and cane in the other, he seemed oblivious to the gunfire and incoming artillery shells.

Hunkered by the seawall, Major Tabb also watched him, "striding along with his walking stick and ignoring the stray small-arms fire and the fragments of mortar and artillery shells. His calm, businesslike demeanor was certainly a staying influence on all who saw him. He also rousted out a lot of laggards from the shelter of the wall and got them moving forward to join their units."

The first Sherman tanks were now ashore and returning fire. The navy control officer for Utah Beach, Commodore James Arnold, dashed for cover behind them. "They offer a world of security to a man in the open who may have a terribly empty sensation in his guts," he said later. As the tanks maneuvered, Arnold chose to make his "headquarters" in a shell crater.

He was in it barely a minute when "an army officer wearing the single star of a brigadier" jumped in to duck the blast of an 88. "Sons-abuzzards," exclaimed the general. As he and the commodore untangled he said, "I'm Teddy Roosevelt. You're Arnold of the navy. I remember you at the briefing at Plymouth."

Into Arnold's headquarters scampered two lieutenant colonels, Conrad Simmons and Carlton MacNeeley. While they and Ted studied a map, the fourth wave of troops was coming in. Wading ashore with them was Col. James Van Fleet. When he joined the officers in Arnold's hole at 0940, he radioed to General Barton on the *Bayfield*, "I am ashore with Colonel Simmons and General Roosevelt, advancing steadily."

Ted said, "Van, we're not where we're supposed to be."

A brief, lively discussion ensued on the subject of what to do about the mistake.

As Van Fleet recalled, there were two options. "Should we try to shift our entire landing force more than a mile down the beach, and follow our original plan? Or should we proceed across the causeways immediately opposite where we had landed?"

Ted answered, "We'll start the war from right here."

In an unpublished memoir Van Fleet said that he'd made the decision to stay put. But as Stephen Ambrose wrote in the chapter devoted to Utah Beach in his book *D-Day June 6, 1944: The Climactic Battle of World War II*, "The important point was not who made the decision but that it was made without opposition or time-consuming argument. It was the right decision and showed the flexibility of the high command." Ambrose's Utah Beach chapter found its title in the words attributed to Ted. He noted that with those words Roosevelt "became a legend." That he did is evidence of the power of the time-honored maxim of journalism, and the allure of the romance of history found by those who write it: "When in doubt as to what is true and what is legend, print the legend."

There is no disputing that in those first moments of confusion on Utah Beach, Brigadier General Roosevelt was an inspiring figure to all who saw him. Among them was Harper Coleman, a member of Heavy Weapons Company H of the 8th Infantry Regiment. "When we came ashore," he said, "we had a greeter. Brigadier General Theodore Roosevelt was standing there waving his cane and giving out instructions, as only he could. If we were afraid of the enemy, we were more afraid of him and could not have stopped on the beach had we wanted."

Forty-six years earlier in Cuba at the foot of Kettle Hill in the San Juan Heights, Col. Theodore Roosevelt had challenged a cowering soldier by asking, "Are you afraid to stand up when I am on horseback?" In the next moment the man was hit by a Spanish bullet that cut through him lengthwise. "I, who was on horseback in the open, was unhurt," TR noted, "and the man lying flat on the ground in the cover beside me was killed."

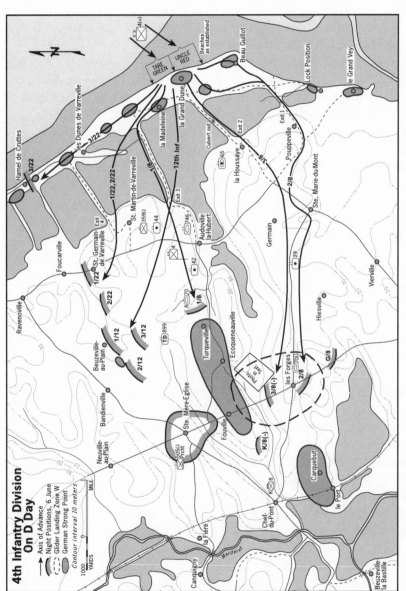

4th Infantry Division On D Day

- Axis of Advance
- Night Positions, 6 June
- Glider Landing Zone, W
- German Strong Point

Contour interval 10 meters

The immediate objective of Ted's 4th Division after landing at the wrong spot on Utah Beach was to get off the beach as fast as possible. Because Germans had destroyed a culvert it caused a huge backup of vehicles, which for a while turned Ted into a traffic cop.

There is no knowing whether this incident as told by TR to his name-sake was in Ted's mind as he prowled Utah Beach with his cane, cheer-ing on the wet, scared soldiers who found themselves face to face with him as they came ashore. What is known is that no man who saw him that morning could forget the spectacle.

John F. Ahearn, commander of Company C, 70th Tank Battalion, was in the second tank to land on Utah. Looking around for key landmarks, he realized immediately that he was in the wrong place. Then he saw General Roosevelt on the beach and reported to him. "He told me to go on with my mission to secure the lateral parts of the beach," Ahearn noted, "and to get inland as fast as we could."

Captain Mabry was now ashore. His uniform was soaked with seawa-ter and spattered by the blood and specks of flesh from the pulverized body of one of his men who'd been hit on the top of his head by a mor-tar round. Standing at the waterline, Mabry had a glimpse of Ted far-ther up the beach "walking along waving his walking cane and encour-aging troops to keep moving."

Sergeant Richard Cassidy of the 237th Engineer Combat Team was clearing obstacles. He also looked up and saw Ted "walking up and down with his cane." Cassidy shouted to one of his men, 'Go knock that bas-tard down, he's going to get killed.'"

The GI bellowed, "Don't you know who that is?"

"Yes, it's Roosevelt," said Cassidy, "and he is going to get killed."

Ted moved on while Cassidy's team blew up the obstacles.

Organized as a beach-obstacle task force (BOTF) commanded by Maj. Herschel E. Linn, the demolition teams were made up of navy and army units with a mission to destroy all water and land obstructions. They found what they'd been told to expect and had the entire beach cleared in an hour. They were then used as needed. Out of their 400 men six died and 39 were wounded.

When later waves of troops reached the beach, including the 12th In-fantry Regiment, they were met by Ted welcoming them, according to Malcolm Williams of the 12th, with a big grin and "How do you boys like the beach?"

The job ahead of them in an area in which they had not expected to fight was to reduce enemy strongpoints quickly and get off the beach by moving inland as fast as possible to make room for succeeding waves of troops and equipment. But everything went so fast that Ted and his of-ficers were confronted with traffic jams. The original plan envisaged leav-

ing the beach by Exits 2 and 3. But because Exit 3 was close to enemy artillery positions, all traffic was funneled into Exit 2. The situation was
complicated by a blown-up bridge over a small stream. The road was also
covered by a German antitank gun. When a tank moved forward, it struck
a mine. The second took a hit from the gun and was knocked out. The
third blasted the gun.

Minutes later, Major Tabb and a BOTF platoon were busy building a
steel overpass called a "treadway." Thirty feet in length and capable of
supporting any tactical loads, it was in place by noon. Tabb was able to
boast of having made the first bridge built by army engineers in the invasion of France.

With clearing of beach obstacles completed, gaps had to be blown in
the seawall and lanes opened through the dune line behind it. When
that task was completed the BOTF was no longer needed and dissolved.
Tabb's 237th turned to improving the Exit 2 roadway, now the main supply route for advanced elements of the 4th Division to move toward the
town of Ste. Marie-du-Mont. At 7:45 P.M. the 3d Battalion, 8th Infantry,
passed through Exit 2 to head inland. To the north, at Exit 3, the 8th
Battalion came under heavy artillery, but it advanced toward its goal of
reaching Turqueville by evening.

On the south the mission of the 2d Battalion under Col. Carlton Mac-
Neeley was to advance toward Pouppeville and relieve elements of the
101st Airborne Division, which had parachuted in during the night. The
men of Company E who had been accompanied on their landing by their
brigadier general had made it through without losing a man. Combined
with F and G companies they proceeded toward Pouppeville and made
contact with the 3d Battalion, 501st Parachute Infantry.

At midnight Colonel Van Fleet radioed to General Barton, "Defense
is not stubborn."

This report and others assured other generals up the chain of command, from Maj. Gen. J. Lawton Collins to Bradley, Montgomery, and
Eisenhower, that at least a foothold was secured on the Cotentin Peninsula and that it had been achieved with less difficulty than had been
feared. As reports of casualties came in, the high command could hardly
believe them. The 8th and 22d regiments had a dozen killed, 106
wounded. The 12th suffered 69 casualties, mostly from mines. The 4th
Division had lost twenty times more men in the submarine attack on the
training exercise at Slapton Sands. Half a century after the generals assessed D day on Utah Beach, Stephen E. Ambrose looked back with the

clear vision of time passed and wrote that D day was a smashing success for the 4th Division for many reasons, not the least being German reliance on mines, flooded areas, and fixed fortifications instead of high-quality troops. As important as was the air and sea bombardment, and naval shelling through the day, Ambrose wrote, "Credit belonged, too, to General Roosevelt and his colonels."

In fifteen hours on D day the Americans had landed more than 20,000 men and 1,700 vehicles, and swiftly moved inland.

The same could not be said for Omaha Beach.

29

Although Eleanor Alexander Roosevelt did not know it, on June 6, 1944, she was the only wife and mother whose husband and son were in action in Normandy. Like millions of Americans on the night of June 5 she had gone to bed feeling that the anxiously anticipated invasion of France was probably imminent. Unable to get to sleep for a long time, and then too fitful to stay asleep for more than a few minutes at a stretch, she was awake and listening to her bedroom radio when the official announcement was broadcast at 3:33 A.M.

A family prayer came to mind. She said it quietly: "O Lord, support us this day until the shadows lengthen and the evening falls."

Later that day she listened to the radio as FDR prayed on behalf of the nation, "Almighty God: Our sons, pride of our nation, this day have set upon a mighty endeavor. . . ."

He said, "These men are lately drawn from the ways of peace." They were fighting not for the lust of conquest. They were fighting to end conquest, to liberate. They yearned for the end of battle, for their return to the haven of home. Some would never return, and for them he prayed, "Embrace these, Father, and receive them, Thy heroic servants, into Thy kingdom."

The radio also brought a recording by General Eisenhower. Everyone in the USA who had read a newspaper or magazine or been to the movies and seen a newsreel would recognize the face and the famous Ike grin. Almost no one in the general public ever heard his voice. He read his order of the day to the men under his command: "Soldiers, Sailors, and Airmen of the Allied Expeditionary Force: You are about to embark upon the Great Crusade, toward which we have striven these many months.

The eyes of the world are upon you. The hopes and prayers of liberty-loving people everywhere march with you. . . . Your task will not be an easy one. Your enemy is well trained, well equipped, and battle-hardened. He will fight savagely. But this is the year 1944. . . . The tide has turned. The free men of the world are marching together to victory. I have full confidence in your courage, devotion to duty, and skill in battle. We will accept nothing less than total victory. Good luck! And let us all beseech the blessing of Almighty God upon this great and noble undertaking."

New York's mayor Fiorello La Guardia told reporters who'd flocked to his residence, Gracie Mansion, at 3:40 A.M., "We can only wait for bulletins and pray for success. It is the most exciting moment in our lives."

Much later in the day there was a radio broadcast of a recording made by war correspondent George Hicks on board the U.S. Navy's *Ancon* lying just off the beaches at the time of the invasion. Listeners heard not only his amazingly calm description of the invasion, but the sounds of the naval guns, the roar of an enemy plane attacking the armada, and the ack-ack-ack of antiaircraft guns trying to shoot it down.

Somewhere in all of that noise, Eleanor knew, were her cherished fifty-seven-year-old husband and beloved twenty-four-year-old son. At this time she did not know that Ted had persuaded General Barton to let him go in with the first wave. Ted's letter containing his offhand disclosure of this would not reach her until much later.

Tuning in radio news bulletins and reading newspapers, Eleanor and the rest of America followed developments described as happening "somewhere in France" as best they could while trying to figure out where their loved ones were by reading between the lines. Suddenly, people who'd had no idea where to find Normandy on a map were talking like experts of towns with unpronounceable names that were under attack. In bits and pieces, cleared and "sanitized" by military censors, they learned a little of what had happened on June 6 at places named Sword, Juno, Gold, Utah, and Omaha.

What was not said was that the assault on Omaha Beach had started poorly and quickly deteriorated. Of 446 Liberator bombers assigned to soften up the defenses, only 329 arrived, but most of them dropped their loads too far inland. The result was that the men coming ashore would not be able to count on the enemy being left dead, wounded, stunned, disoriented, and dispirited, as the Germans were at Utah. Some amphibious tanks were launched nearly four miles offshore and sank. Navy-fired rockets designed to provide a curtain of fire mostly fell short.

When the first wave came in, the men who were not immediately killed or wounded by withering crossfire were left dazed and disorganized. Many were in the wrong sector. By the nightfall there were more than thirty-four thousand ashore, but they were desperately clinging to ground that went no more than a mile inland. More than a thousand men were dead and many more wounded.

"Omaha Beach was," wrote General Bradley thirty years later, "a nightmare."

On June 7 the people at home were told of "opposition less than expected" and that the troops were ten miles in. On the eighth the news was that beaches had been cleared. More troops and supplies were "pouring onto the Continent." A battle was raging at the city of Caen. The next day's newspapers had a picture of General Eisenhower in profile, snapped as he visited pacified beachheads that swarmed with men and supply trucks.

On D day plus 1, Utah Beach received 10,735 men, 1,469 vehicles, and a little over 800 tons of supplies, for a two-day total of 32,000 troops, 3,200 vehicles, and 2,500 tons. But the plan had called for much more (39,722, 4,372, and 7,000 respectively). Slow progress was also being made by the 82d Airborne in securing a bridgehead over the Merderet River. This kept the 4th Division from crossing the stream to capture Valognes and continue northwest toward its goal of quickly seizing Cherbourg. There had also been a delay in linking Utah and Omaha, raising the frightening prospect of the Germans driving a wedge into the gap between VII Corps on Utah and V Corps on "Bloody Omaha," as it was now being called.

Stretching from Port-en-Bessin on the east to Pointe du Hoc on the west, Omaha terrain was not easy. Firm sand at waterline and then shingle formed a beach backed by a seawall, a V-shaped tank trap, flat swampy area, and steep, high bluffs. Five draws sloped up from the beach to a plateau. All of this was honeycombed with cannon in pillboxes, mortars, machine-gun nests, and an extensive system of trenches that lived up to the boast of their designer, Rommel, that on the England-facing coast of France he'd built a wall that would thwart any Allied invasion.

From the shape of things as Eisenhower personally assessed the situation on his visit to the Omaha sector on June 7, 1944, it appeared that Rommel's boast was partially justified. Ike and his generals stared at an alarming gap between the V and VII that, if not closed, could mean the doom of the entire enterprise. He ordered Bradley to make sealing the opening top priority. To accomplish this V Corps would have to thrust westward through Isigny to close the gap as VII Corps blocked the route of German reinforcements by capturing the inland town of Carentan and a strategic causeway across marshes and tactically inundated areas.

Aerial reconnaissance photos indicated that the population had been evacuated. But the attacking Americans ran into unexpectedly fierce resistance. The plan was to encircle the town. In one counterattack the Germans charged through an orchard and threatened to rout GIs south and east of a farmhouse. Withering machine-gun fire drove the Germans back. Further action by the enemy strained the American positions almost to the breaking point. Four days after Bradley had ordered Carentan taken, it remained a German pocket of resistance. Consequently, on the night of June 11–12 it was set ablaze by U.S. artillery, naval batteries, mortars, and several tank-destroyer guns. With the town in flames the Americans closed in on all sides, but this pincers movement closed too late to catch the bulk of the German defenders. They'd escaped during the nighttime bombardment.

With the capture of Carentan, VII Corps acquired a bastion against a German attack in the gap between Omaha and Utah, and a vital communication link with V Corps. But on June 13 elements of the German 37th and 38th Panzer Grenadier Regiments and the 17th Tank Battalion combined with other units in an attempt to retake the town. The surprise action so unnerved the generals at First Army headquarters that armor was sent to repel it. Late in the morning and in early afternoon, tanks of the 2d Armored Division's Combat Command A rumbled along the Carentan-Baupte Road, followed by the 502d Parachute Infantry, while another task force came from another direction. This coordinated maneuver by tanks, foot soldiers, and artillery threw the Germans back, at a German loss of 300 men. Securing of Carentan on June 14 removed the threat posed by the Utah-Omaha gap, allowing the linkup of the beachheads and eliminating any chance of the D-day invaders being driven back into the sea.

The objective now for Eisenhower and his generals was to wheel VII Corps west and north to destroy the German army in the Cotentin Peninsula and capture the greatest prize of the assault on Normandy: the port of Cherbourg. The original plan provided that in the advance up the thumb-shaped peninsula the right flank of Ted's 4th Division be secured by the 90th Division. But difficulties in achieving early goals of the landings required a change in that scheme, assigning the 90th the task of cut-

ting across the width of the peninsula and advancing north in conjunc-
tion with the 4th to Cherbourg. This would seal off a southerly escape
route for the Germans.

The dual problem for the German high command was to create the
maximum delay in the American plan to cut Cotentin crosswise and then
advance northward, and to keep the best of Germany's troops in the region, the 77th Division, from being trapped and decimated. And there

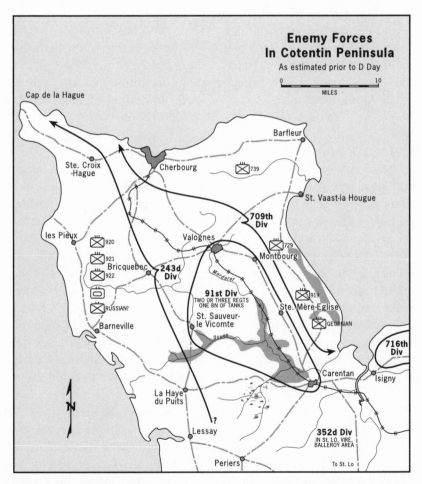

The invasion and its progress were heralded by the U.S. Armed Forces newspaper
the *Stars and Stripes*. Americans on the home front followed developments in newspapers, on the radio, and in newsreels, all of which received heavily censored reports.

was an order to the commander of the Germans in the Cotentin from Adolf Hitler himself that Cherbourg must be held at all costs.

"The possession of Cherbourg," said the Führer from Berlin to Generalleutnant Karl-Wilhelm von Schlieben, "is decisive."

German abandonment of the peninsula was foreclosed on June 17 when the 9th Division completed its mission of bottling up the enemy.

Congratulations on this achievement were sent to the men of the 9th from an unexpected source of compliments on American fighting ability. General Bernard Law Montgomery used a cowboy term. He thanked the GIs for "roping off" the peninsula.

At a meeting between Bradley and General Collins it was decided that the push to Cherbourg would be made by three divisions moving abreast, the 9th on the left, the 79th in the center, and the 4th on the right. The attack was to commence just before dawn on June 19. In a conference with Ted and division regimental officers General Barton ordered that the 8th and 12th Infantry Regiments would capture the town of Montebourg. A railway center, it was expected to be strongly defended by 1,000 to 1,500 hardened veterans of battle.

The Americans would also have to contend with a new type of terrain. In advancing north they found themselves in hilly country that grew higher around Cherbourg. Much of the country was broken by ridges and valleys with streams. In the vicinity of the target city they would find a steep outcropping of bare rock. It was ideal ground to mount a defense. The enemy had deeply and densely fortified it.

The GIs who fought northward against varying degrees of resistance arrived in front of "Fortress Cherbourg" on June 12. That night General Collins issued an ultimatum by radio and messenger to General von Schlieben and his soldiers. The Germans would have until 0900 on June 22 to surrender. While awaiting the answer, the 4th Division held ground that isolated the city from the east. If the surrender demand was ignored, the division's 12th Infantry was to capture the heavily defended suburb of Tourlaville.

The ultimatum expired without a word from von Schlieben. H-Hour for the Americans was set for two o'clock in the afternoon, to be preceded at 1240 by bombing and strafing by four squadrons of rocket-firing Typhoons, followed by six squadrons of Mustangs, all from the Second Tactical Air Force (of the Royal Air Force). Then would come twelve groups of U.S. Ninth Air Force fighter-bombers (P-47s, P-38s, and P-51s), a total of 562 planes. This would be followed by prolonged artillery barrages.

The air assault was the first large-scale usage of medium and fighter-bombers in close support of ground forces. Because it was a first there were failures in coordination. The effects were far less than hoped. The bombing was so scattered that some bombs fell behind U.S. lines. The main impact was on German communication lines and troop morale.

Neither did the U.S. ground plan go well. There were difficulties on the left, center, and right. Fighting was still raging on June 24. But the situation in Cherbourg had become desperate. In an intercepted message General von Schlieben advised his superiors, "Communications to several battalions no longer available. Phosphorus shells have put eight battalions out of action. Completely crushed by artillery fire."

On June 25 a German medical officer, adjutant of the naval hospital, came out from the besieged fortress with a captured American air force officer and begged that the hospital be spared from shelling and that blood plasma be sent for wounded American prisoners inside the city. He was given the plasma and sent back alone carrying another demand for surrender that had the tone of a message that might have been sent in the time of knights in armor and castles: "The Fortress Cherbourg is now surrounded and its defenses have been breached."

The note advised the Germans that the city was now isolated and "you are outnumbered and it is merely a question of time when Cherbourg must be captured. The immediate unconditional surrender of Cherbourg is demanded."

Again there was no compliance. Determined to show that the city had indeed obeyed the order from the Führer to fight on at all costs, and to deny the enemy spoils of war, the Germans began destroying assets, blowing up the Amcot Aircraft Works and the Gare Maritime. But when American tanks were brought up to fire point-blank at several pillboxes, nearly 350 Germans fled their fortifications and surrendered to men of the 4th Division.

On June 27 all organized resistance ended. More than 10,000 prisoners were taken, including nearly 3,000 wounded Germans in two hospitals. To carry out Hitler's "last stand" order the Germans had been forced to use every man available regardless of his military specialty. "With their backs to the sea," wrote a U.S. Army historian, "they showed little disposition for a last-ditch fight."

The timetable in the master plan for capturing Cherbourg called for it to happen on D plus 8. It fell into American hands on D plus 25. In the fight to meet the objective VII Corps had more than 22,000 casualties (2,800 killed, 5,700 missing, 13,500 wounded). The Germans lost an undetermined number of men and 39,000 were captured.

An infuriated Führer blamed this on his general and in meetings with top-ranking officers of the Wehrmacht held up Wilhelm von Schlieben as the very model of a poor commander.

An unexpected prize for Ted's 4th Division in the conquest of Cherbourg was the capture of a complex of bunkers and ammunition and supplies storage rooms known as "the arsenal." In addition to weapons it yielded 50 sides of beef and 300 sides of pork. It was the first fresh meat the GIs had tasted in a month.

In choosing a military governor for the captured port city, General Eisenhower and his high command agreed that no one in the European Theater was better suited to the job than the man who had been governor general of both Puerto Rico and the Philippines. Ted set up his headquarters in a cellar lit by a single oil lamp.

Eventually, he relinquished the desk job and returned to his troops. They'd given him a truck that he described in a letter written to Eleanor on July 10. Calling it his "little home," he wrote, "It was captured from the Germans by one of our units and given to me by them. The ordnance [unit] has done it over and I've got a desk and bed in it. The inside is painted white. Show [his driver] is having a time fixing it up. He's put a headboard on the bed, made from the back of an old French chair. He's found a place for my footlocker and bag. He's put in an electric light. I feel positively a softie."

He continued:

The truck arrived yesterday at a most opportune moment, for [my] old chassis had begun to feel the strain of these last few years of combat. I was a pretty sick rabbit, and it had been raining for God knows how long. It still is, for that matter. I got in and was dry after I'd screwed up enough energy to take off my drenched clothes. The Doc came and said with a little embarrassment that my troubles were primarily from having put an inhuman strain on a machine that was not exactly new. Anyhow, he gave me something to make me sleep, and this morning I was almost as good as new.

It's getting late and tomorrow we attack again—as we will day after tomorrow. Artillery is already firing nearby—the heavies—and every salvo shakes this paper. I'm glad you've liked my letters.

The part about the doctor was untrue. He'd not seen one.

The day after writing to her, he got a visit from someone to whom he was sure he could speak about his health without it making its way to the high command. It was Quentin. He'd dropped in once before, looking "fit, healthy, and unscathed, but filthy," as Ted had written to Eleanor on the occasion.

On July 11 Quentin knocked on the open door of the truck at 7:30 in the evening. They talked until after ten, "having a wonderful time," according to Quentin. The father-and-son conversation was about "everything—home, the family, my plans, the war, having a swell time." At some point during the gabfest Ted said that after nearly two years of steady combat under terrible conditions, he had begun to get "very tired." Then he confessed that he had been having heart attacks. Quentin was shocked. He asked about them and told Ted to "lay low."

To be sure he would, Quentin spoke to Ted's doctor. He also told Stevie that the next time Ted was "sick" to "hold him down" until the doctor came. When Quentin got back to the 1st Division around two in the morning, he was told his father was dead of a heart attack.

Rushing back to 4th Division HQ, he found the entire division staff waiting for him. They offered him "all the help they could" and all of them were "absolutely swell." To inform Eleanor of the death he had the assistance of the war correspondents who were covering both the 1st and 4th Divisions. They cleared away red tape so that Quentin could get a message back to Sagamore Hill through press channels. The reporters then flashed the news to the United States that the son and namesake of the twenty-sixth president of the United States, the man who looked so much like his father and had emulated the colonel of the Rough Riders by becoming a hero in two world wars—was gone.

The newspapers at home were also informed by the office of the Supreme Headquarters of the Allied Expeditionary Forces that at the moment of Brig. Gen. Ted Roosevelt's death, there was on Ike's desk a set of orders dated July 14, 1944, naming Ted commander of the 90th Division, U.S. Army, and recommending promotion to the rank of major general.

Also pending at SHAEF was a "strong" recommendation of a battalion commander, a regimental commander, and division commander that for Ted's valor on Utah Beach on D day he be awarded the Congressional Medal of Honor.

Ted was buried on July 14, Bastille Day, coincidentally the twenty-sixth anniversary of the death of Ted's brother and the uncle and namesake whom Quentin never knew. Burial was in the official cemetery at Ste. Mère-Eglise. An army band played Chopin's "Funeral March." A half-track carried the coffin, followed by a sergeant and seven enlisted men to lift it on and off the vehicle. The "family" was Quentin, Marcus "Stevie" Stevenson, and Kurt Show. The honor company was chosen from "old-timers," one from each unit in the division. At the graveside the band played "The Son of God Goes Forth to War." Artillery boomed in the distance, not only in salute, but firing shells at the enemy. A squad of riflemen fired three volleys. Two buglers sounded taps, echo fashion.

Quentin told his mother it was "a warrior's funeral."

Saluting as honorary pallbearers were other great figures of battle-fields—six generals, including J. Lawton Collins, Raymond "Tubby" Barton, Omar Bradley, and George S. Patton.

The general who had ordered Ted relieved of duty in Sicily was asked years later to name the bravest act he had ever known in more than forty years of military service. Omar Bradley had four words: Ted Roosevelt . . . Utah Beach. George Patton would note in his diary that Gen. Ted Roosevelt was the bravest soldier he ever knew.

On the night of Ted's death Quentin had written to Eleanor, "The lion is dead."

The letter continued:

There is no one today, there probably has been no one, who had so full a life. He had great material successes, but the part that really counted was the unfailing, complete loyalty which was felt for him by the people that he felt counted. To him, to me, that counted a thousand times more than any further gain or achievement. To me he was much more than simply a father, he was an amazing combination of father, brother, friend, and comrade in battle. . . . The day he died he spent with his front-line battalions.

"It was," Quentin said, "like the magnificent climax of a great play."

Epilogue

In the days following Ted's death tributes were offered, laudatory editorials written, and memorial services held across the nation. Newspapers published accounts of his life and years in civil government and in the military. Articles recorded that Theodore Roosevelt Jr. had earned more medals for valor in his two wars than any other American officer. Photographs showed him at attention as a French general pinned one of them on his uniform in World War I; in a training camp in 1941, showing recruits how to use a bayonet; and standing in his jeep "Rough Rider."

There were photos of Generals Bradley and Patton looking grim at the funeral. Articles reported that as the coffin was being lowered into the grave, Frenchmen from both world wars showered it with red roses.

Newsreels showed Ted in his roles as a gubernatorial candidate, as assistant secretary of the navy, governor of both Puerto Rico and the Philippines, and general. The journalist A. J. Liebling said that while Ted's father had been a dilettante soldier and first-class politician, his son had been the reverse. A dabbler in the electoral process, Ted had been a peerless warrior.

At a memorial held at Oyster Bay on July 18 an army honor guard carried flags with the battle ribbons of his units.

In Washington, D.C., the army chief of staff, George C. Marshall, received and signed off on General Eisenhower's endorsement of recommendations for awarding Ted the Medal of Honor. Congress ratified unanimously and sent the gold medallion with its light-blue neck sash to President Roosevelt for presentation.

The citation, in the name of the president on behalf of the Congress, read:

For gallantry and intrepidity at the risk of his life and beyond the call of duty on 6 June 1944, in France. After 2 verbal requests to accompany the leading assault elements in the Normandy invasion had been denied, Brig. Gen. Roosevelt's written request for this mission was approved and he landed with the first wave of the forces assaulting the enemy-held beaches. He repeatedly led groups from the beach, over the seawall, and established them inland. His valor, courage, and presence in the very front of the attack and his complete unconcern at being under heavy fire inspired the troops to heights of enthusiasm and self-sacrifice. Although the enemy had the beach under constant direct fire, Brig. Gen. Roosevelt moved from one locality to another, rallying men around him, directed, and personally led them against the enemy. Under his seasoned, precise, calm, and unfaltering leadership, assault troops reduced beach strong points and rapidly moved inland with minimum casualties. He thus contributed substantially to the successful establishment of the beachhead in France.

When FDR presented it to Eleanor at the White House on September 22, 1944, he told her, "His father would have been proudest."

Author's Note and Sources

I was delighted that you did not use footnotes, I believe they distract from the narrative.

       —TR, in a letter to an author who'd
       sent him a copy of his book

Without the determination and dedication of Mrs. Theodore Roosevelt Jr. to record her life with her beloved Ted in a book of "reminiscences," published in 1958 and titled *Day Before Yesterday,* writing a biography of her husband would have been difficult, perhaps impossible. That no one had done so before my undertaking amazed me. But in looking for Ted Roosevelt beyond Eleanor's book, I discovered his name in the pages of biographies and memoirs of most of the leading personalities of politics, government, and warfare throughout the first half of the century that encompassed all but twelve years of Ted's life. In D-day stories he was necessarily written large. He was such an important, fascinating, compelling, and heroic figure on June 6, 1944, that in the 1962 epic motion picture based on Cornelius Ryan's D-day book, *The Longest Day,* the film's producer, Darryl F. Zanuck, in a film with an all-star international cast, chose one of the most celebrated names in the movies to portray him. Even though Ted looked nothing like the tall and lanky Henry Fonda, one of the most American of actors with an "aw-shucks" manner that marked his roles as young Abraham Lincoln and "Mister Roberts" was perfectly cast to say the most famous words voiced on a D-day beach, "We'll start the war from right here."

Credit for discerning that a biography of Ted Roosevelt was long overdue belongs to my literary agent, Jake Elwell. Although I had authored two books on Ted's father, covering TR's two years as head of New York City's police department *(Commissioner Roosevelt)* and TR as founder, leader, and hero of the Rough Riders *(Colonel Roosevelt),* when Jake proposed that I do a book on TR's namesake, I knew little more about Ted's part in Wold War II than what I had seen of him on a movie screen. In searching for whatever might have been written about him, I quickly discovered Eleanor's autobiography. After she (and I) first met Ted Roosevelt on the platform of the New Haven railway station when she was nineteen and he was twenty, I saw that because his amazing life had unfolded in the shadow of a luminous father my book about him would follow the thread that ran through his life—the need he felt to measure up to his father's history and fulfill TR's expectations for his namesake.

It was inevitable in writing Ted's story that it be entwined with those of his siblings, especially brothers Kermit, Archie, and Quentin. My great good fortune in that aspect was the publication of a book on the very subject of TR's four sons. Thanks to the author of *The Lion's Pride*, Edward J. Renehan Jr., I gained not only insights from his book as I set out on my task, but help in the direction of resources related to Ted.

Similar invaluable assistance in the initial phase of my research was found in classic and more recent biographies of TR by Joseph Bucklin Bishop (TR's letters to his children), David H. Burton, Hermann Hagedorn, William Henry Harbaugh, Alvin Harlow, Harold Howland, Nathan Miller, Elting E. Morison's *The Letters of Theodore Roosevelt*, Edmund Morris, and H. W. Brand; and TR's own writings.

For details of what Ted did on Utah Beach, and a general overview on what had occurred on D day, I turned to the book that had inspired Zanuck's movie and gave it its title. Cornelius Ryan's *The Longest Day* was the first book on the twenty-four hours that shifted the tide of history, and it became the standard followed by later Normandy historians. Many of them found raw material in the results of a decade-long project of the Eisenhower Center at the University of New Orleans. Inspired and led by Stephen E. Ambrose, its director and president of the National D-Day Museum in New Orleans, the center collected remembrances of June 6, 1944, and events leading up to the invasion from 1,400 men and women who were there—the citizen soldiers, sailors, and airmen; officers and enlisted. Anyone tackling the task of writing about D day is indebted to Ambrose, the center, and the books of the subject that have flowed from that unique archive. Among volumes that draw on it are Ambrose's *D-Day June 6, 1944: The Climactic Battle of World War II*, and Ronald J. Drez's *The Voices of D-Day: The Story of the Allied Invasion Told by Those Who Were There*.

I am also grateful to Gerald Astor for his massive work, *The Greatest War: Americans in Combat 1941–1945*, and his chapters on D day, and for sharing with me a tape made by George L. Mabry Jr. He related anecdotes concerning Ted's encounter with the two men, big and small, of a mortar team on their way to board their ship and Ted's experiences when joining the men of E Company on their way to earning the distinction of being the first Americans to set foot on a Normandy beach. Oral history accounts of Ted's actions on the beach and after the landings were also found in Astor's book.

For the official United States Army's history of the taking of Utah Beach I consulted *Utah Beach to Cherbourg*, part of the American Forces in Action Series of the Historical Division of the Department of the Army. Maps contained in this book are drawn from maps in that publication.

My appreciation and gratitude also go to Wallace Finley Dailey, curator, the Theodore Roosevelt Collection, Houghton Library of the Harvard College Library, Harvard University, for many of the photographs of Ted at various periods of his life.

With Eleanor's autobiography as a guide to the life and times of Theodore Roosevelt Jr., I found valuable material in contemporary periodicals, magazines, and newspapers as they traced his activities from school days to his career as a businessman, as a soldier in World War I, his role in realizing the American Legion, his service in the New York State Assembly, his run for governor, his search for the elusive *Ovis poli*, his term as assistant secretary of the navy, the effect on him of Teapot Dome, his governorship of Puerto Rico and the Philippines, his brief connection to America First, reenlistment in the army and his service through North Africa and Sicily, to Utah Beach, and a posthumous Congressional Medal of Honor.

The award of America's highest accolade for military valor above and beyond the call of duty that FDR presented to Eleanor was the first to be given to a Roosevelt. Ted would hold the distinction until January 16, 2001. On that date, in the Roosevelt Room of the White House, President Bill Clinton, on behalf of Congress, finally awarded TR the Medal of Honor that had been denied him for the exploits of his crowded hour at the San Juan Heights in July 1898. It was accepted on behalf of the Roosevelt family by TR's great-grandson, Tweed Roosevelt, grandson of Ted's brother Archie. The medal was returned to the White House for permanent display in the Roosevelt Room, along with TR's Nobel Peace Prize.

"This is what we as a country stand for," said Ted's great-grandnephew in accepting the Medal. "Peace and honor."

President Clinton said, "TR was a larger-than-life figure, who gave our nation a larger-than-life vision of our place in the world."

Fifty-six years after Ted earned his Medal of Honor, the father to whose expectations Ted had spent a lifetime trying to measure up joined Ted in a rare category of American history. Ted became the second Medal of Honor recipient whose father also earned one. The first was Douglas MacArthur, given it in 1942 for his service in the Philippines. His father, Arthur, had been recommended for it following heroic deeds in action at Missionary Ridge in 1863, but because of red tape did not receive it for another twenty-seven years. The only other president whose son earned the MOH was Rutherford B. Hayes. Lieutenant Colonel Webb C. Hayes got it in the same year TR was denied it. Hayes was given it for bravery in the 1898 Philippine Insurrection.

Although Ted could not write his own life story, he did produce autobiographical works that were revealing of how his character had been shaped by TR. His 1929 *All in the Family* is a treasure of Roosevelt family lore, tradition, and customs from which Ted learned and benefited while growing up on Sagamore Hill, and continued in the rearing of his own children. *East of the Sun and West of the Moon* is not only an account of the hunt for the *Ovis poli* and other creatures of Central Asia, but a portrait of Ted and Kermit as brothers bound together by their love for one another and a need for vigorous and even dangerous adventures instilled in them by their ever strenuous and daring father.

Measuring up to the colonel was an enterprise in which Kermit would ultimately fail. His widow, Belle, died in 1968 at the age of seventy-six. Whether Kermit's suicide was his admission that he'd failed to live up to TR's expectations, or a doom ordained by the alcoholism that had claimed the uncle after whom he was named, is unknowable. Yet the Roosevelt spark that had led Kermit to Africa and Brazil with TR and into the Himalayas with Ted was passed on to Kermit's son and namesake. Called Kim, he grew up to be one of the master operatives of the Central Intelligence Agency, as did his cousin Archibald Roosevelt Jr. (Archie's son and Ted's nephew). As a CIA agent in the early 1950s Kim was instrumental in the overthrow of an anti-West government in Iran and the restoration to its "Peacock Throne" of Shah Reza Pahlevi. Kim was also a friend of a British intelligence agent with whom he shared the nickname Kim, until Kim Philby was exposed as a Soviet spy and defected to Moscow. Kermit Roosevelt Jr. died on June 8, 2000.

Another grandson of TR to have a long career with the CIA was Ted's son Cornelius. An MIT scientist, he never married and died in 1991 at the age of seventy-six.

His cousin Archie worked on behalf of the CIA in Istanbul, Madrid, and London until he retired in 1974 to become a vice president and director of international relations for the Chase Manhattan Bank in Washington, D.C. His wife, Selwa Showker "Lucky" Roosevelt, served as the chief of protocol at the State Department during the Ronald Reagan presidency. In 1988 Archie published *For Lust of Knowing: Memoirs of an Intelligence Officer*. It adhered so strictly to his CIA secrecy oath that he did not identify countries in which he'd served. When he died of congestive heart failure at his Maryland home in 1990, his representative in Congress, Mary Rose Oakar, took the floor of the House of Representatives to laud him for "a full life" and "twenty-seven years as a public servant to our country." To the *Congressional Record* she added the obituary that had appeared in the *Washington Post*. It cited the "grandson of President Theodore Roosevelt" as "a soldier, scholar, linguist," who had viewed his calling "in the faceless, anonymous half-world of nuance and seemingly random fact with a hardheaded realism leavened by a kind of romanticism that has echoes of an earlier time."

In noting the passing of TR's grandson and son of the Archie who'd dared the Japanese to shoot him as he stood in a small reconnaissance boat in New Guinea, Representative Oakar spoke to the members of the House on an auspicious forty-sixth anniversary—June 6, 1990.

The father of the man she praised, Archibald Bulloch Roosevelt, outlived his brother Ted by forty-six years. Archie came home from the war to found the Wall Street firm Roosevelt and Cross, a brokerage specializing in municipal bonds, and to take an active part in supporting Alcoholics Anonymous, perhaps in memory of Kermit. After Archie's wife was killed in an auto accident in which Archie was driving, he withdrew to his winter home in Florida, evidently blaming himself for Grace's death. He died of a stroke on October 13, 1979. It was his grandson Tweed who received TR's Medal of Honor from President Clinton.

Ted's sister Ethel died on December 3, 1977. She'd outlived her doctor-husband Dick Derby by fourteen years. She devoted much of her time to the Theodore Roosevelt Memorial Association, later renamed the Theodore Roosevelt Association, based at Sagamore Hill.

It was there that Ted's mother, Edith Carow Roosevelt, had died in 1948.

Her daughter-in-law, Eleanor Alexander Roosevelt, also died at Oyster Bay, at the age of seventy-five, in 1960. The house she had hoped to share with Ted and that they had called Old Orchard, but in which they'd lived together only three years, was made part of the Sagamore Hill National Historic Site.

Quentin Roosevelt II came home from the war and took a job with Pan American Airlines, but the position was also cover for his work with the CIA in arranging airlifts of food and other supplies for anticommunist forces in China. On December 21, 1948, while he was on a commercial flight from Shanghai to Hong Kong, his plane crashed into a mountain in circumstances deemed mysterious. He had three daughters, one of whom became an expert on Chinese culture and the wife of William Weld, who was governor of Massachusetts from 1990 to 1997. Another daughter became an anthropologist with the Field Museum, sponsor of Ted's search for the *Ovis poli*.

Ted's daughter, Grace Green Roosevelt, died at age eighty-two. Her brother Theodore Roosevelt III (Teddy) became the father of Theodore IV and grandfather of Theodore V.

The first child of TR, Alice Lee Roosevelt, known to Ted and his brothers as they grew up as "Sister," and "Auntie Sister" to their children, became the toast of Washington as the wife of Nick Longworth, and remained so long after his death in 1931. Still famous for her lively expressions, she supposedly said to a guest at one of her parties, "If you have nothing good to say about anyone, come and sit by me."

Alice died on February 20, 1980. At age ninety-six, she'd outlived all of TR's children.

Ted and his brother Quentin were reburied at Sagamore Hill.

Selected Bibliography

Ambrose, Stephen E. *D-Day June 6, 1944: The Climactic Battle of World War II*. New York: Simon & Schuster, 1994.

Astor, Gerald. *The Greatest War: Americans in Combat, 1941–1945*. Novato, California: Presidio Press, Inc., 1999.

Bishop, Joseph Bucklin, ed. *Theodore Roosevelt's Letters to His Children*. New York: Charles Scribner's Sons, 1919.

Blumenson, Martin. *Patton: The Man Behind the Legend, 1885-1945*. New York: William Morrow, 1985.

Brands, H. W. *TR: The Last Romantic*. New York: Basic Books, 1997.

Churchill, Allen. *The Roosevelts: American Aristocrats*. New York: Harper & Row, 1965.

Department of the Army, Historical Division. *Utah Beach to Cherbourg*. Washington, D.C.: Department of the Army, 1947.

D'Este, Carlo. *Decision in Normandy: The Unwritten Story of Montgomery and the Allied Campaign*. London: Collins, 1983.

Drez, Ronald J., ed. *Voices of D-Day: The Story of the Allied Invasion, Told by Those Who Were There*. Baton Rouge: Louisiana State University Press, 1994.

Gilbert, Martin. *The First World War: A Complete History*. New York: Henry Holt and Company, Inc., 1994.

Hagedorn, Hermann. *The Roosevelt Family of Sagamore Hill*. New York: The Macmillan Company, 1954.

Harbaugh, William Henry. *Power and Responsibility: The Life and Times of Theodore Roosevelt*. New York: Farrar, Straus and Cudahy, 1961.

Harrison, Gordon. *Cross-Channel Attack*. Washington, D.C.: Office of the Chief of Military History, Department of the Army, 1951.

Hastings, Max. *Overlord: D-Day and the Battle for Normandy*. New York: Simon & Schuster, 1984.

Jeffers, H. Paul. *Colonel Roosevelt: Theodore Roosevelt Goes to War, 1897–1898*. New York: John Wiley & Sons, 1996.

———— *Commissioner Roosevelt: The Story of Theodore Roosevelt and the New York City Police, 1895–1897*. New York: John Wiley & Sons, 1994.

Liebling, A. J. "Reporter at Large." *New Yorker,* July 8 and 15, 1944.

Longworth, Alice Roosevelt. *Crowded Hours*. New York: Charles Scribner's Sons, 1933.

McCullough, David. *Mornings on Horseback*. New York: Simon & Schuster, 1981.

Miller, Nathan. *F.D.R: An Intimate History*. New York: Doubleday & Company, Inc., 1983.

———— *Theodore Roosevelt: A Life*. New York: William Morrow, 1992.

———— *The Roosevelt Chronicles: The Story of a Great American Family*. New York: Doubleday & Co., 1979.

Morris, Edmund. *The Rise of Theodore Roosevelt*. New York: Coward, McCann & Geoghegan, Inc., 1979.

Pringle, Henry F. *Big Frogs*. New York: Macy-Masius/The Vanguard Press, 1928.

Pyle, Ernie. *Ernie's War: The Best of Ernie Pyle's World War II Dispatches*, edited by David Nichols. New York: Random House, 1986.

Renehan, Edward J. *The Lion's Pride: Theodore Roosevelt and His Family in Peace and War*. New York: Oxford University Press, 1998.

Roosevelt, Kermit, ed. *Quentin Roosevelt: A Sketch with Letters*. New York: Charles Scribner's Sons, 1921.

Roosevelt, Theodore. *Theodore Roosevelt: An Autobiography*. New York: Macmillan, 1913.

Roosevelt, Theodore, Jr. (Ted). *All in the Family*. New York: G. P. Putnam's Sons, 1929.

———— *Average Americans*. New York: G. P. Putnam's Sons, 1920.

———— and Kermit Roosevelt. *East of the Sun and West of the Moon*. New York: Charles Scribner's Sons, 1926.

———— *Rank and File: True Stories of the Great War*. New York: Charles Scribner's Sons, 1928.

———— and Grantland Rice. *Taps: Selected Poems of the Great War*. Garden City, New York: Doubleday, Doran, 1932.

Roosevelt, Mrs. Theodore R., Jr. *Day Before Yesterday: The Reminiscences of Mrs. Theodore Roosevelt Jr.* Garden City, New York: Doubleday & Company, Inc., 1959.

Ryan, Cornelius. *The Longest Day*. New York: Popular Library, 1959.

Schriftgiesser, Karl. *The Amazing Roosevelt Family, 1613–1942*. New York: Wilfred Funk, 1942.

Sommers, Martin. "The Longest Hour in History." *Saturday Evening Post,* July 8, 1944.

Vellavielle, Michel de. *D-Day at Utah Beach*. Coutances, Normandy, 1982.

Weigley, Russell. *Eisenhower's Lieutenants: The Campaigns of France and Germany, 1944–1945*. Bloomington, Indiana: Indiana University Press, 1981.

Index